Essential Readings ON Comprehension

Compiled and introduced by Diane Lapp and Douglas Fisher

INTERNATIONAL
Reading Association
800 BARKSDALE ROAD, PO BOX 8139
NEWARK, DE 19714-8139, USA
www.reading.org

The International Reading Association attempts, through its publications, to provide a forum for a wide spectrum of opinions on reading. This policy permits divergent viewpoints without implying the endorsement of the Association.

Executive Editor, Books   Corinne M. Mooney
Developmental Editor   Charlene M. Nichols
Developmental Editor   Tori Mello Bachman
Developmental Editor   Stacey L. Reid
Editorial Production Manager   Shannon T. Fortner
Design and Composition Manager   Anette Schuetz

Project Editor   Christina Lambert

Cover   Design, Linda Steere

The publisher would appreciate notification where errors occur so that they may be corrected in subsequent printings and/or editions.

Library of Congress Cataloging-in-Publication Data

Essential readings on comprehension / compiled and introduced by Diane Lapp and Douglas Fisher.
   p. cm.
 Includes bibliographical references.
 ISBN 978-0-87207-807-9
 1. Content area reading. 2. Reading comprehension. I. Lapp, Diane. II. Fisher, Douglas.
 LB1050.455.E85 2009
 428.4'3—dc22

2009013933

Contents

About the Editors

Diane Lapp, EdD, is a distinguished professor of education in the Department of Teacher Education at San Diego State University (SDSU), San Diego, California, USA. She has taught in elementary and middle schools and is teaching English at Health Sciences High and Middle College, San Diego, California. Her major areas of research and instruction have centered on struggling readers and their families who live in urban, economically disadvantaged settings. Diane directs and teaches field-based preservice and graduate programs and courses. She was the coeditor of California's literacy journal *The California Reader*. She also has authored, coauthored, and edited many articles, columns, texts, handbooks, and children's materials on reading and language arts, including *Teaching Reading to Every Child*, a reading methods textbook in its fourth edition; *Content Area Reading and Learning: Instructional Strategies*; *Accommodating Differences Among English Language Learners: 75 Literacy Lessons*; *Handbook of Research on Teaching the English Language Arts*; and *Handbook of Research on Teaching Literacy Through the Communicative and Visual Arts* (Vol. 1 & 2).

Diane has also chaired and cochaired several International Reading Association (IRA) and National Reading Conference committees, including IRA's Early Literacy Committee. Her many awards include Outstanding Teacher Educator and Faculty Member in the Department of Teacher Education at SDSU, Distinguished Research Lecturer from SDSU's Graduate Division of Research, and IRA's 1996 Outstanding Teacher Educator of the Year. She is a member of the Reading Hall of Fame. Diane can be reached at lapp@mail.sdsu.edu.

Douglas Fisher, PhD, is a professor of language and literacy education in the Department of Teacher Education at San Diego State University (SDSU), California, USA, and a classroom teacher at Health Sciences High and Middle College, San Diego, California. He is the recipient of an International Reading Association (IRA) Celebrate Literacy Award, the Farmer Award for excellence in writing from the National Council of Teachers of English, and a Christa McAuliffe Award for excellence in teacher education from the American Association of State Colleges and Universities. He is a past chair of IRA's Adolescent Literacy Committee.

Doug has published numerous articles on reading and literacy, differentiated instruction, and curriculum design as well as books such as *In a Reading State of Mind: Brain Research, Teacher Modeling, and Comprehension Instruction* (with Nancy Frey and Diane Lapp), *Creating Literacy-Rich Schools for Adolescents* (with Gay Ivey), *Better Learning Through Structured Teaching: A Framework for the Gradual Release of Responsibility* (with Nancy Frey), and *Teaching English Language Learners: A Differentiated Approach* (with Carol Rothenberg). He has taught a variety of courses in SDSU's teacher-credentialing program as well as graduate-level courses on English-language development and literacy. An early intervention specialist and language development specialist, he has taught high school English, writing, and literacy development to public school students. Doug can be reached at dfisher@mail.sdsu.edu.

Introduction

Diane Lapp and Douglas Fisher

lthough 20 years separate the findings of Durkin (1978/1979) and Pressley and colleagues (1998), results from both these classic studies found that classroom teachers, especially those in the upper grades, did not teach comprehension but instead asked students postreading questions to determine if they understood what they had read. In 2000, Duke suggested that when teachers do provide direct comprehension instruction they usually do so using narrative texts; however, Pappas and Barry (1997) found that students often prefer to read expository or information text.

Based on our work with teachers at various grade levels over the last several decades, we believe that the majority of classroom teachers, similar to those in these classic studies, have always been intent on teaching comprehension but are not exactly sure what that entails. Fortunately, there have been many excellent books and articles published recently that can support teachers in their efforts to teach comprehension explicitly, so that students will develop skills in critical understanding of a variety of text types.

The Purpose of This Resource

Our goal in designing this resource is to offer a sort of "one-stop shopping" for you related to comprehension instruction. First, we provide a description or definition of comprehension that we hope will help you see possible areas of focus for your instruction. Second, we offer an overview of research that highlights factors that contribute to readers' successful comprehension of a wide array of texts. Finally, we draw from existing publications to compile the collection of readings included in this book, and we include extensive recommendations for other resources (including lessons, research-to-practice articles, books, YouTube videos, a DVD, and podcasts) that support successful comprehension instruction. Also included at the end of this introduction is a reference list to support further reading, where we've highlighted articles we consider "must reads" by means of asterisks. Overall, our goals with this resource are to define comprehension, note the processes one must engage to comprehend, identify what it means to teach comprehension, and then offer resources to help you support your students as they learn these very important processes of understanding.

What Is Comprehension?

To better understand the complexity of this question we often use the following text. A sailing instructor gave this to Diane during her first sailing lesson. You read it and see if you comprehend enough to feel confident about doing what it describes.

Raising the Mainsail

Step 1: Remove your mainsail from its bag and spread it out on the deck.

Step 2: Locate the three corners of your sail—head (top), tack (bottom inside), and clew (bottom outside).

Step 3: Attach the tack to the base of the mast with the forestay.

Step 4: Attach the bottom of the mainsail to the boom, if applicable.

Step 5: Release the halyard from its cleat.

Step 6: Attach the halyard to the headboard at the head of the mainsail.

Step 7: Feed the mainsail into the groove in the mast.

Step 8: Take the slack out of the halyard and secure it into a cleat.

Step 9: Tie the sheet to the clew of the boom with a bowline.

Step 10: Coil your lazy sheets flat and lay them in the cockpit or hang them on a cleat.

Step 11: You are now ready to raise the mainsail.

If you're confused, you are feeling exactly how Diane felt. At her first sailing lesson, she was told to read these instructions and then to attempt to rig the mainsail. This happened well after she had learned to read. In fact, it was her move to California's Pacific coast to start teaching at San Diego State University that had prompted her desire to learn to sail. She had gone to the sailing class with great enthusiasm, with many successes both as a reader and student, but with no experience sailing boats.

Are you thinking that you could do better with raising the mainsail if the text had supports like pictures, diagrams, and a glossary? This is exactly what Diane thought, so off she went to the bookstore to get a less difficult text, one that had illustrations and definitions.

What we can learn from Diane's experience and her subsequent actions is that she had lots of prior knowledge about how to help herself comprehend text but very little prior knowledge or background that would help her understand the language or procedures of sailing. What we can also realize from Diane's experience is that comprehension or meaning making is about the reader's ability to interact with information; it is about both the information in the text (in this case, a sailing manual) and also the reader's (in this case Diane's) background experiences with the topic and language of the text (sailing), her purpose for reading (to learn how to do something), and motivation (she was highly motivated to sail). Comprehension involves the ability to draw from all these areas to coconstruct meaning from text.

Because Diane was a skilled learner, she did not give up. Unfortunately, this isn't the case for many readers who find themselves assigned to read texts with which they are unable to interact. When this happens, teachers must first determine what is causing the student's inability to connect and then what can be done to remedy this. If teachers make this two-step process transparent to students—first, determining what supports are needed, and second, figuring out how they can best be acquired—students will start to understand how to support their own comprehension.

Extrapolating from Diane's experiences we can see that comprehension requires the reader to be fluid in putting into action multiple processes, including decoding words and then fluently recognizing their meaning first in sentences and then in increasingly longer text passages. To comprehend more deeply and critically, the reader must also engage his or her background knowledge of the topic, recognize and know how to use any text features (text structure, illustrations, graphs, etc.) to support and enhance meaning construction, situate the text in relation to other thematically related texts, and contest how it is culturally, historically, or politically positioned. When the reader is unable, for whatever reason, to perceive and understand the text, additional instructional supports are needed.

What's Involved in Comprehension and Comprehension Instruction?

Effective teachers understand the complexity of the processes involved in comprehending as well as the instructional routines that support students as they develop the ability both to understand and critically evaluate a wide array of texts and also to recognize and take action when they do not understand. Although we discuss various processes involved in comprehension individually, we do not mean to suggest that readers use them one at a time. Instead, proficient readers draw on a wide repertoire of processes or cognitive strategies, often simultaneously, to support their comprehension of text.

Being able to comprehend and critically respond to what is being read depends on the reader's ability to engage background knowledge about the text's topic and the language used and to apply skills and strategies to decode and assign meaning to words with a level of fluency that supports meaning making. The readings and recommendations in this resource focus on the interaction between text and reader, beginning with activating background knowledge. Of course, the processes involved in decoding, reading fluency, and vocabulary development are critical for comprehension, but these topics are explored in depth in other resources. For convenience, we have included recommended readings on these topics in the Appendix.

How Important Is Background Knowledge?

As you know from reading about Diane's experience with the sailing text, her background knowledge about rigging a mainsail as well as her understanding of the specialized vocabulary of sailing and sailboats had to be developed in order for her to comprehend the text.

Although the work of Anderson and Pearson (1984) helped us to realize that the more prior knowledge readers have about the topic of a text, the fuller will be their comprehension, McKoon and Ratcliff (1992) note that readers do not always use their prior knowledge to support comprehension. Subsequent studies by Pressley et al. (1992) and Stanovich and Cunningham (1993) show that background knowledge, which is developed in part through wide reading, can be activated to support comprehension when readers interrogate themselves and the text, asking why things are happening. Through textual interrogation before, during, and after reading, readers draw on their prior knowledge to make sense or monitor their understanding of what they are reading. Questioning techniques such as Question–Answer Relationship (QAR), ReQuest, or reciprocal questioning support readers in this process.

Included Readings
- "QAR: Enhancing Comprehension and Test Taking Across Grades and Content Areas," by Taffy E. Raphael and Kathryn H. Au
- "Expansion Modules for the ReQuest, CAT, GRP, and REAP Reading/Study Procedures," by Anthony V. Manzo

Additional Recommended Resources
- "Guided Comprehension: Self-Questioning Using Question-Answer Relationships," a lesson plan by Sarah Dennis-Shaw at Read WriteThink.org (www.readwritethink.org/lessons/lesson_view.asp?id=227)
- "Request Reciprocal Teaching," a lesson plan by Frede Stier at Educator's Reference Desk (www.eduref.org/Virtual/Lessons/Language_Arts/Reading/RDG0006.html)

What Cognitive Strategies Do Readers Use to Support Their Comprehension?

Pressley and Afflerbach (1995) found that, in addition to using knowledge of language, vocabulary, and past experience, proficient readers also make use of a repertoire of strategies. They preview the text to get an overview of what will be read, set purposes that keep them focused, make predictions and then check them as they read, use context clues to figure out vocabulary, create mental visuals to help them understand and remember, ask questions of themselves and the text to connect prior and new information, synthesize large chunks of information to support remembering, underline and take notes about points they consider important, reread and monitor their speed to ensure their understanding, reflect and revise their knowledge based on new insights gained, continually evaluate the truth or worth of the information, summarize to support remembering the major thesis, and then apply and expand the knowledge. They do not use one cognitive strategy at a time but rather, as they monitor their comprehension, they use them in the configurations needed.

But the goal is not to produce strategic readers who can simply name the processes that are occurring in their minds. Instead, the goal is to produce readers who can automatically deploy the cognitive strategies. In their discussion of skilled versus strategic readers, Afflerbach, Pearson, and Paris (2008) emphasize the reader's actions and the extent to which they are automatic or deliberate. In their words, "reading skills operate without the reader's deliberate control or conscious awareness…[t]his has important, positive consequences for each reader's limited working memory" (p. 368). Strategies, on the other hand, are "effortful and deliberate" (p. 369) and occur during initial learning and when the text becomes more difficult for the reader to understand. Identification of the skills that are thought to be most important by researchers was first noted by Davis in 1944. (This is an article you'll want to be sure to read. Much of what we know today about reading skills versus strategies began with this study.)

In addition to teaching students to question themselves and the text, other cognitive strategies that have been found to be of major significance to a reader's understanding are creating mental representations of what is being read, summarizing, and recognizing and organizing text structures (Pearson & Dole, 1987; Pearson & Fielding, 1991; Pressley, Johnson, Symons, McGoldrick, & Kurita, 1989). These should be taught continuously through teacher modeling, explanation, and scaffolded support.

Visualizing, or creating a mental model while reading, involves cognitively constructing a graphic or picture based on what is already known and what is derived while reading. If the reader is able to construct a mental image from what is read, his comprehension will be enhanced; by attending to illustrations in the text, comprehension will be enhanced still further (Gambrell & Jawitz, 1993).

Included Readings

- "A Picture Is Worth a Thousand Words: Using Visual Images to Improve Comprehension for Middle School Struggling Readers," by Anne Nielsen Hibbing and Joan L. Rankin-Erickson

Additional Recommended Resources

- "Mind Pictures: Strategies That Enhance Mental Imagery While Reading," a lesson plan by Susan Ruckdeschel at Read WriteThink.org (www.readwritethink.org/lessons/lesson_view.asp?id=792)

Summarizing involves presenting the key ideas or main points of a text or experience in a briefer form. In the included reading "Teaching Summarization as a Content Area Reading Strategy," author Rosalie Friend illustrates that a student must be able to process the ideas presented in the text, consider their relationships to one another, eliminate redundancy, and then make generalizations about the ideas to produce a thorough summary. The National Reading Panel (National Institute of Child Health and Human Development, 2000) found from an evaluation of existing research that summarization is a very important comprehension strategy when it is bundled with question generating and question answering. Harvey and Goudvis (2000) illustrate in their work that summarizing, which involves restating the text in a significant but briefer version, is a part of synthesizing, which involves moving beyond creating a summary by generating a new perspective or insight. Seeing the big idea, or main point, of a text helps children to summarize what they are reading.

Included Readings

- "Getting the Big Idea: A Neglected Goal for Reading Comprehension," by Sean A. Walmsley
- "Teaching Summarization as a Content Area Reading Strategy," by Rosalie Friend

Additional Recommended Resources

- "Understanding the Big Idea," an audio podcast based on Sean Walmsley's article (www.reading.org/downloads/podcasts/CA-Walmsley.mp3)
- "Strategies for Reading Comprehension: Summarizing," an overview and

downloadable instructional resources at ReadingQuest.org (www.readingquest.org/strat/summarize.html)

- "Summarization," an overview and description of strategies from FOR-PD (for-pd.ucf.edu/strategies/stratsummarization.html)
- "Guided Comprehension: Summarizing Using the QuIP Strategy," a lesson plan by Sarah Dennis-Shaw at ReadWriteThink.org (www.readwritethink.org/lessons/lesson_view.asp?id=231)
- "GIST: A Summarizing Strategy for Use in Any Content Area," a lesson plan by Che-Mai Gray at ReadWriteThink.org (www.readwritethink.org/lessons/lesson_view.asp?id=290)
- "Guided Comprehension in Action: Teaching Summarizing With the Bio-Cube," a lesson plan by Alexandria Gibb and Danielle Bevilacqua at ReadWriteThink.org (www.readwritethink.org/lessons/lesson_view.asp?id=1028)
- "Summarization Station: Reading to Learn," a lesson plan by Jenni Anderson (www.auburn.edu/~murraba/guides/andersonrl.html)

Visual representations of *text structure* help students organize and remember information presented in a text. Text maps, which are also referred to as webs, and concept, pictorial, or other graphic organizers provide a way to display organized relationships or patterns among the key ideas and terms in a text. Griffin, Malone, and Kame'enui (1995) found that students' comprehension, recall, and information transfer were enhanced after being given explicit instruction in how to design and use graphic organizers and then practice using them.

Included Readings
- "Teaching Expository Text Structure Awareness," by Susan Dymock
- "Guidelines for Implementing a Graphic Organizer," by Donna M. Merkley and Debra Jefferies

Additional Recommended Resources
- *Guiding Readers Through Text: Strategy Guides for New Times,* by Karen Wood, Diane Lapp, James Flood, and Bruce Taylor (and, with this book, part of the IRA Library: Comprehension package; find more information at www.reading.org/General/Publications/Books/bk681.aspx)
- "Teaching Tip: Jim Burke on Using Graphic Organizers," a video clip (www.youtube.com/watch?v=-k7Yuo4uMhw)
- "Scaffolding Comprehension Strategies Using Graphic Organizers," a lesson plan by Susan Ruckdeschel at ReadWriteThink.org (www.readwritethink.org/lessons/lesson_view.asp?id=95)
- "Strategies for Reading Comprehension: History Frames/Story Maps," an overview and instructional resources from ReadingQuest.org (www.readingquest.org/strat/storymaps.html)
- "Graphic Organizers," an overview and instructional resources from the North Central Regional Educational Laboratory (www.ncrel.org/sdrs/areas/issues/students/learning/lr1grorg.htm)
- www.graphic.org, a website index of links to online resources related to graphic organizers
- Ready-to-use graphic organizers from TeacherVision (www.teachervision.fen.com/graphic-organizers/printable/6293.html?_R=1)
- Downloadable graphic organizers from SoftSchools.com (www.softschools.com/graphic_organizers/)

What Instructional Routines Can Teachers Use to Support Comprehension Instruction?

To avoid confusion about the word *strategy*, we use the phrase *instructional routine* when discussing the use of classroom time. This allows students and teachers to distinguish between cognitive strategies (and subsequently automatized skills) that happen in the reader's mind and instructional routines we use to facilitate those strategies and skills. There are a number of instructional routines that can be used by teachers across grade levels and disciplines to ensure that students develop meaning-making habits.

Evidence from research over several decades indicates that *teacher modeling* positively affects student performance and achievement (e.g., Afflerbach & Johnston, 1984; Duffy, 2003; Olson & Land, 2007). Modeling provides students with examples of the thinking and language demands required by the task at hand. In essence, students get to peer inside the mind of an expert reader (the teacher) to see how that person thinks about, processes, and solves a problem.

Included Readings

- "Shared Readings: Modeling Comprehension, Vocabulary, Text Structures, and Text Features for Older Readers," by Douglas Fisher, Nancy Frey, and Diane Lapp
- "'You Can Read This Text—I'll Show You How': Interactive Comprehension Instruction," by Diane Lapp, Douglas Fisher, and Maria Grant

Additional Recommended Resources

- *In a Reading State of Mind: Brain Research, Teacher Modeling, and Comprehension Instruction,* a book–DVD combination resource by Douglas Fisher, Nancy Frey, and Diane Lapp (and, with this text, part of the IRA Library: Comprehension package; find more information at www.reading .org/General/Publications/Books/bk777 .aspx)
- "Fisher, Frey, and Lapp on Modeling During Shared Reading," an audio podcast (www.reading.org/downloads/podcasts/ FisherFreyLapp.mp3)
- "Scaffolding Comprehension Strategies Using Graphic Organizers," a lesson plan by Susan Ruckdeschel at ReadWriteThink. org (www.readwritethink.org/lessons/ lesson_view.asp?id=95)

Like teacher modeling, *reciprocal teaching* is a highly effective instructional routine for developing comprehension. Evidence on the effectiveness of reciprocal teaching dates back more than 20 years (Palincsar, 1984), and more recent research is investigating how it can be applied to diverse student populations (e.g., Alfassi, 1998; Takala, 2006). The effectiveness of reciprocal teaching probably relates to the fact that it provides students with practice in four cognitive strategies for comprehending texts (summarizing, predicting, clarifying, and questioning) as well as with feedback and support from peers.

Included Readings

- "Interactive Teaching to Promote Independent Learning From Text," by Annemarie Sullivan Palincsar and Ann L. Brown

Additional Recommended Resources

- "Reciprocal Revision: Making Peer Feedback Meaningful," a lesson plan by Donna Vorreyer at ReadWriteThink.org (www.readwritethink.org/lessons/lesson _view.asp?id=403)

Writing to learn differs from other types of writing, especially the writing process approach typically followed in writers' workshop, because the writer does not go through multiple refinements toward an intended final product. Instead, it is meant as an opportunity for students to recall, clarify, and question what they know and what they still wonder about. Writing to learn "involves getting students to think about and to find the words to explain what they are learning, how they understand that learning, and what their own processes of learning involve" (Mitchell, 1996, p. 93). As Jenkinson (1988) explains, writing to learn "should be a process in which writers discover what they know and do not know about their topics, their language, themselves, and their ability to communicate with specific audiences" (p. 714).

Included Readings

- "Using Writing to Enhance Content Area Learning in the Primary Grades," by Evelyn T. Cudd and Leslie Roberts
- "We Learn What We Do: Developing a Repertoire of Writing Practices in an Instant Messaging World," by Gloria E. Jacobs

Additional Recommended Resources

- "Strategic Reading and Writing: Summarizing Antislavery Biographies," a lesson plan by Sarah Dennis-Shaw at ReadWriteThink.org (www.read writethink.org/lessons/lesson_view .asp?id=1017)

What Might the Future Hold for Comprehension Instruction?

We have noted throughout each segment of this introduction that comprehension development is best supported through wide, purposeful reading and effective, explicit instruction. Realizing this, educators must share with their students an ever-expanding collection of text types as well as ways to gain meaning from them. The end goal of this instruction is that every student will be well prepared to meet the new literacy challenges that will present themselves throughout the 21st century. Two additional areas that you may want to consider as you plan your instruction are digital and critical literacies. In addition to the readings on these topics that we've included in this resource, be sure to see the references we've identified in the Appendix.

The majority of today's students feel quite comfortable navigating digital technologies to gain, share, and modify information related to both in- and out-of-school activities. Many are also quite nimble at digitally navigating the social networks and accessing the products and services of Web 2.0. One concern, noted by DeBell and Chapman (2006) and others, is that educators must ensure that students have access to computer technology at school to reduce the "digital divide" that exists among students who do and who do not have Internet access at home. This request to educators seems no more profound than suggesting that in schools there must be many types of texts placed in the hands of each student. The complexity relates to the instruction that must be provided. As Kress (2004) notes, literacy for the 21st century is multimodal and nonlinear, with meaning being derived with great immediacy from multiple layers of visual images, sound, and text simultaneously. Access to digital technologies provides students with a growing range of tools not merely to retrieve information but also to share their ideas (Meyer, Chall, Onofrey, & Rose, 1999). How these technologies can be integrated with classroom learning is a topic on the minds of educators, many of whom are not expert with technology themselves. Educators are, however, experts at planning engaging instruction that promotes learning for all their students. How this instruction looks today may change tomorrow because we live in exciting times with new media being introduced on a regular basis.

As Flood and Lapp (1995) noted more than a decade ago, our shared goal as educators must continue to be to use our students' engagement and interest in multimodalities and multiple sign systems to support their learning and allow them to interpret, communicate, and participate in the 21st century. Multimodal instruction and learning offers possibilities of success for all students (Gee, 2000; New London Group, 1996; Warschauer & Ware, 2008) because its expansiveness supports opportunities to develop and bridge multiple forms of literacy, including out-of-school literacies (home, personal, sports, cultural, technology/media, and popular culture), transformative literacies (critical literacy and social justice literacy), and authentic academic literacies (functional literacy and problem-solving literacy). The following resources provide examples of how to bring multimodal learning into your curriculum.

Included Readings

- "Recentering the Middle School Classroom as a Vibrant Learning Community:

Students, Literacy, and Technology Intersect," by Dana L. Grisham and Thomas D. Wolsey

- "Reading Literature, Reading Text, Reading the Internet: The Times They Are a'Changing," by Linda B. Gambrell

Additional Recommended Resources

- "Hoax or No Hoax? Strategies for Online Comprehension and Evaluation," a lesson plan by Deborah Kozdras and James L. Welsh at ReadWriteThink.org (www.readwritethink.org/lessons/lesson_view.asp?id=1135)
- "Book Report Alternative: Comic Strips and Cartoon Squares," a lesson plan by Traci Gardner at ReadWriteThink.org (www.readwritethink.org/lessons/lesson_view.asp?id=195)
- "Points of View in the News," a lesson plan at National Geographic Xpeditions (www.nationalgeographic.com/xpeditions/lessons/18/g68/pointsnews.html)
- The Media Literacy Clearinghouse (www.frankwbaker.com/default1.htm)

When readers are critically literate, they do not passively accept the messages in texts but rather act as active participants in the reading process, questioning, examining, and disputing the power relations between authors and readers. *Critical literacy* promotes reflection, transformation, and action by investigating issues of position and power (Freire, 1970, McLaughlin & DeVoogd, 2004). Critical literacy practices are dynamic, flexible, and can be adapted to reading multiple forms of texts. To be critically literate means that the reader is able to use a sociocultural lens to evaluate information by analyzing it through issues of power, culture, class, and gender. This adds an additional dimension, a sociocultural perspective of analysis, to what has been traditionally thought of as critical reading. Critical literacy complements critical reading by asking the reader, no matter his or her age, to go beyond questioning the text's intention and

authenticity by confronting the stance, values, and thinking that lie beneath a literal interpretation of text, author, and self.

This is powerfully illustrated in the included reading by Karen Spector and Stephanie Jones, who described how a group of secondary students read the popular Goodrich and Hacker play about Anne Frank along with different editions of her diary, and who also viewed a thematically related video. Through these multiple texts and lively conversations, they came to challenge their original beliefs about Anne and their insights were greatly expanded. A person is considered to be critically literate when she or he uses insights and draws on multiple viewpoints automatically while reading, watching, and thinking about a text or situation. In the lessons revolving around Anne Frank, digital literacy could have been integrated with Internet research and culminating work to create a webpage with text, graphics, and links to offer a personal final analysis, opinion, or call to action in relation to the Holocaust or a current situation of discrimination.

Vasquez (2004) describes a preschool lesson where 3- to 5-year-old children redesign the packaging of a fruit candy snack after a conversation about advertising and appealing to the consumer. As a part of the conversation, the children also looked at the manufacturer's website for the product and discussed what was presented at the site. (To further understand how critical literacy can be a part of daily life, be sure to listen to the podcast by Vasquez listed below under Additional Recommended Resources.)

Xu (2007) takes us inside a second-grade classroom where the teacher and her students discuss the value of US$10 during a math lesson. In their discussion, they come to realize that the value may be somewhat dependent on what else the owner has; from this they move to a focus on what US$100 would mean to those affected by Hurricane Katrina. They conclude by initiating a fundraising drive to contribute to the American Red Cross. This example shows that while learning the value of money as a math concept, students can also come to a critical understanding of money as a social concept.

Behrman (2006) and Stribling (2008) also offer many ideas for both elementary and secondary instruction that involve students analyzing texts from a critical stance. Some of these include reading and comparing supplementary texts (e.g., online texts), reading and comparing the presented premises of multiple texts, reading from a resistant perspective, producing "countertexts" that show an alternate perspective, conducting student choice research projects (e.g., creating a webpage), and taking social action on a self-selected issue.

Included Readings

- "Constructing Anne Frank: Critical Literacy and the Holocaust in Eighth-Grade English," by Karen Spector and Stephanie Jones

Additional Recommended Resources

- "A Tale of Differences: Comparing the Traditions, Perspectives, and Educational Goals of Critical Reading and Critical Literacy," an article by Gina Cervetti, Michael J. Pardales, and James S. Damico at Reading Online (www.readingonline.org/articles/art_index.asp?HREF=/articles/cervetti/index.html)
- "Investigating Junk Mail: Negotiating Critical Literacy at the Mailbox," a lesson plan by Lisa Storm Fink and Sharon Roth at ReadWriteThink.org (www.readwritethink.org/lessons/lesson_view.asp?id=321)
- "Critical Literacy: Women in 19th-Century Literature," a lesson plan by Elizabeth Nolan Conners at ReadWriteThink.org (www.readwritethink.org/lessons/lesson_view.asp?id=1009)
- "Book Sorting: Using Observation and Comprehension to Categorize Books," a lesson plan by Renee Goularte at ReadWriteThink.org (www.readwritethink.org/lessons/lesson_view.asp?id=145)
- "Defining Critical Literacy," an audio podcast by Vivian Vasquez from Critical Literacy in Practice (www.bazmakaz.com/clip/2007/11/19/defining-critical-literacy_show-51/)

The Reason for Meaning Making

Comprehension—meaning making or understanding—is a complex process that happens in a reader's mind and thus has been hard to expose. Thankfully, over the past several decades, teachers and researchers have uncovered a great deal of information about the processes involved in comprehension. In addition, we now have a number of instructional routines verified as useful in developing students' comprehension repertoires. We know, for example, that graphic organizers, teacher modeling, writing to learn, and reciprocal teaching have a positive impact on student understanding.

Of course, we are still learning. As the world changes and we embrace the technological innovations of our time, new processes and new instructional routines will likely develop. As they do, teachers will adapt so that their students have access to the best information possible and to the best ways of making sense of it. This collection represents the current knowledge of a professional organization devoted to helping teachers teach all children in the world to read, to understand, and to think critically. Isn't this what it means to be free?

References

* Indicates a highly recommended, "must read" article.

Afflerbach, P., & Johnston, P. (1984). On the use of verbal reports in reading research. *Journal of Reading Behavior, 16*(4), 307–322.

Afflerbach, P., Pearson, P.D., & Paris, S. (2008). Clarifying differences between reading skills and reading strategies. *The Reading Teacher, 61*(5), 364–373. doi:10.1598/RT.61.5.1

Alfassi, M. (1998). Reading for meaning: The efficacy of reciprocal teaching in fostering reading comprehension in high school students in remedial reading classes. *American Educational Research Journal, 35*(2), 309–332.

*Anderson, R.C., & Pearson, P.D. (1984). A schema-theoretic view of basic processes in reading. In P.D. Pearson, R. Barr, M.L. Kamil, & P. Mosenthal (Eds.),

Handbook of Reading Research (pp. 255–291). White Plains, NY: Longman.

Behrman, E.H. (2006). Teaching about language, power, and text: A review of classroom practices that support critical literacy. *Journal of Adolescent & Adult Literacy, 49*(6), 490–498. doi:10.1598/JAAL.49.6.4

Davis, F.B. (1944). Fundamental factors of comprehension in reading. *Psychometrika, 9*(3), 185–197. doi:10.1007/BF02288722

*DeBell, M., & Chapman, C. (2006). Computer and internet use by students in 2003 (NCES 2006–065). U.S. Department of Education. Retrieved January 12, 2009, from scholar.google.com/scholar?q=DeBell+%26+Chapman+2003+computer+use&hl=en&client=firefox-a&channel=s&rls=org.mozilla:en-US:official&um=1&ie=UTF-8&oi=scholart.

Duffy, G.G. (2003). *Explaining reading: A resource for teaching concepts, skills, and strategies.* New York: Guilford.

Duke, N.K. (2000). For the rich it's richer: Print environments and experiences offered to first-grade students in very low- and very high-SES school districts. *American Educational Research Journal, 37*(2), 441–478.

Durkin, D. (1978/1979). What classroom observations reveal about reading comprehension instruction. *Reading Research Quarterly, 14*(4), 481–533. doi:10.1598/RRQ.14.4.2

Flood, J., & Lapp, D. (1995). Broadening the lens: Towards an expanded conceptualization of literacy. In K. Hinchman, D. Leu and D. Kinzer (Eds.) *Perspectives on Literacy Research and Practice* (pp. 1–6). Chicago: 44th Yearbook of the National Reading Conference.

Freire, P. (1970). *Pedagogy of the oppressed.* New York: Herder and Herder.

Gambrell, L.B., & Jawitz, P.B. (1993). Mental imagery, text illustrations, and children's story comprehension and recall. *Reading Research Quarterly, 28*(3), 264–276. doi:10.2307/747998

Gee, J.P. (2000). Discourse and sociocultural studies in reading. In M.L. Kamil, P.B. Mosenthal, P.D. Pearson, & R. Barr (Eds.), *Handbook of Reading Research* (Vol. 3, pp. 195–207). New York, Lawrence Erlbaum.

Griffin, C.C., Malone, L.D., & Kame'enui, E.J. (1995). Effects of graphic organizer instruction on fifth-grade students. *The Journal of Educational Research, 89*(2), 98–107.

Harvey, S., & Goudvis, A. (2000). *Strategies that work: Teaching comprehension to enhance understanding.* York, ME: Stenhouse.

Jenkinson, E.B. (1988). Learning to write/writing to learn. *Phi Delta Kappan, 69*(10), 712–717.

Kress, G. (2004). Reading images: Multimodality, representation and new media. Retrieved January 12, 2009, from, www.knowledgepresentation.org/BuildingTheFuture/Kress2/Kress2.html

McKoon, G., & Ratcliff, R. (1992). Inference during reading. *Psychological Review, 99*(3), 440–466. doi:10.1037/0033-295X.99.3.440

*McLaughlin, M., & DeVoogd, G. (2004). *Critical literacy: Enhancing students' comprehension of text.* New York: Scholastic.

Meyer, A., Chall, J.S., Onofrey, J.F., & Rose, D.H. (1999). *Learning to read in the computer age.* Cambridge, MA: Brookline.

Mitchell, D. (1996). Writing to learn across the curriculum and the English teacher. *English Journal, 85*(5), 93–97. doi:10.2307/820728

National Institute of Child Health and Human Development. (2000). *Report of the National Reading Panel. Teaching children to read: An evidence-based assessment of the scientific research literature on reading and its implications for reading instruction (NIH Publication No. 00–4769).* Washington, DC: U.S. Government Printing Office.

New London Group. (1996). A pedagogy of multiliteracies: Designing social futures. *Harvard Educational Review, 66*(1), 60–92.

Olson, C.B., & Land, R. (2007). A cognitive strategies approach to reading and writing instruction for English language learners in secondary school. *Research in the Teaching of English, 41*(3), 269–303.

Palincsar, A.S. (1984). Reciprocal teaching of comprehension-fostering and comprehension-monitoring activities. *Cognition and Instruction, 1*(2), 117–175. doi:10.1207/s1532690xci0102_1

Pappas, C.C., & Barry, A. (1997). Scaffolding urban students' initiations: Transactions in reading information books in the read-aloud curriculum genre. In Karolides, N.J. (Ed.), *Reader response in elementary classrooms: Quest and discovery* (pp. 215–236). Hillsdale, NJ: Erlbaum.

Pearson, P.D., & Dole, J.A. (1987). Explicit comprehension instruction: A review of research and a new conceptualization of instruction. *The Elementary School Journal, 88*(2), 151–165. doi:10.1086/461530

Pearson, P.D., & Fielding, L. (1991). Comprehension instruction. In R. Barr, M.L. Kamil, P.B. Mosenthal, & P.D. Pearson (Eds.), *Handbook of reading research* (Vol. 2, pp. 815–860). White Plains, NY: Longman.

*Pressley, M., & Afflerbach, P. (1995). *Verbal protocols of reading: The nature of constructively responsive reading.* Hillsdale, NJ: Erlbaum.

Pressley, M., Johnson, C.J., Symons, S., McGoldrick, J.A., & Kurita, J.A. (1989). Strategies *that improve children's memory and comprehension of text. The Elementary School Journal, 90*(1), 3–32. doi:10.1086/461599

Pressley, M., Wharton-McDonald, R., Hampson, J.M., & Echevarria, M. (1998). Literacy instruction in 10 fourth- and fifth-grade classrooms in upstate New York. *Scientific Studies of Reading, 2*(2), 159–191. doi:10.1207/s1532799xssr0202_4

Pressley, M., Wood, E., Woloshyn, V.E., Martin, V., King, A., & Menke, D. (1992). Encouraging mindful use of prior knowledge: Attempting to construct explanatory answers facilitates learning. *Educational Psychologist*, *27*(1), 91–110. doi:10.1207/s15326985ep2701_7

Stanovich, K.E., & Cunningham, A.E. (1993). Where does knowledge come from? Specific associations between print exposure and information acquisition. *Journal of Educational Psychology*, *85*(2), 211–229. doi:10.1037/0022-0663.85.2.211

Stribling, D.M. (2008). Using critical literacy practices in the classroom. *The New England Reading Association Journal*, *44*(1), 34–38.

Takala, M. (2006). The effects of reciprocal teaching on reading comprehension in mainstream and special (SLI) education. *Scandinavian Journal of Educational Research*, *50*(5), 559–576. doi:10.1080/00313830600953824

Vasquez, V. (2004). *Negotiating critical literacies with young children*. Mahwah, NJ: Erlbaum.

Warschauer, M., & Ware, P. (2008). Learning, change, and power: Competing frames of technology and literacy. In J. Coiro, M. Knobel, C. Lankshear, & D.J. Leu (Eds.), *Handbook of research on new literacies* (pp. 215–240). New York: Taylor & Francis.

Xu, S. (2007). Critical literacy practices in teaching and learning. *The New England Reading Association Journal*, *43*(2), 12–22.

QAR: Enhancing Comprehension and Test Taking Across Grades and Content Areas

Taffy E. Raphael and Kathryn H. Au

Promoting high levels of literacy for all children is a core responsibility for today's teachers. In this article, we describe the potential of Question Answer Relationships (QAR) for helping teachers guide all students to higher levels of literacy. We set this description within the current instructional and assessment context, with a particular focus on what it means to teach to high levels of literacy and why it is especially important to ensure that such instructional activities reach all students.

Educators agree that students must meet high standards for literacy achievement. In a democratic society, success depends on an informed citizenry who can participate effectively in the democratic process—reading a wide range of materials, interpreting and evaluating what they read, drawing conclusions based on evidence, and so forth. Furthermore, with increasing accountability at the district, state, and national levels, U.S. teachers know that they are often judged on the basis of how well their students perform on mandated, high-stakes tests. And certainly high levels of achievement in literacy are important for learning across the curriculum, for independence in engaging with print for personal satisfaction, and for success in an increasingly information-based economy.

But what does it mean to achieve high levels of literacy? Recent national panels and current reviews detailing what it means to comprehend text help inform us about current policies and future trends (e.g., Pressley, 2002; Snow, 2002; Sweet & Snow, 2003). For example, the RAND report (Snow), commissioned by the U.S. Department of Education, identifies literacy proficiency as reached when a

> reader can read a variety of materials with ease and interest, can read for varying purposes, and can read with comprehension even when the material is neither easy to understand nor intrinsically interesting.... [P]roficient readers...are capable of acquiring new knowledge and understanding new concepts, are capable of applying textual information appropriately, and are capable of being engaged in the reading process and reflecting on what is being read. (p. xiii)

This same view is reflected in the current National Assessment of Educational Progress (NAEP; Donahue, Daane, & Grigg, 2003), the only federally funded large-scale testing program in the United States, and the framework for the NAEP 2009 reading assessment (National Assessment Governing Board, 2004) pushes the definition for proficiency even further. For example, students will be expected to read comfortably across genres within fiction, nonfiction, procedural texts, and poetry. They will be required to successfully answer questions, 70% to 80% of which call for the integration, interpretation, critique, and evaluation of texts read independently. Traditional questions that simply require readers to locate and recall information

Reprinted from Raphael, T.E., & Au, K.H. (2005). QAR: Enhancing comprehension and test taking across grades and content areas. *The Reading Teacher*, 59(3), 206–221. doi: 10.1598/RT.59.3.1

will constitute only a third to a fourth of the questions that students will face. Over half of the higher level questions will require students to provide a short or extended written response rather than simply to select from multiple-choice options. To be judged as proficient in reading fiction, students must demonstrate that they can think deeply about and write in response to questions that address themes and lessons, elements of plot structures, and multiple points of view. To demonstrate high levels of literacy when reading nonfiction, students will need to draw on their knowledge of text organization (e.g., description, causal relationships, logical connections) and be able to identify important details in texts, graphs, photos, and other materials.

The kind of strategic knowledge assessed on national and state tests, now and in the future, is central to the achievement of high levels of literacy. In this context, the gap between the literacy achievement of mainstream students and students of diverse backgrounds must be a central concern (Au, 2003). Students of diverse backgrounds differ from mainstream students in terms of their ethnicity, socioeconomic status, or primary language (Au, 1993). In the United States, for example, students of diverse backgrounds may be African American, Latino American, or Native American in ethnicity; come from low-income families; or speak African American Vernacular English or Spanish as their primary language.

As displayed in Table 1, the existence of an achievement gap between students of diverse backgrounds and mainstream students is underscored by 2002 reading results (Grigg, Daane, Jin, & Campbell, 2003). These results show that, as a group, students of diverse backgrounds have fallen four years behind their mainstream peers in reading achievement by the time they reach grade 12. The average 12th-grade black student's score (267) is at the same level as the average 8th-grade Asian/Pacific Islander student (267), and slightly below that of the average 8th-grade white student (272). Similarly, an average 12th-grade Hispanic student's score (273) is only 1 point above that of an average 8th-grade white student. This gap is present as students move through the elementary grades, and it only becomes worse.

Many theories have been proposed to explain the literacy achievement gap, identifying factors within and beyond the purview of the classroom teacher. We focus here on an area that falls within the control of individual classroom teachers and their school colleagues: diverse students' currently limited opportunities for high-quality instruction in reading comprehension. Research shows that, in comparison to their mainstream peers, students of diverse backgrounds tend to receive a great deal of instruction in lower level skills and little instruction in reading comprehension and higher level thinking about text (Darling-Hammond, 1995; Fitzgerald, 1995). This emphasis on lower level skills frequently results from lowered expectations for the achievement of students of diverse backgrounds, reflecting the mistaken belief that these students are less capable of higher level thinking than mainstream students (Oakes & Guiton, 1995). Using this misguided logic leads to the erroneous conclusion that instruction in lower level skills is a better match to the abilities of students of diverse backgrounds.

These stereotypes of students of diverse backgrounds are especially harmful at a time of rising standards for reading performance. As noted earlier, a high proportion of test questions—within the next five years, approximately three quarters to four fifths of questions on the NAEP reading assessment—require students to use higher level thinking, such as making reader–text connections or examining the content and structure of the text (National Assessment Governing

Table 1
Average 2002 NAEP Reading Scores

Ethnicity	Grade 4	Grade 8	Grade 12
White	229	272	292
Black	199	245	267
Hispanic	201	247	273
Asian/Pacific Islanders	224	267	286

Board, 2004; Donahue et al., 2003). As indicated above, studies suggest that many students of diverse backgrounds are not receiving the kind of comprehension instruction that would prepare them to perform well on assessments that are increasingly oriented toward higher level thinking with text. It is clear from research that all students need instruction in reading comprehension, especially the kind that focuses on the strategies required to answer and generate challenging questions (Taylor, Pearson, Peterson, & Rodriguez, 2003).

In our work with schools enrolling a high proportion of students of diverse backgrounds, we find that teachers often experience difficulty making the desired changes to instruction. Typically, these teachers have become accustomed to instruction focused on lower level skills rather than on higher level thinking and reading comprehension. Or they are unsure of how to teach different comprehension strategies in a way that allows students to see how the strategies work together to facilitate an understanding of the text. The consequences of weak instruction for all students, but particularly for those of diverse backgrounds, may extend far beyond testing, likely limiting their opportunities for higher education, employment, and overall advancement in society.

In summary, current practice and future trends place increasingly heavy demands on teachers to ensure that all of their students achieve high levels of literacy. Teachers may feel overwhelmed by the challenges of bringing students to these high levels of literacy, due to uncertainty about how to teach reading comprehension strategies to foster the integration, interpretation, critique, and evaluation of text ideas. The challenges are compounded by the fact that students of diverse backgrounds often enter classrooms reading far below grade level.

We believe QAR provides a framework that offers teachers a straightforward approach for reading comprehension instruction with the potential of eventually closing the literacy achievement gap. QAR can serve as a reasonable starting point for addressing four problems of practice that stand in the way of moving all students to high levels of literacy:

- The need for a shared language to make visible the largely invisible processes underlying reading and listening comprehension.
- The need for a framework for organizing questioning activities and comprehension instruction within and across grades and school subjects.
- The need for accessible and straightforward whole-school reform for literacy instruction oriented toward higher level thinking.
- The need to prepare students for high-stakes testing without undermining a strong focus on higher level thinking with text.

Two decades ago, research showed that QAR could reliably improve students' comprehension (Raphael & McKinney, 1983; Raphael & Pearson, 1985; Raphael & Wonnacott, 1985). In the two decades since, literacy educators in a broad range of settings have demonstrated its practical value and shared their experiences in professional journals (e.g., Mesmer & Hutchins, 2002), textbooks (e.g., Leu & Kinzer, 2003; Reutzel & Cooper, 2004; Roe, Smith, & Burns, 2005; Vacca et al., 2003), and on the World Wide Web (e.g., www.smsd.org/schools/diemer/ and http://gallery.carnegiefoundation.org/collections/castl_k12/yhutchinson/). In the remaining sections of this article, we discuss the reasons underlying the "staying power" of QAR and its usefulness across a variety of settings. We frame our discussion in terms of the four problems of practice the QAR framework can address.

Making the Invisible Visible Through QAR

The vocabulary of QAR—In the Book, In My Head, Right There, Think & Search, Author & Me, and On My Own—gives teachers and students a language for talking about the largely invisible processes that constitute listening and reading comprehension across grades and subject areas. Teachers know the value of modeling and thinking aloud to make visible the thought processes involved in higher levels of thinking, but it can be frustrating trying to convey complex ideas without a shared vocabulary. Thus, QAR first and foremost provides teachers and students with a much-needed common language.

How many times and in how many classrooms have conversations (such as the one that follows) taken place when students answer questions after reading or listening to text? In this fifth-grade classroom, students have read and are now writing answers to questions about *Hatchet* (Paulsen, 1987). Brian, the main character, is the lone survivor of a plane crash. He has as his only tool a hatchet. The teacher, Ms. Bendon, notices Alex looking upset as he reads and rereads the text. (Pseudonyms are used for teachers and students.)

Ms. Bendon: Alex, you look like you might need help. What can I do for you?

Alex: I don't get it.

Ms. Bendon: Can you tell me what it is that you don't get?

Alex: I don't know. I just don't get it.

Ms. Bendon: Can you tell me the question you are having trouble with?

Alex: [Turns to the page of questions sitting to the side, and points to the question, "How do you think Brian's hatchet might come in handy?"].

Ms. Bendon: OK, let's think about this. What could you do to help answer this question?

Alex: [shrugs]

Ms. Bendon: [taking the book from Alex] I think you know a lot to help you answer this question. Just think about this some more and I'm sure you'll be able to think of some reasons.

Alex: OK.

Ms. Bendon knew that Alex had background knowledge about hunting, survival strategies, and the use of hatchets and other tools. Thus, she walked away believing that Alex would be fine, because she had cued him to reflect on his background knowledge rather than refer to the text. But instead we see Alex move the question page aside and go back to his already frustrating re-reading strategy; to him, the process of answering the question remains mysterious. He may believe the right answer is found only in the text. He may not want to take risks by using his own knowledge and experience. He may not realize the importance of using his background knowledge in question-answering activities. There are many possibilities for why he "doesn't get it," but they remain unidentified and unarticulated in the absence of a language framework to talk about questioning and related strategies. The original articles written to introduce QAR explained the common vocabulary, but they did not provide guidance about the best approach for introducing this language. Over the years, it has become increasingly clear that there are advantages to introducing QAR language in terms of three binary comparisons: In the Book versus In My Head, Right There versus Think & Search, and Author & Me versus On My Own.

Too often, students of diverse backgrounds are denied access to the language needed to discuss strategies and questions, because the lessons they receive focus largely on lower level skills. We have observed that lessons in the reading programs often used in these classrooms tend to be based on texts that do not challenge or interest students. Questions tend to be limited to the Right There category, and students are not taught strategic or critical thinking. The classroom examples that follow show how teachers can move away from these limitations to provide more effective instruction, especially for students of diverse backgrounds.

Developing QAR's Shared Language

In QAR classrooms during the first few days of school, Ms. Bendon and other teachers introduced students to the basic principle underlying

QAR: that generating and answering questions draws on two core sources of information. As illustrated in Figure 1, these sources are the texts that we read and our background knowledge and experiences; or, in the language of QAR, information that is In the Book or In My Head, respectively. Teachers use QAR language as they emphasize the importance of both sources of information. Furthermore, teachers use QAR language to help students learn to use strategies effectively. For example, they explain how skimming or scanning might lead to details for an In the Book QAR (a typical locate/recall strategy) or how using clues from the title and chapter headings can point to relevant background knowledge for answering an In My Head QAR (a relatively simple interpret/integrate/infer task).

Students like Alex may still say, "I don't get it," but they are more able to describe the strategies they've used and the kind of help they need.

For example, Alex could explain that he has tried three In the Book strategies—rereading, skimming, and scanning—but can't find an answer explaining how a hatchet could help. Ms. Bendon could convey that this is an In My Head QAR and, thus, there are more effective strategies to use for this particular question. Once freed from his focus on the text, Alex could be directed to consider his background knowledge. Furthermore, he could help a peer, Samuel, who has never used tools such as hatchets or gone hunting with family members. Faced with the same question, Samuel could tell Ms. Bendon, "I know it's an In My Head but I went to my head and there's nothing there. Can I talk to Alex?" Armed with QAR language, students can communicate about what they are doing and request the help they need to answer or ask questions effectively.

Students learn about QAR through the comparisons illustrated in Figure 1. To differentiate among the QARs, teachers emphasize the source of information needed to answer the question. Mr. Blanco, a sixth-grade teacher, begins QAR instruction by analyzing the differences between In the Book and In My Head QARs. The text in the lesson is an adapted newspaper article about a heroic gorilla who rescued a toddler at a zoo (Bils & Singer, 1996). Mr. Blanco and his students read short segments, each followed by two questions, one In the Book, one In My Head. The article begins,

> A crowd of visitors at Brookfield Zoo looked on in horror Friday afternoon as they watched a toddler tumble more than 15 feet into a pit, landing near seven gorillas. But as zoo patrons cried out for help, expecting the worst for the 3-year-old boy lying battered on the concrete below, an unlikely hero emerged. (Bils & Singer, p. 1)

The two questions Mr. Blanco asks students to answer and analyze are (1) What caused the visitors to look on in horror? and (2) What do you think makes a hero an unlikely one?

Answering the first question requires readers to use the information in the first two sentences of the text, that a toddler fell 15 feet into a gorilla pit. The horror might be attributed to the length of the fall, the toddler landing in the midst

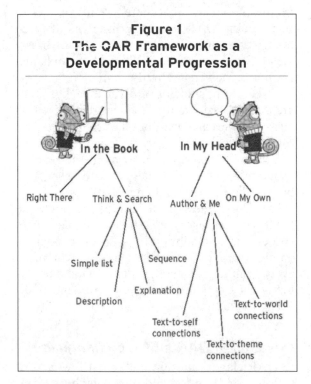

Figure 1
The QAR Framework as a Developmental Progression

In the Book

In My Head

Right There   Think & Search   Author & Me   On My Own

Simple list   Sequence

Description   Explanation

Text-to-self connections

Text-to-theme connections

Text-to-world connections

Note. From Raphael and Au (2001, pp. 4 and 5). Used by permission of the publisher, McGraw-Hill/Wright Group.

of the gorillas, or the toddler lying battered, but the limited information relevant to answering the question is in the text. In contrast, answers to the second question will vary considerably, depending on the background knowledge and experiences of the reader.

QAR instruction should not wait until students are able to read independently. Ms. Rodrigues, a first-grade teacher, introduces her students to the QAR language through listening comprehension activities during her read-aloud program. Like Mr. Blanco, she begins by introducing the categories of In the Book and In My Head. She reads a book's title to her class, then holds up the book and fields the children's comments and questions. She focuses children's attention on the relationships among what they know, the information provided by the text, and their questions. She records children's questions on sticky notes, which she puts on the cover of the book, then asks students to consider sources for answering their questions. She then models how their questions require information from their heads or from the text, introducing the formal language of In the Book and In My Head using a large wall chart.

For example, early in the year, Ms. Rodrigues displayed the cover of the text, *Anansi and the Magic Stick* (Kimmel, 2001). The students looked closely at the cover and began to make comments and ask questions. Martin looked closely at the illustrations on the cover and asked, "Why is there a tomato floating on the water?" Ms. Rodrigues wrote his question on a sticky note and placed it, along with other students' questions, on the front cover. She then asked the students to think about where the information to answer their questions might come from. For Martin's question, Viola suggested that "he could look inside the book when he is reading it and maybe it will say." Ms. Rodrigues reinforced that as one possibility, then asked, "What if you finish reading the book, and you still don't really have an answer? What if the book doesn't exactly tell you?" In this way she introduced the possibility that not all questions may be answered in the text. The students then read the story and paused to talk about relevant information for answering their questions.

Following the reading, Ms. Rodrigues created a two-column chart, with In the Book and In My Head each heading a column. She modeled how to think about the questions they had asked in terms of the source of information needed for answers, placing a sticky note for each question in the appropriate column on the chart.

Regardless of grade level and whether students read independently or participate in shared readings or read alouds, teachers introduce students to the language of QAR by analyzing the differences between questions with answer sources in the book and those where the answer source is students' own heads. Shorter texts work quite effectively for characterizing basic differences between these two information sources, but as students become more experienced with QARs, this simple distinction is not sufficient to capture the range of strategies used to answer and generate questions related to text. Thus, teachers build on In the Book and In My Head by introducing the four core QARs.

Once students are confidently and accurately identifying In the Book QARs, teachers introduce its subcategories, Right There and Think & Search. Similarly, when students are confident and accurate with In My Head QARs, teachers introduce its subcategories, Author & Me and On My Own (see Figure 2 for definitions of each).

Longer passages (e.g., 3–5 paragraphs) are used for this instruction so that students can more easily see the differences between Right There and Think & Search, as well as between Author & Me and On My Own responses.

Mr. Blanco conducted QAR instruction within a unit on immigration. For these QAR lessons, he used the following passages from a short biography of Cesar Chavez, displayed on an overhead transparency:

Cesar Chavez moved from Arizona to California with his family when he was ten years old. He and his family worked as migrant farm laborers. Chavez attended more than thirty-eight schools during his childhood. After eighth grade, he worked full-time to help his family until he left home to fight in World War II.

When he returned home after the war, Chavez learned all he could about labor law and worked at

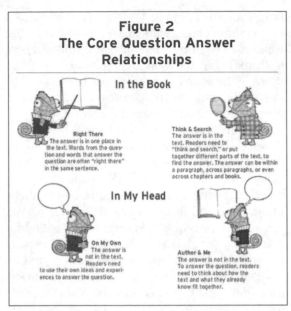

Figure 2
The Core Question Answer Relationships

In the Book

Right There
The answer is in one place in the text. Words from the question and words that answer the question are often "right there" in the same sentence.

Think & Search
The answer is in the text. Readers need to "think and search," or put together different parts of the text, to find the answer. The answer can be within a paragraph, across paragraphs, or even across chapters and books.

In My Head

On My Own
The answer is not in the text. Readers need to use their own ideas and experiences to answer the question.

Author & Me
The answer is not in the text. To answer the question, readers need to think about how the text and what they already know fit together.

Note. From Raphael and Au (2001, pp. 4 and 5). Used by permission of the publisher, McGraw-Hill/Wright Group.

organizing protest marches for the rights of farm laborers. In 1962 he organized the National Farm Workers Association, called La Causa, in Fresno, California. La Causa wanted to stop using dangerous chemicals in the fields. "Our belief is to help everybody, not just one race," Chavez said.

Most farm owners refused to negotiate with La Causa. Some reacted with violence, and local police usually supported the owners. Chavez urged protesting workers to leave their guns and knives at home. "If we used violence, we would have won contracts long ago," he said, "but they wouldn't be lasting because we wouldn't have won respect."

La Causa called for Americans to boycott, or refuse to buy, lettuce and grapes to show their sympathies for the workers. The boycotts were so successful that owners agreed to contracts with the workers.

By the time Chavez died in 1993 he had helped create better lives for thousands of people. Senator Robert F. Kennedy called Chavez "one of the heroic figures of our time." (Raphael & Au, 2001, p. 15)

Mr. Blanco used two questions, written on chart paper, to introduce Right There and Think & Search QARs: (1) How many schools did Chavez attend as a child? and (2) How did Chavez create better lives for thousands of people?

He used a "transfer of control" model of instruction (see Au & Raphael, 1998; Pearson, 1985), beginning by thinking aloud about the information source for the first question. While saying he thought this was an In the Book QAR, he highlighted the words *schools* and *attended* in the first paragraph. He then described scanning the sentence they appeared in for a number that would make sense to answer the question. He circled *thirty-eight* as he said aloud, "This is the answer to the first question." Then he wrote on the chart paper, "Chavez attended 38 schools as a child." He used a similar process of modeling, highlighting, and displaying an answer to the second question, highlighting better working conditions, getting higher pay, and learning to use boycotts rather than violence.

Mr. Blanco then spoke about his own analysis of the differences in what it took to answer the two questions, drawing on the definitions in Figure 2 (Raphael & Au, 2001). He talked about how much more difficult a Think & Search QAR can be for many reasons. Think & Search QARs require that readers find *all* the information that is relevant to the question and then integrate that information into one coherent answer. This is more challenging than finding a detail in the text to respond to a Right There question. Over time and through many examples, Mr. Blanco's students learned to apply the heuristic that their teacher had taught them to reading, social studies, science, and other school subjects, and to a variety of tasks—from answering end-of-chapter questions in their content area subjects to generating inquiry questions for research projects and good discussion questions for student-led book clubs.

To illustrate the differences between the In My Head QARs—Author & Me and On My Own—Mr. Blanco began with the following two questions about the Chavez biography: (1) List characteristics you most admire about Cesar Chavez and describe why you think these are admirable, and (2) Whom do you admire in your family, and why do you admire them? Continuing the same instructional approach, he paired these two questions to illustrate the key difference between Author & Me and On My Own. While both QARs require that readers use information from their background knowledge, to answer an Author & Me, readers need to have read and understood the text. Unless they had prior knowledge, most students would be unable to list admirable characteristics of Cesar Chavez without having read the selection. However, an On My Own QAR does not require students to read the text. For example, students could describe a family member they admire without reading or understanding the biography.

Organizing Comprehension Instruction Through QAR

QAR instruction can be adjusted for use across grade levels and content areas because of the way the categories form a progression of difficulty. This provides an opportunity to coherently frame specific instruction in QAR, as well as more general instruction in the range of high-level comprehension strategies students learn across grade levels.

The use of QAR as a framework for comprehension across the grades and school subjects may be particularly helpful in schools serving many students of diverse backgrounds. Often, under the pressure to raise test scores, teachers in these schools have been implementing highly structured programs focusing on lower level skills. Teachers usually report that they see gains in lower level skills, such as word identification, but not in comprehension and higher level thinking. QAR provides a means for teachers to gain or regain a focus on instruction in comprehension strategies in their classrooms.

Initially, teachers introduce In the Book and In My Head QARs. In early primary grades, some teachers may use only these two categories and may depend on teachers in later grade levels to introduce the next level of categories. Others may begin with the two categories but choose to introduce the next level once certain students understand the two sources well. Research has shown that by second grade, students comfortably learn

to distinguish between Right There and Think & Search QARs (Raphael & McKinney, 1983). Further, research studies have demonstrated that fourth graders understand the differences among the four core QARs (e.g., Raphael & Wonnacott, 1985). Introduction of the core categories varies depending on the knowledge of the teacher as well as the progress of students. However, anecdotal data from teachers such as Ms. Rodrigues suggest that, with appropriate instruction, even young students are able to talk about all four QARs.

Across grade levels and subject areas, teachers continue to use the QAR categories to frame listening and reading comprehension strategy instruction (see Table 2). Although there are exceptions (e.g., reciprocal teaching, transactional strategy instruction, Questioning the Author), many approaches to comprehension instruction are based on teaching individual strategies. However, readers functioning at high levels of literacy use strategies in combination and apply different approaches to strategic thinking, depending on the genre or difficulty of the texts. Understanding how strategies interrelate can be quite abstract for students faced with the need to apply several strategies, as well as quite demanding for teachers in terms of providing effective instruction. Table 2 conveys how QAR can be used to help students see the relationships among the strategies they are learning and the task demands represented by different questions. Table 3 shows how questions asked typically vary across the reading cycle.

Thinking about QAR in this way provides a framework that students can use to link strategies at appropriate points in the reading cycle—whether during their language arts instruction or in other school subjects. Furthermore, the framework guides teachers' modeling of question-asking practices before (e.g., eliciting relevant background knowledge), during (e.g., focusing on important information, locating key terms, making inferences about key plot events or character motivation), and after reading (e.g., considering themes, building arguments about author intent supported by text evidence). Understanding and control of strategies learned helps readers engage

Table 2
Using QAR to Frame Comprehension Strategy Instruction

QAR	Sample comprehension strategies
On My Own	1. Activating prior knowledge (e.g., about genre, experiences, authors) 2. Connecting to the topic (e.g., self-to-text)
Right There	1. Scanning to locate information 2. Note-taking strategies to support easier recall of key information 3. Using context clues for creating definitions
Think & Search	1. Identifying important information 2. Summarizing 3. Using text organization (e.g., comparison/contrast, problem/solution, list, explanation) to identify relevant information 4. Visualizing (e.g., setting, mood, procedures) 5. Using context to describe symbols and figurative language 6. Clarifying 7. Making text-to-text connections 8. Making simple inferences
Author & Me	1. Predicting 2. Visualizing 3. Making simple and complex inferences 4. Distinguishing fact and opinion 5. Making text-to-self connections

in the high levels of literacy for which they are accountable in their day-to-day classroom literacy activities and in high-stakes assessments at the district, state, and national levels.

Whole-School Reform Through QAR

The efforts of an individual teacher to provide effective comprehension strategy instruction can certainly contribute to improvements in students' achievement. However, more than one year of instruction by an individual teacher is usually required to bring students of diverse backgrounds to high levels of literacy and to ensure their continued success as readers. There has been increasing recognition that to have the strongest effect on students' literacy development, we should look to the school as the unit of change (Cunningham & Creamer, 2003) and

organize professional development to promote teacher learning that leads to a coherent, schoolwide approach to literacy instruction. Coherence is central to students' literacy success on informal and high-stakes assessments (Newmann, Smith, Allensworth, & Bryk, 2001; Taylor et al., 2003). Coherent efforts are particularly needed for increasing the access of students of diverse backgrounds to the kind of reading comprehension instruction that will close the literacy achievement gap.

In the United States, under the influence of the federally funded Comprehensive School Reform program of 2001, many schools—enrolling considerable numbers of students of diverse backgrounds—purchased packaged programs that emphasized lower level skills (Viadero, 2004). The problem with reform efforts based on packaged programs is that they do not foster the kinds of conversations among teachers within and across grades that can lead to coherent and

Table 3
Using QAR to Frame Questioning Within the Reading Cycle

Before reading	**On My Own** From the title or the topic, what do I already know that can connect me to the story or text? **Author & Me** From the topic, title, illustrations, or book cover, what might this story or text be about?
During reading	**Author & Me** What do I think will happen next? How would I describe the mood of the story and why is this important? **Think & Search** What is the problem and how is it resolved? What role do [insert characters' names] play in the story? What are the important events? (literary, informational) **Right There** Who is the main character? (literary) Indentify the topic sentence in this paragraph. (informational) What are some words that decribe the setting? (literary)
After reading	**Author & Me** What is the author's message? What is the theme and how is it connected to the world beyond the story? How can I synthesize the information with what I know from other sources? How well does the author make his or her argument? How is the author using particular language to influence our beliefs? **Think & Search** Find evidence in the text to support an argument.

cohesive literacy instruction. Research (e.g., Anders & Richardson, 1991; Duffy, 2004; Taylor, Pearson, Peterson, & Rodriguez, 2005) suggests that a schoolwide approach based on collaboration and long-term commitment is more effective than top-down models or packaged programs designed as a "quick fix." Our observations suggest that schools serving students of diverse backgrounds often prefer to rely on packaged programs rather than undertaking the long-term professional development efforts that are likely to be more effective. The reasons that such schools favor packaged programs include large numbers of inexperienced teachers, high rates of teacher turnover, and a lack of the expertise or funding needed to carry out systematic, multiyear professional development.

As a framework that is relatively simple and straightforward, yet applicable across grade levels and subject areas, QAR has potential for schoolwide professional development. The QAR framework helps organize comprehension instruction within and across grade levels and serves as a bridge between study of the language arts and other subjects. The application is clear for both day-to-day classroom activities as well as high-stakes assessments. In addition, it is not based on a particular ideology (e.g., it can be applied within basal reading instructional programs or literature-based instruction or content area instruction). The QAR framework can be a starting point for conversations that lead teachers to think deeply about reading comprehension instruction to promote sustained changes in practice.

For example, teachers at one of the largest elementary schools in Hawaii use QAR to frame comprehension instruction in their ongoing efforts to improve their students' reading achievement. To implement a schoolwide focus on reading comprehension, teachers mapped their end-of-year targets for student learning in terms of grade-level benchmarks related to state standards. The QAR framework laid out in Figure 1 helps a school with such mapping. In this case, the first-grade teachers agreed to teach In the Book and In My Head QARs. The third-grade teachers agreed to teach their students all four of the core categories. Teachers in the fourth through sixth grades agreed to emphasize Think & Search, which students could use with both fiction and nonfiction texts.

At this school, teachers in special education as well as in general education use the language of QAR. One of the special education teachers developed approaches for teaching her students about QARs by drawing on multiple modalities. She created rhythmic chants for In the Book and In My Head. She used sentence strips so that students could physically match questions and answers. She created charts for each category to help students better understand the meaning of "sources of information." As shown in Figure 3, one of the charts was developed as students brainstormed places that information comes from before it eventually ends up in our heads. She then helped students identify which of these information sources could be read, putting an *R* in the box by the source.

Having the common language of QAR can help teachers know how to proceed when they are seeking to improve comprehension instruction. For example, when examining the results of their classroom-based assessments, the first-grade teachers at this school noticed that their students had trouble making inferences. As they discussed the problem, one of the teachers had an idea. She explained to the other teachers that the problem might lie in the fact that they had been teaching only the QAR categories of In the Book and In My Head. However, to answer questions requiring inferences, children needed to know the category of Author & Me. At the time, Author & Me was being introduced to students in later grades, but the first-grade teachers decided that they should begin teaching it.

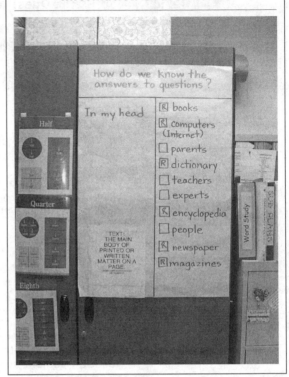

Figure 3
Information Source Chart

Note. Photograph by the authors.

Consistent QAR instruction across the grades and school subjects establishes the foundation for improved reading and listening comprehension. By the time students are in intermediate grades, those who have received consistent QAR instruction develop sophisticated strategies to analyze questions and use appropriate strategies and language for formulating good answers. For example, Kathy Highfield documented students' use of QARs from third through fourth grade (Highfield, 2003). She found several examples of students' theorizing about how questions work as well as appropriate strategies for answering questions. For example, students in her classroom discovered that the word *you* may signal that the question is either an On My Own or Author & Me, while they also recognized that this is not always the case.

Highfield (2003) found that students learned to value skimming or rereading strategies to locate specific information in the text for Right There QARs (and the occasional Think & Search), while simultaneously recognizing the role of their prior knowledge in answering questions. They even began to debate individual differences in the way QARs might apply as they read and responded to questions. Toward spring of fourth grade, Highfield eavesdropped as two students debated whether a question represented a Right There or an On My Own QAR. After the debate had gone on for a few minutes, one student explained that for her, it was an On My Own because she already knew the information to answer the question, but for her peer, it was a Right There, because she didn't already have the information and had to get it from the book. Such metacognitive knowledge about questioning and related strategies supports students in their day-to-day work with text, as well as when they must take a high-stakes test.

Accountability and Test Preparation Through QAR

Educators in U.S. schools are under increasing pressure to improve students' reading performance, as measured by scores on standardized and state reading tests. This pressure is greatest in schools with histories of low test scores, and these are schools that often have high proportions of students of diverse backgrounds. In their attempts to raise test scores, these schools inadvertently lower the quality of educational experiences. For example, one common response is to narrow the curriculum to focus on tested subjects such as reading and math, to the exclusion of subjects such as science, social studies, the arts, and physical education (Smith, 1991). Another common response, often months prior to spring testing, is to spend the bulk of instructional time on test preparation.

Test preparation typically takes the form of having students complete workbook exercises with items of a form and content ostensibly similar to those on upcoming tests. In general, students practice by reading short passages and responding to multiple-choice items. Most test preparation packages involve little or no instruction by the teacher. The problem with practice-only activities is that students who have not already acquired reading comprehension strategies gain little or nothing from the large amounts of time spent on these activities. Some students will muddle through as best they can, using the coping techniques at their disposal, while other students simply quit trying altogether. Teachers in schools following these practices have reported to us that many students of diverse backgrounds experience burnout and discouragement. These students lack motivation by the time large-scale testing actually occurs. For these reasons, practice-only test preparation activities cannot be expected to improve the test scores of most students of diverse backgrounds, much less help them to become better readers and thinkers.

With QAR as the framework for teaching listening and reading comprehension strategies, within a rich curriculum in language arts and other school subjects, teachers can help students be strategic when faced with the texts and tasks on high-stakes tests. As we described earlier, the trend in national assessments is toward ever higher levels of literacy, moving away from a heavy emphasis on locating and recalling information to require that students integrate ideas across texts, draw inferences, critique, and evaluate.

To illustrate this trend, we present an analysis of the 12 questions on a fourth-grade NAEP reading selection, "Watch Out for Wombats!" (Donahue et al., 2003). An overview of the questions and their characteristics is presented in Table 4. There are 6 multiple-choice questions, 5 short constructed responses, and 1 extended constructed response. For 4 of the multiple-choice questions, the QAR is Right There. For 1 of the remaining multiple-choice questions, the QAR is Author & Me, and for the other, Think & Search. Thus, even multiple-choice questions on the NAEP may go beyond simple forms of comprehension. With the 5 short constructed response items, 3 reflect the Think & Search QAR, while 1 is an Author & Me and the other a Right There. For the extended constructed response, the QAR

Table 4
Analysis of NAEP Sample Passage Questions

Question	Format	QAR and Strategies
1. This article mostly describes how....	Multiple choice	Think & Search • Identifying important information • Summarizing • Making simple inferences
2. Where do wombats live?	Multiple choice	Right There • Scanning to locate information
3. Describe one way in which wombats and koalas are similar and one way in which they are different.	Short constructed response	Think & Search • Visualizing • Identifying important information • Using text organization to identify relevant information • Summarizing
4. Use the information in this passage to describe marsupials.	Short constructed response	Think & Search • Visualizing • Identify important information • Using text organization to identify relevant information • Summarizing
5. Where do wombats usually live?	Multiple choice	Right There • Scanning to locate information
6. Choose an animal, other than a koala, that you know about and compare it to the wombat.	Short constructed response	Author & Me • Visualizing • Making simple and complex inferences (to compare) • Making text-to-self connections
7. Why are wombats not often seen by people?	Multiple choice	Right There • Scanning to locate information
8. Describe the sleeping area of wombats.	Short constructed response	Right There • Scanning to locate information • Note-taking to support easier recall
9. To get food, the wombat uses its....	Multiple choice	Right There • Scanning to locate information
10. What would a wombat probably do if it met a person?	Multiple choice	Author & Me • Predicting • Making simple and complex inferences
11. Why has Australia set up animal reserves to protect the wombat?	Short constructed response	Think & Search • Identifying important information • Using text organization to identify relevant information • Making simple inferences
12. Give two reasons why people should not have wombats as pets. Use what you learned in the passage to support your answer.	Extended constructed response	Author & Me • Identifying important information • Making complex inferences • Visualizing

Note. Questions retrieved June 14, 2005, from http://nces.ed.gov/nationsreportcard/ITMRLS/search.asp?picksubj=Reading

is Author & Me. In total, students are required to answer 5 Right There items, 3 Author & Me items, and 4 Think & Search items. This analysis shows the shift toward higher level comprehension in current assessments and also highlights the fact that there is not a simple one-to-one correspondence between question format and QAR in current reading assessments. Specifically, multiple-choice questions do not always have a QAR of Right There. It is clear that teachers who want their students to perform well on reading tests would be wise to provide instruction in all the QARs and the reading strategies associated with them, as listed in Table 2. Instruction should foster students' independence in the application of QARs and reading strategies, as well as a mindset toward critical evaluation.

Through QAR instruction, teachers do not need to teach to a particular test but instead are able to unpack the task demands of different types of questions and alert students to these demands as appropriate to the different tests students face. For example, in 2003 on the Illinois State Achievement Test, many students were not successful when required to write an extended response. The state's definition for success required that students meet the following criteria:

- Demonstrate an accurate understanding of important information in the text by focusing on the key ideas presented explicitly or implicitly.
- Use information from the text to interpret significant concepts or make connections to other situations or contexts logically through analysis, evaluation, inference, or comparison/contrast.
- Use relevant and accurate references; most are specific and fully supported.
- Integrate interpretation of the text with text-based support (Illinois State Board of Education, 2004).

Many students simply wrote a personal response without making explicit connections to the text. Others wrote about the text but did not include any personal connections. Simply writing an extended essay was not sufficient. To be successful, students needed to identify the QAR as Author & Me and compose a written response including both text ideas and a personal connection.

Concluding Comments

We believe QAR addresses four troubling problems of practice today, particularly involving students of diverse backgrounds who often receive little literacy instruction oriented to promoting high levels of thinking about text. First, QAR can help address the lack of a shared language among teachers and students for improving questioning practices, whether in the day-to-day life of the classroom, in students' activities outside of school, or in high-stakes testing situations. Second, QAR can bring coherence to literacy instruction within and across grade levels by providing a framework for a developmental progression for comprehension instruction. As a framework, QAR provides a means for organizing comprehension strategy instruction. Third, QAR provides a focal point to begin sustained efforts for whole-school reform aimed at higher standards for literacy learning and teaching. It is difficult to find points of contact that bring teachers from kindergarten through middle school to the table with the same high levels of interest. Yet all readers at all grades can benefit from learning to think in terms of information sources for answering and asking questions. Fourth, QAR provides a responsible approach to preparing students for high-stakes tests at different grade levels and in a variety of subject areas, without detracting from the high-quality instruction that leads to high levels of literacy.

Using the QAR framework can provide benefits to schools, teachers, and students for a relatively small amount of time and effort. For schools, the benefit comes in the chance to pull the grade levels together around reading comprehension instruction. For teachers, the benefit is found in the opportunity to improve instruction around questioning activities and reading comprehension. For students, the benefit lies in gaining access to reading comprehension and higher level thinking with text—an opportunity often unavailable to those of diverse backgrounds.

References

Anders, P., & Richardson, V. (1991). Research directions: Staff development that empowers teachers' reflection and enhances instruction. *Language Arts, 68,* 316–321.

Au, K.H. (1993). *Literacy instruction in multicultural settings.* Fort Worth, TX: Harcourt Brace Jovanovich College.

Au, K.H. (2003). Literacy research and students of diverse backgrounds: What does it take to improve achievement? In C.M. Fairbanks, J. Worthy, B. Maloch, J.V. Hoffman, & D.L. Schallert (Eds.), *52nd yearbook of the National Reading Conference* (pp. 85–91). Oak Creek, WI: National Reading Conference.

Au, K.H., & Raphael, T.E. (1998). Curriculum and teaching in literature-based programs. In T.E. Raphael & K.H. Au (Eds.), *Literature-based instruction: Reshaping the curriculum* (pp. 123–148). Norwood, MA: Christopher-Gordon.

Bils, J., & Singer, S. (1996, August 17). Gorilla saves tot in Brookfield Zoo ape pit. *Chicago Tribune,* p. 1.

Cunningham, J.W., & Creamer, K.H. (2003). Achieving best practices in literacy education. In L.M. Morrow, L.B. Gambrell & M. Pressley (Eds.), *Best practices in literacy education* (2nd ed., pp. 333–346). New York: Guilford.

Darling-Hammond, L. (1995). Inequality and access to knowledge. In J.A. Banks & C.A.M. Banks (Eds.), *Handbook of research on multicultural education* (pp. 465–483). New York: Macmillan.

Donahue, P., Daane, M., & Grigg, W. (2003). *The nation's report card: Reading highlights 2003* (NCES 2004-452). Washington, DC: National Assessment of Educational Progress.

Duffy, G.G. (2004). Teachers who improve reading achievement: What research says about what they do and how to develop them. In D.S. Strickland & M.L. Kamil (Eds.), *Improving reading achievement through professional development* (pp. 3–22). Norwood, MA: Christopher-Gordon.

Fitzgerald, J. (1995). English-as-a-second-language reading instruction in the United States: A research review. *Journal of Reading Behavior, 27,* 115–152.

Grigg, W.S., Daane, M.C., Jin, Y., & Campbell, J.R. (2003). *The nation's report card: Reading 2002* (NCES 2003-521). Washington, DC: U.S. Department of Education, Institute for Education Sciences.

Highfield, K. (2003). *QAR and test preparation in a fourth grade classroom.* Unpublished dissertation, Oakland University, Rochester, MI.

Illinois State Board of Education. (2004). *Extended-response reading rubric.* Retrieved June 14, 2005, from www.isbe.net/assessment/readrubric.htm

Kimmel, E.A. (2001). *Anansi and the magic stick.* Ill. J. Stevens. New York: Holiday House.

Leu, D.J., & Kinzer, C.K. (2003). *Effective literacy instruction: Implementing best practice K–8* (5th ed.). Upper Saddle River, NJ: Pearson Education.

Mesmer, H.A.E., & Hutchins, E.J. (2002). Using QARs with charts and graphs. *The Reading Teacher, 56,* 21–27.

National Assessment Governing Board. (2004). *Reading Framework for the 2009 National Assessment of Educational Progress* (Contract No. ED-02-R-0007). Washington, DC: American Institutes for Research.

Newmann, F.M., Smith, B.S., Allensworth, E., & Bryk, A.S. (2001). Instructional program coherence: What it is and why it should guide school improvement policy. *Education, Evaluation, and Policy Analysis, 23,* 297–321.

Oakes, J., & Guiton, G. (1995). Matchmaking: The dynamics of high school tracking decisions. *American Educational Research Journal, 32,* 3–33.

Paulsen, G. (1987). *Hatchet.* New York: Puffin Books.

Pearson, P.D. (1985). Changing the face of reading comprehension instruction. *The Reading Teacher, 38,* 724–738.

Pressley, M. (2002). Comprehension strategies instruction. In C.C. Block & M. Pressley (Eds.), *Comprehension instruction: Research based best practices* (pp. 11–27). New York: Guilford.

Raphael, T.E., & Au, K.H. (2001). *SuperQAR for testwise students: Teacher resource guide, Guide 6.* Chicago: McGraw-Hill/Wright.

Raphael, T.E., & McKinney, J. (1983). An examination of 5th and 8th grade children's question answering behavior: An instructional study in metacognition. *Journal of Reading Behavior, 15,* 67–86.

Raphael, T.E., & Pearson, P.D. (1985). Increasing students' awareness of sources of information for answering questions. *American Educational Research Journal, 22,* 217–236.

Raphael, T.E., & Wonnacott, C.A. (1985). Heightening fourth-grade students' sensitivity to sources of information for answering comprehension questions. *Reading Research Quarterly, 20,* 282–296.

Reutzel, D.R., & Cooper, R.B. (2004). *Teaching children to read: Putting the pieces together* (4th ed.). Upper Saddle River, NJ: Pearson Education.

Roe, B.D., Smith, S.H., & Burns, P.C. (2005). *Teaching reading in today's elementary schools* (9th ed.). Boston: Houghton Mifflin.

Smith, M.L. (1991). Put to the test: The effects of external testing on teachers. *Educational Researcher, 20,* 8–11.

Snow, C.E. (2002). *Reading for understanding: Toward an R&D program in reading comprehension.* Santa Monica, CA: RAND.

Sweet, A.P., & Snow, C.E. (Eds.). (2003). *Rethinking reading comprehension: Solving problems in teaching of literacy.* New York: Guilford.

Taylor, B.M., Pearson, P.D., Peterson, D.P., & Rodriguez, M.C. (2003). Reading growth in high-poverty classrooms: The influence of teacher practices that encourage cognitive engagement in literacy learning. *The Elementary School Journal, 104,* 3–28.

Taylor, B.M., Pearson, P.D., Peterson, D.P., & Rodriguez, M.C. (2005). The CIERA school change framework: An evidenced-based approach to professional development and school reading improvement. *Reading Research Quarterly, 40,* 40–69.

Vacca, J.L., Vacca, R.T., Grove, M.K., Burkey, L., Lenhart, L., & McKeon, C. (2003). *Reading and learning to read* (5th ed.). Boston: Allyn & Bacon.
Viadero, D. (2004, April 21). Reform programs backed by research find fewer takers. *Education Week,* 1–5.

Questions for Reflection

• In what ways can you imagine extending your use of QARs into content area subjects in addition to the social studies examples in the article? Think about texts in science or math, for example. What features do they include that lend themselves to this approach?

• Think about the high-stakes tests used in your school, district, or state. How do they compare in format to the NAEP sample given in Table 4? How might you use QAR to help prepare your students for the high-stakes tests that they face this year? Would QAR be equally helpful across subject areas in which students are tested?

• QAR is a language for talking with your students to take the mystery out of activities that involve questions. How might you use QAR language to take the mystery out of common classroom activities that involve questions, such as engaging in inquiry or preparing for student-led or teacher-student discussions of text?

Expansion Modules for the ReQuest, CAT, GRP, and REAP Reading/Study Procedures

Anthony V. Manzo

Too often, teaching techniques once shared with the profession are not updated or expanded to achieve new goals. I would therefore like to share with others some improvements made on four earlier study/learning procedures: ReQuest, the CAT game, GRP, and REAP.

Teachers who are already using these procedures will, I hope, be interested in the newer suggestions, and perhaps other teachers will be stimulated also to go back to the original descriptive articles—all of which appeared in earlier issues of this very journal—and try the techniques with their own students.

Most of the modifications noted here are in the direction of increasing student metacognition and independence. Metacognition is a heightened awareness of personal thought processes and is considered a significant factor in better monitoring and regulating one's own reading, language, thinking skills, and general behavior. A brief postscript (more of a metamusing) will note the potential significance of metacognition to any educational theory and practice.

ReQuest '69 vs. '85: Change the Question

Once a purpose for reading has been evolved using the Reciprocal Questioning Procedure (Manzo, 1969), it is now recommended that the teacher should not ask the purpose question first, as was previously recommended, but should ask this more strategic question: "Did we raise (evolve) the best question or purpose for which to read this selection?"

This self-evaluative question helps to better mobilize three of the more valuable features of the ReQuest Procedure: (1) It puts emphasis upon acquiring a *strategy* for reading and learning more than just "getting through" the selection at hand; (2) it gives the student an opportunity to reciprocally influence the direction of the lesson and therefore rewards self-monitoring behaviors; and (3) the newly emphasized requirement to think and talk on this elevated level causes the student to be more mindful of the language and thought patterns of the teacher and other more language sophisticated students (where the procedure is used in a group setting). In this way students begin to emulate question-answering as well as question-asking behaviors. This use of modeling contributes to the learning of complex cognitive, language, and social skills in a holistic and robust manner.

The inspiration for using modeling to improve social thinking and language skills came from social and imitation learning theory. This theory structure is still not used very much in the development of cognitive and potentially metacognitive skills (see Bandura, 1977; Miller & Dollard, 1941).

Reprinted from Manzo, A.V. (1985). Expansion modules for the ReQuest, CAT, GRP, and REAP reading/study procedures. *Journal of Reading, 28*(6), 498-502.

CAT '70 vs. '85: Emphasize Allusions

There is a good chance that the Cultural Academic Trivia game (Manzo, 1970) has been forgotten by many readers, so this update is both a reminder and a recommendation for its expanded use.

Students are told that an index card containing a word, name, or commonly acknowledged fact is to be their legitimate admission ticket to class each Monday. These cards are then shuffled and a game is played each week. Points are given by the teacher based upon whether a player gives a response that is a simple association, information, or an allusion. It is the qualitative scoring and emphasis upon the value of allusions as a form of vocabulary which constitutes the expansion feature of CAT '85. Here is an example:

Stimulus: "Geraldine Ferraro"?

1 point (association level response): "A woman in U.S. politics."

2 points (information level responses): "A Congresswoman," "A vice-presidential candidate of the Democratic Party," "An Italian-American candidate for high office."

3 points (allusion level responses): "A symbol of progress in the stature of women in American life," "An indication of the growing acceptance of ethnic Americans into the American mainstream and of the changing nature of that mainstream."

CAT is more timely today than at first publication due to the popularity of the game Trivial Pursuit as well as the broader acknowledgement of the roles of prior knowledge and anaphoria, or understanding parenthetical expressions, in effective communication.

Emphasis upon learning common allusions, and how to create and use these, should contribute to metaphoric thinking and therefore to effective reading, speaking, and writing. In this way CAT, too, heightens metacognitive growth by increasing awareness of our use of allusions in receptive and expressive thinking.

GRP '75 vs. '85: Add Step 9

The Guided Reading Procedure (Manzo, 1975) is cited most frequently as a means for improving unaided recall and organizational skills. Occasionally it is remembered for its emphasis upon the (meta) attitudinal factors of awareness of the need to be more self-determinately accurate and self-correcting in reading. The growing understanding and appreciation of the role of metacognitive (and attitudinal) level functioning now makes it easier to suggest a more definitive step for achieving this end.

Essentially, a ninth step is added to create GRP '85. It amounts to posing the following question on occasion to the class: "Have you learned something about the best ways to read and to learn from today's lesson activity?" The point of the question, however one might actually phrase it, is to have students probe more consciously for an understanding of the role and importance of self-determination as a factor in *personal* reading-learning outcomes.

This question is best reserved for those teachable moments when an especially telling GRP lesson has come together. The insights and resolutions reached can be considerable and durable.

REAP '76 vs. '85: Add 3 Types of Annotations

The Read, Encode, Annotate, and Ponder Procedure (Eanet & Manzo, 1976) is based upon the proposition that the charge to write one of several specified types of annotations following silent reading raises the act from a passive to a more active thought process. This proposition recently has been further supported by Rumelhart (1978) and others.

Inherent in this proposition is the belief that the act of writing, and of reading the annotations of others, stimulates students to think and write in ways which may have occurred to them but appeared too ill formed or unconventional to be expressed.

Now, as emphasis upon creative production, self-directed learning, and metacognitive awareness continues to grow, it is more feasible to suggest still other annotation models for REAP users. Three are described and illustrated here. The illustrations are based upon the same passage from *Summerhill* (Neill, 1960) as can be found in the original article describing REAP.

One of the original annotation forms, the thesis annotation is stated first as a reminder of the major precept of Neill's blueprint for an "unrestrained" approach to education and moral development.

Thesis annotation (REAP '76): An incisive précis-like statement of the root idea of the article or book. For example: "Children have natural needs. Moral instruction conflicts with natural needs. This contradiction causes delinquent behavior. Eliminate moral instruction."

The probe annotation (REAP '85): Focus is given to practical points and questions which deserve further exploration before a reasoned judgment can be reached. Emphasis is given to *verification*, *consequences*, and *alternatives*. For example: "Has Neill's system of education been tested against more traditional approaches? What would be the full consequences to schools and students if such a system were to be adopted? Are there other ways to resolve the dilemma he poses?"

Personal view annotation (REAP '85): This annotation form answers the question "How do personal experiences, views, and feelings stack up against the thesis or main idea?" For example: "I have known at least a few persons who struck me as being inherently troubled and therefore inclined to be delinquent. It seems as if it takes the lives of several other persons to keep them 'straight.' Modifying education to meet their needs might not be possible, fair, nor cost-effective in human terms."

The inventive annotation (REAP '85): An intentionally constructive point of view is taken, one drawn from another context or synthesized for the occasion. For example: "Children need both structure and freedom. Replace *moral* instruction with *ethical* instruction. Ethics flows from a profound understanding of natural human needs rather than religious beliefs. Fundamental human needs also are more common across time and cultures and, therefore, more appropriate for a complex society."

Notably, REAP '85 encourages some strongly introspective and risky thinking. The justification is simple, however: The times are risky, life is more complex and complicated than ever before, and it is time to deal more directly and candidly with what we read and really think, or at least think we think. The new REAP forms offer a potential outlet for reducing the kinds of (mis-) apprehensions which tend to warp comprehension, effective thinking, writing, and personal-social adjustment.

On a purely practical level, it seems proper to wonder whether such annotation forms can be learned and generated by students and at what age and grade levels. Field experience and imitation learning theory suggest that these can be learned more easily than one might think, because once a model is presented of candid and creative thinking, it no longer is an abstraction or an unknown. Of course, most everyone, teachers included, will tend to be a little clumsy with some of these representations initially. There are few models of invention and candor to emulate. This paucity should be overcome, however, as teacher demand and student determination to be inventive are converted into some exemplary levels of constructive writing.

Presently, study is underway of the best age at which to teach each annotation type and of the effect of each annotation form (old and new) upon reading comprehension, creative and critical thinking, and apprehension or perception and mind set. Collective growth in ability to generate these new forms is expected to contribute to "world view," as Chall recently called the highest level of reading progress (Chall, 1983).

Related efforts to better measure such stages of progress toward reading maturity also are progressing. A broad spectrum battery of experimental tests spanning aspects of reading, language, thinking, social-emotional and learning style factors is available at no cost for use in research and evaluation (Manzo & Casale, 1981, 1983).

Metacognition as an Affective Feature

The growing popularity of metacognitive theory deserves further reflection in itself, if we reading professionals are to grasp more fully what it is that we are doing, and why.

Metacognitive theory seems to stem from an essentially psychoanalytic idea that wherever conscious expression is given to subconscious thoughts, the individual will be better able to monitor and self-correct patterns of thought and behavior. This is an affective feature of education.

The joining of this affective feature to the more behavioristic skills-and-practice tradition of education offers promise of more penetrating and generative methods of instruction. This union also should help to reverse a recurring problem noted by Krathwohl, Bloom, and Masia (1964, p. 16), authors of the prevailing Taxonomy of the Affective Domain, namely that there is a noticeable "erosion of affective objectives [from their initially intended levels] in most all courses and educational programs [observed]."

References

Bandura, A. (1977). *Social learning theory*. Englewood Cliffs, NJ: Prentice Hall.

Chall, J. (1983). *Stages of reading development*. Englewood Cliffs, NJ: Prentice Hall.

Eanet, M.G., & Manzo, A.V. (1976, May). REAP—A strategy for improving reading/writing/study skills. *Journal of Reading, 19*, 647–652.

Krathwohl, D., Bloom, B., & Masia, B. (1964). *Taxonomy of educational objectives. Handbook II: Affective domain*. New York: David McKay.

Manzo, A.V. (1969, November). The ReQuest Procedure. *Journal of Reading, 13*, 123–126.

Manzo, A.V. (1970, February). CAT—A game for extending vocabulary and knowledge of allusions. *Journal of Reading, 14*, 367–369.

Manzo, A.V. (1975, January). Guided Reading Procedure. *Journal of Reading, 18*, 287–291.

Manzo, A.V., & Casale, U.P. (1981). A regression analysis of conventional and "mature comprehension." In G. McNintch (Ed.), *First yearbook of the American Reading Forum*. Athens, GA: American Reading Forum.

Manzo, A.V., & Casale, U. (1983, April–June). A preliminary description and factor analysis of a broad spectrum battery for assessing "pgoress toward reading maturity." *Journal of Reading Psychology, 4*, 181–191.

Miller, N.E., & Dollard, J. (1941). *Social and imitation learning theory*. New Haven, CT: Yale University Press.

Neill, A.S. (1960). *Summerhill*. New York: Harcourt Brace Jovanovich.

Rumelhart, D. (1978). *Schemata: The building blocks of cognition* (Tech. Rep. No. 79). San Diego, CA: Center for Human Information Processing, University of California.

Questions for Reflection

- This article was published in 1985 and updates articles published earlier in the 20th century. If you have used any of the strategies it describes, think about how you have or could update them still further to meet current teaching contexts. What has changed in your classroom, and how have your instructional strategies kept pace?

- One of the benefits of the REAP activity is that it engages students during their own silent reading. How might discussion be woven in as a postreading activity to further engage students? How could such discussion be structured or guided to deepen reading comprehension?

A Picture Is Worth a Thousand Words: Using Visual Images to Improve Comprehension for Middle School Struggling Readers

Anne Nielsen Hibbing and Joan L. Rankin-Erickson

We are surrounded by visual imagery through television, movies, videos, computers, and illustrated texts. The use of these sources of images is obvious as one walks through a school. Classrooms in the United States often have computers, televisions, and VCRs. School classrooms, media centers, and computer labs are filled with visual images. Unfortunately this bombardment of visual images does not necessarily transfer to students' ability to create mental images that support reading comprehension. We have found that our students who lack the ability to create visual images when reading often experience comprehension difficulties. For these students the adage "A picture is worth a thousand words" is particularly relevant as they maneuver their way through the informational maze of learning from text. We asked our students to reflect upon that quote and write their thoughts in their journals. These middle school reluctant readers responded with comments such as the following (all comments are presented as written by students):

- A picture helps me by showing what's going on.
- In my textbooks when they show pictures it helps me see what they are talking about.

- If you look at a picture, it puts more ideas in your head.
- If you have a picture it may take a thousand words to get the true meaning of the picture.

These statements indicate the students' understanding of the supportive roles pictures play in helping them understand what they read.

We noticed that many of our reluctant and low-ability readers with comprehension difficulties were not able to describe the pictures in their minds as they read. Over our years of teaching we've had several students who claimed to "see nothing" as a result of their reading. This is not surprising given the issues faced by many of our students, specifically, limited vocabulary, little background knowledge about many topics, lack of understanding of the relationships represented in the language of the text, and lack of awareness that attempting to visualize what is happening might be helpful. Students are confronted regularly with the continuous images of television or video that create the visual representation for them. Students may become dependent on the action sequence of images because these images provide a concrete representation of actions, ideas, time, and space. Gaining meaning from an action sequence, as in television or video, is very

Reprinted from Hibbing, A.N., & Rankin-Erickson, J.L. (2003). A picture is worth a thousand words: Using visual images to improve comprehension for middle school struggling readers. *The Reading Teacher, 56*(8), 758-770.

different than using one's own concrete external experiences to create internal visual images that support comprehension.

As scholar-practitioners, we have paid close attention to the development of imagery skills in our students. We have noticed that the strategic use of visual material can enhance reading experiences for reluctant and low-ability readers and, indeed, can help them become more proficient creators of internal visual imagery that supports comprehension. In this article we discuss instructional tools appropriate for middle-level students that use external visual images to build comprehension and are supported by the research on mental imagery. We present a summary of points practitioners will want to consider when using sketches, illustrations, picture books, and movies with reluctant and low-ability middle school readers.

Pictures in the Mind—Mental Imagery

The role of imagery in making sense of text has its theoretical roots in the work of Allan Paivio and his colleagues (Clark & Paivio, 1991; Paivio, 1971, 1983, 1986; Sadoski, Paivio, & Goetz, 1991). From this perspective, knowledge is represented both verbally and nonverbally in what is referred to as a dual-coding system, including both verbal and nonverbal representations of knowledge. Verbal representations of knowledge are composed of words (the verbal code) for objects, events, and ideas. The imagery or nonverbal system represents knowledge in "nonverbal representations that retain some resemblance to the perceptions giving rise to them" (Pressley & McCormick, 1995, p. 71). For example, the words *hot dog* may evoke a series of verbal representations—"something you eat in a bun," "made of ground animal parts," "high in preservatives," and so on. *Hot dog* may also evoke nonverbal images that share some features with the actual perception or experience. Nonverbal images may include a visual image of a particular hot dog (the one I drooled over yesterday), an olfactory image (the smell of hot dogs on a grill),

a visual image of a context where hot dogs have been eaten (the baseball game when my son's team lost), emotional responses related to an event that included hot dogs (the disappointment team parents shared watching their sons leave the field), or other nonlinguistic images associated with *hot dog*. According to dual-coding theory, it is possible to have nonverbal images only or images that also include associated words.

The concept of dual coding, or the coding of knowledge in both verbal and nonverbal representations, suggests that the elements of both systems are intricately connected. This connection between the verbal and nonverbal coding systems allows us to create images when we hear words and to generate names or descriptions of things we see in pictures. In fact, there is some evidence that successful readers do this automatically and that the inability to make verbal and nonverbal connections quickly and efficiently is related to learning disabilities (Swanson, 1989).

We have observed that creating a mental image of what is read is a natural process for our more proficient readers. In fact, when images do not come easily to our proficient readers, they see it as a warning that there is a breakdown in comprehension and are aware of the need to use a fix-up strategy (e.g., reread, adjust rate of reading, refocus). In contrast, many of the low-ability and reluctant readers with whom we have worked do not automatically create images or are unable to do so even with conscious effort. Rather than creating images associated with meaning, many of our struggling readers are focusing on the decoding of words. When asked about the reading that he had just completed, Shaun (pseudonym) put it this way, "I don't know what happened, I was too busy reading the words."

The more we encountered students like Shaun, the more we became aware of the specific challenges faced by our low-ability readers. Shaun happened to have difficulty with comprehension because he labored at decoding. In contrast, some students read the words fluently but still lacked the ability to create mental images that related to the text. In cases like this, there may be problems in the verbal or nonverbal coding systems or their ability to function in an integrated fashion. Consequently, connections between words and images may not be made, thus putting comprehension at risk.

Research on mental imagery demonstrates that comprehension of text is enhanced when students are prompted or taught to use mental imagery. For example, learners who were instructed to create mental images of events in sentences learned two to three times as much as learners who read aloud the sentences repeatedly (Anderson, 1971). When children are taught to generate mental images as they read, they experience greater recall and enhanced abilities to draw inferences and make predictions (Gambrell, 1981; Gambrell & Bales, 1986; Pressley, 1976; Sadoski, 1983, 1985). Suzuki (1985) identified implications for educators in her review of the imagery research. Specifically, she determined that there is evidence that prompting students to use imagery and verbal elaboration has a powerful effect on learning and remembering. For greatest benefits, the type of prompting needs to be related to the age of the learner. Younger learners may need demonstrations, whereas older learners may require "try-to-imagine" instructions only. Suzuki also found evidence that even the most proficient older adolescent readers may need help in transferring strategic behavior from one task requiring imagery to other tasks requiring imagery.

Television in the Mind— A Strategy for Imaging

As teachers of reluctant and low-ability readers, we have encountered students who lack the ability to create pictures in their minds. Therefore, we have incorporated several strategies to help students become aware of the imaging process. One strategy we use is an analogy of a television in the mind. This analogy helps students to realize that there should be more going on in the reading process than just "barking the words." We talk about the television screen that we "watch" as we read, and we use think-alouds to talk about the pictures on our mental screen as we read. We emphasize the need for the pictures to match the words. We explain that when the pictures and words do not match (e.g., a student's mind wanders to picturing the dance on Friday night rather than picturing the actions of the text) it is as if the channel has been switched from the "story" channel to the "dance" channel. We teach students they need to do something when this "channel switching" happens, such as refocus or reread in order to "get back on the right channel" and create an appropriate mind picture.

In our work with struggling readers, we have learned that sometimes the words and pictures may not match, not only because of a lack of focused attention or the struggle to decode words but also because of a limited vocabulary or background knowledge. For example, when reading *SOS Titanic* (Bunting, 1996), Clarissa (pseudonym) expressed puzzlement when she read, "The deck steward gestured toward the serving cart that held silver teapots, sugars and creamers, cups and saucers" (p. 83). Clarissa did not understand the use of the word *saucer* in relation to *cups and saucers*. She was imaging as she read, but her image of *saucer* was tied to outer space and not to dishes. We observed another instance of confusion due to lack of experience when Teyen (pseudonym), a student whose first language was not English, looked bewildered after reading "They gave up the firewood business after Hal got his Caterpillar paid off" from *A Killing Freeze* (Hall, 1988, p. 94). The student said it did not make sense, "because a *caterpillar* is a fuzzy worm before it turns into a butterfly." After Teyen was shown a picture of a *Caterpillar tractor* he could resume his reading with understanding. These students were aware of the "static" caused by mental pictures that did not make sense and, unlike many reluctant readers, asked for clarification.

Our reluctant and struggling readers often felt they had read when their eyes had passed over the words. This type of reading can result in the lack of a picture or a fuzzy picture on the mental TV screen. When students become aware of the lack of an image or "static" from a current image, they can then be taught to use fix-up strategies such as changing their rate, rereading, refocusing attention, or asking for clarification to overcome the confusion. The ability to regain an image related to the text becomes an indication that comprehension is back on track. The research on mental imagery (Gambrell, 1981) confirms that students may need to be prompted repeatedly to focus on their mental images, or "television in the mind," as a way to monitor comprehension. In addition to prompting, teachers may need to teach and model the fix-up strategies to use when the picture is missing or fuzzy. We have found that this modeling and prompting must be an ongoing process. Students may not engage in these processes independently—at least not until they see the value and feel the success of doing so.

Drawings in the Classroom

There are times when students cannot create a picture in the mind due to lack of background knowledge or the complexity of the text. Clarissa achieved instant understanding simply by being told that, in the context of the story, a saucer was a "little plate that a cup sat on." For Teyen, a verbal description of a Caterpillar as a "vehicle used in road building" did not trigger understanding. However, after seeing a picture of a Caterpillar tractor he not only could create an image in his mind of what this was but also could see why it was important to the meaning of the text. Sometimes a verbal description is sufficient and other times an actual picture may be necessary to reach understanding.

Some students experience confusion due to lack of understanding of critical features in the setting or spatial relationships between characters or items discussed in the text. We have found that a drawing or quick sketch made by the teachers is a useful tool to help create understanding. For example, one seventh-grade student responded to a paragraph in *Earthquake Terror* (Kehret, 1996) by stating, "I don't get what's going on." Others from her class of low-ability readers (i.e., students scoring in the bottom quartile on a standardized achievement test) nodded in agreement at her expressed confusion. The paragraph described the making of a small shelter in the woods by using the trunk of a downed maple tree and three small

alders to form the walls and roof of the shelter. The paragraph read as follows,

> After stripping off as many of the lower branches as he could, he laid the root end of the alder on top of the downed maple's trunk. He did the same thing with the other two alders. Next he gathered pine and cedar boughs.... He laid them on top of the alders, forming a crude roof. He placed the alder branches that he had removed across the far end of the shelter, propping them up to form a back wall. The shelter was shaped like half a tent, with an opening at one end. (pp. 46–48)

After the teacher drew a step-by-step sketch of what was happening, the students voiced understanding. See Figure 1 for the drawing.

In the text *Watchdog and the Coyotes* (Wallace, 1995), the author took pages to describe the setting and the meeting of the three main characters, dogs who lived side by side. Once again some students were having trouble envisioning the setting. The students understood this important part of the novel after the teacher drew a diagram illustrating the spatial layout of the dogs' neighborhood. A simple sketch can be worth a thousand words for some students.

Just as teacher-generated drawings help students visualize events and relationships portrayed in text, drawings done by students can inform the teacher about what students are or are not understanding about a text. When reading a novel aloud to students, we give them the option to just listen, or listen and create drawings based on the text being read. We have learned that these drawings provide a visible and explicit record of learning (McConnell, 1993).

Some students elected to produce drawings as they listened to the novel *The Night Crossing* (Ackerman, 1994), an adolescent novel dealing with the Holocaust. As we examined the drawings (see Figures 2, 3, and 4) it became clear that there was great variability in what the students were portraying. Drawings in Figures 2 and 3 represented scenes directly from the novel being read, whereas the drawing in Figure 4 may have had something to do with the topic of the Holocaust but had no direct connection to the events included in the day's reading. Drawings

Figure 1
A Teacher-Drawn Sketch in Response to Students' Questions About *Earthquake Terror*

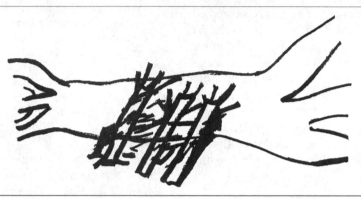

Figure 2
Student Drawing, True to Text, While Listening to *Night Crossing*

Figure 3
Student Drawing, True to Text, While Listening to *Night Crossing*

Figure 4
Student Drawing, Unrelated to Text Events, While Listening to *Night Crossing*

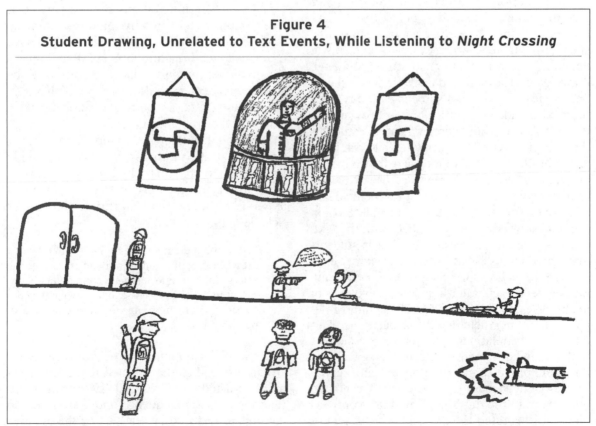

that are related to the topic but not the text should prompt the teacher to question students to see if they are comprehending the text or simply drawing something from related background knowledge but not tied to the events of the text. As Peeck (1987) pointed out, a student's failure to produce complete or accurate drawings can reveal comprehension gaps at an early stage in the learning process. We occasionally have had students who spent a great deal of time drawing superfluous details to cover up their lack of understanding of the text. For example, Figure 4 alerted us to question the student about his understanding of what had been read. His detailed drawing of Hitler speaking did relate to the events of World War II but had nothing to do with the day's reading. This drawing became the starting point of a conversation that cleared up his confusion about important events and relationships in the text.

In addition to informing the teacher of students' understandings, drawings can also aid in retention of information (Snowman & Cunningham, 1975). But as Peeck (1987) cautioned, drawings need to be accurate, and time spent drawing needs to be evaluated in terms of net gain. One way we have structured students' drawings is to have them quickly draw one sketch on a series of television screens each day after the read-aloud. This builds on our television in the mind analogy and communicates to students that the purpose of this drawing is to track the action of the story and to represent the main idea or events of each day's reading. The drawings of the previous days provide an excellent source of information to help students activate background knowledge and reconnect with the text. The drawings also serve as a tool to help students make predictions about the subsequent reading.

Figure 5 shows the television screen drawings of one student after four consecutive days of reading *Night John* (Paulsen, 1993). Frame 1 depicts the setting, including the layout of the plantation and the relationship of the slaves' quarters to the main house and the fields. Frame 2 shows one event of the chapter, the slaves being served dinner out of a trough. Although this was not the only event in the day's reading, this event was one that illustrated the day-to-day treatment of the slaves that was key to the overall meaning of the chapter. Frame 3 illustrates the significant event of the "trading" that went on between the main characters—that of secretly exchanging the knowledge of how to write the letter *A* for tobacco. The final frame shows the hanging of a slave, one of the risks, discussed in the chapter, for slaves who break the rules. These drawings show not only the student's understanding of specific events in the text but also an understanding of the larger issues represented by these events.

Illustrations in the Text

In addition to prompting image making and using drawings to support imagery, it is important for teachers to consider the role text illustrations and book cover illustrations play in the reading process. Illustrations frequently serve an affective or motivational function for students. Peeck's (1987) review of the affective–motivational effects of illustrations shows many positive outcomes. Specifically, pictures can make reading a text more enjoyable, result in positive attitudes toward reading in general and toward illustrated text in particular, and can influence the time readers are willing to spend on a text. All of these effects are particularly beneficial for students who are reluctant readers.

Beyond the affective and motivational functions, illustrations also may serve to provide knowledge to students who are reading about things that are not part of their experience, as with Teyen and the Caterpillar picture. As Schallert (1980) stated,

Pictures help the reader learn and comprehend a text when they illustrate information central to the text, when they represent new content that is important to the overall message, and when they depict structural relationships mentioned in the text. (pp. 513–514)

The role of illustrations may be more critical for struggling readers than skilled readers. For example, Rusted and Coltheart (1979) confirmed that poor readers frequently move from text to pictures to text as they read, using the pictures

Figure 5
Student Drawings Following Read-Aloud of *Night John* on Four Consecutive Days

Frame 1

Frame 2

Frame 3

Frame 4

as a tool for understanding. In contrast, good readers pay little attention to the illustrations during their reading. Goldstein and Underwood (1981) confirmed that less competent readers are influenced to a greater degree by text illustrations. For readers who struggle, pictures operate beyond the decoration function (Levin, Anglin, & Carney, 1987), serving as a tool to create or confirm understanding. An example of this was when a small group of students reading *Slam* (Myers, 1996) repeatedly looked back at the cover to verify points in the novel. The cover

depicts a young man holding a basketball in one arm, staring through a chain-link fence. Students turned to the cover when Slam, the main character, was described as being six feet, four inches. One young man turned to the cover when we read, "I remember walking away to the other side of the park and then turning back and looking through the fence to where he was" (pp. 30–31). The next day the student pointed out the cover illustration and retold the incident in the prereading discussion.

Sometimes a picture is *not* worth a thousand words. When the text and illustrations do not match, the illustrations can actually interfere with comprehension and reduce learning (Willows, 1978). We found this to be true when a group of middle school reluctant readers read "A Few Dirty Words" (Scott, 1999), a play dealing with harassment in school. The students nearly rebelled due to the one illustration that accompanied the play. The illustration of two young male basketball players and a female manager appeared four pages into the play. The students had already created an image of the characters based on the text. The images described by the students did not match the illustration. According to the students, the two basketball players pictured were too young and the boys' shorts looked like dresses. There was a noticeable change in the students' attitude from that point on. The play no longer held credibility, and motivation to continue reading it declined. This experience caused us to pay attention to the text-illustration match in the materials we use with our students and to try to use a mismatch productively.

A text-illustration mismatch can be used to engage students more deeply with the text if the students are set up for it. Our experience when reading *Such Nice Kids* (Bunting, 1990) provides an example of this. We knew that the main characters depicted on the cover of this text looked much younger than they were described in the text. In our prereading discussion of the book with a small group of eighth-grade boys, we asked them to make predictions about the ages of the characters. We then asked the boys to look for information as they read that either supported or refuted their predictions. Several times while reading the novel, discussion returned to the cover illustration. The students definitely felt the boys on the cover looked younger than 17, as described in the text. However, they still studied the cover and tried to identify the characters by name. And, regardless of the obvious misrepresentation of age, the readers used other information on the cover to predict what was going to happen. One of our final discussions included an overall critique of the cover illustration based on information in the text. The active and detailed discussion provided evidence that proactive attention to a text-illustration mismatch and supporting discussions can help readers engage more deeply in analysis of the text.

Because novels for adolescents usually present only a cover illustration, we had students read picture books as a way to better understand their use of illustrations. A picture book is defined as a storybook that is "a fiction book with a dual narrative, in which both the pictures and the text work interdependently to tell a story. It is a tale told in two media, the integration of visual and verbal art" (Bishop & Hickman, 1992, p. 2). After students read the picture books, we asked them to write in their journals about how the pictures helped them and what they liked or disliked about the illustrations. Comments such as the following support the view that "pictures in text consistency produce prose-learning benefits" (Levin et al., 1987, p. 53).

- It helped me get a better clue of what's going on. Helped me see what I was reading.
- The pictures toled the rest of the story.
- So I could picture out what the chipmunk was doing—it also helps me read faster.
- I liked tha pictures because it was less to read and so I could just look at tha picture instead of having to picture it in my brain.

These responses confirmed for us that low-ability readers do use illustrations to help them picture story details and to verify their understanding. Students can benefit from the use of illustrations if they are in alignment with the text and if students are making connections that support meaning making.

Picture Books to Build Background Knowledge

Given our students' positive response to picture books, we have used them as a tool to build background knowledge needed for the understanding of adolescent novels taught in the classroom. Specifically, before reading novels dealing with the Holocaust, our students read picture books that dealt with World War II. After reading a self-selected picture book, students filled out comment forms asking questions about reading the picture books. Student comments ranged from general to specific, dealing with three distinct areas: (a) the artwork, (b) the emotions portrayed or evoked, and (c) the increase of specific content knowledge or awareness of details.

Many students critiqued the artwork. Overall, the more realistic or true to the text the illustrations were, the better the students liked them. For example, some students wrote,

- I liked the pictures because they were well-drawn and detailed and colorful.
- He did a good job in drawing them. It looks exactly what I would picture in my mind.
- I liked all of the different colors but all the pictures were kinda blurry and not too clear.
- The pictures were not very colorful. I liked that because it showed how dark and dull the Holocaust was.

In research, Gombrich's (1982) arguments supported the conclusion that pictures are supreme in their capacity to arouse emotions. Many students' comments addressed the emotive power of illustrations and the role illustrations played in helping them understand the emotions of the characters. For example, some students stated the following:

- They (the pictures) helped a lot because I really understood how the boy felt.
- They (the pictures) were very graphic, showed real cruelness.
- I like how they (the pictures) made the people's face sad and happy. You could feel the emotion.
- I could see the emotions on the faces and know what they were going through.

The low-ability reader might not have the memory "pegs" (Gambrell & Jawitz, 1993) for some of the specific details within a text. Visual representations can provide the memory peg needed (Kozma, 1991) to connect with appropriate background knowledge. Specifically, students may not understand the written description until they have the visual representation to link with it. Students' comments expressing expanded understanding of specific details in the picture books on World War II provide evidence of the role illustrations may play for some readers.

- It helped me understand how people can build things so nicely and how the guards would watch them all the time.
- The kids used sticks as guns. They didn't use plastic ones!
- They showd want it was like after the bomb and before.
- In one of the pictures it showed Anne and her sister sitting together with a big blanket around them and they were both bald because the Germans shaved there heads to make things out of. And that showed me that it was cold and sad where they where.

The comments of our students demonstrate that text illustrations support low-ability readers. Students used the illustrations to assist them in understanding what they read and as vehicles to provide additional and supporting information.

Movies as Image Makers

"Seeing is beeter than hearing seeing is beliving," wrote one of our students when asked to write in his journal about his reaction to watching a movie version of a book we had been reading. For this student, the visual images provided by the movie cleared up many of his confusions and helped him "imagine" the reality of what he was reading.

Showing movies in a reading classroom can facilitate different learning goals. Movies in the reading classroom can have many of the positive affective-motivational effects found in illustrations (Peeck, 1987) and can provide students with critical background information and support for understanding related texts. Movies are enjoyable, they motivate the learner, and they can result in positive attitudes toward reading. Movies also can provide time contexts, setting details, and other important situational information for those students who have less prior knowledge of the subject being addressed. Movies can be a language model for individuals who are reading texts that include unfamiliar dialect. Visual representations offer memory pegs that can be used to form associations with information already in long-term memory (Kozma, 1991). Our experiences support the belief that movie images provide information students need to make sense of text. However, the type of movie and how it is used must match the teaching objective and the learning needs of the students. Following are examples of using movies to meet different learning goals.

Before beginning a literature unit about the Holocaust with a class of middle school reluctant readers, we asked students what they knew about the subject. Seven of the 12 students knew nothing about it. The others knew it had to do with Hitler and the killing of many Jewish people. We decided to use movies to help build the background knowledge our students needed if they were going to successfully read *The Devil's Arithmetic* (Yolen, 1988) and *Daniel's Story* (Matas, 1993).

To meet the objective of building background knowledge, the movies we selected were not video versions of the books; rather they were such things as historical documentaries and clips from other fictional and nonfictional movies about the same time period and context. We selected movies that would provide information about the setting; the historical and religious context; the multiple layers of conflict between individuals, communities, races, and religions; and characters—not specific to the books, but rather the roles played by individuals or groups during the Holocaust.

After teaching the Holocaust unit, we asked the students to write in their journals about what they learned. Their knowledge had increased substantially. Many of the "facts" they talked about came from the movies they had seen rather than the books they read. Two students

directly stated that the movies helped them to picture the events from their novels. The movies provided key images to enhance understanding and comprehension, allowing students to then create internal images as they read the novels. When students were asked to write in their journals about whether or not the movies had helped them understand the novels, they echoed many of the same things they had written regarding the support they had gained from picture books. Specific comments included the following:

- When you watch a movie you can get a better picture of what is happening.
- The movies helped us read in our book. It was like visual. I understand visual things better then reading.
- In the book when they talked about the ghetto it did not sound that bad tell you saw it—it was wet and dark...people where dying in the streets. In the books you have to make your own pictures.
- When you watch the movie, a lot of things just click.

Sometimes we have stopped in the middle of a book to watch a movie to help build necessary background knowledge. From the discussion we had related to the novel *Monkey Island* (Fox, 1991), it was evident that the students did not understand that homelessness is a real problem that affects families and children very much like themselves. After seeing a television show based on a family's experiences with homelessness, two middle school students commented in the discussion, "I didn't realize people like me were homeless" and "I thought the homeless were bums." Throughout the remaining discussions of the novel, students often referred to information from the movie. The movie had provided key images with which to connect new information from the novel (Gambrell & Jawitz, 1993). In this case, the movie did more than simply provide cognitive background information regarding the topic of homelessness. The movie provided students with a greater ability to reflect on the judgments they had made due to their lack of accurate information. Students' increased understanding better enabled them to empathize with victims of homelessness and to personally connect with characters and events in the novel.

We know of many teachers who use movies as a "reward" for finishing a class novel or play. After watching a movie version of *To Kill a Mockingbird* (Lee, 1960) in her English class, one struggling reader reported that she finally "got it" (the book). This report and others like it led us to believe that movies based on novels could be used more effectively with struggling readers, especially when the text is difficult and the novel is unfamiliar in vocabulary, language structure, dialect, setting, or time period. Our concern resulted in what we now refer to as the Watch-Read-Watch-Read (W-R-W-R) cycle of novel reading. Several teaching goals can be met with this technique. Specifically, W-R-W-R can be used to build background knowledge prior to reading and as students move through the text. It can also be used as a tool to confirm understanding of previously read text, to teach how to make predictions, to teach how to confirm or deny predictions, and to provide the students with memory pegs to use as they read. In order for this technique to be effective the teacher must be familiar with both the text and the movie, where they match well, and where they differ.

The basic W-R-W-R cycle goes like this:

1. The teacher introduces the novel in whatever motivating manner he or she decides would work best with students. Part of this should include a discussion that helps the teacher gain an understanding of the background knowledge students bring to the text.

2. The teacher explains that the class is going to watch a brief clip of a movie based on the novel they will be reading. The teacher also instructs the students to attend to specific elements of the movie clip. This could include details related to setting, such as climate, rural versus urban, indications of poverty or wealth, or types of homes or buildings present. Students also could be prompted to pay attention to specific characters, their clothing, and their physical features and to try to predict their role in the novel. Students could listen for unique vocabulary or dialect used by the characters. Finally, students could try to get a sense of what problems might be faced by the characters. The teacher draws attention to those aspects of the text that he or she thinks could pose difficulty for students and that are represented in the movie clip.

3. Students watch the first movie clip. It could be a short three- to five-minute viewing or it could last longer, depending on the movie, its match to the text, and what the teacher's goals are. The point to remember is that students need to see enough to help them understand the targeted elements of the text and to motivate them to read, but not so much that they feel they don't have to read.

4. The class processes the critical elements of the movie, with the teacher directing the discussion to the critical elements that will facilitate comprehension. Part of this discussion should include students making predictions about what they will read in the first chapter (or whatever length of reading assignment). The success of this step depends on the teacher knowing what elements of the movie will be most useful to the understanding of the text and helping students "notice" these elements.

5. Students read the parallel text, looking for information that matches what they saw in the movie related to characters, setting, context, and so on. They also read to confirm their predictions related to the action sequence or problems presented in the first clip of the movie.

6. After students read the first assigned text, it is discussed with the specific intent of making the critical elements more salient and pointing out that students can use the images from the movie to add to their understanding.

7. Students watch the second clip of the movie. This clip should cover the material

that students have just read but not go beyond that. This allows readers to see the visual representation of what they have read, to confirm the understanding they gained from reading, and to prepare them for the next section of reading.

8. Students discuss any new understandings and make predictions about the next section of text to be read.

9. The cycle of watch, discuss, read, discuss, watch, discuss, read discuss continues until the novel is complete or students have gained enough background that they can read the rest of the novel independently.

The W-R-W-R cycle is much like the Directed Reading-Thinking Activity developed by Stauffer (1969), with the visual representation provided by the movie inserted prior to each section of reading. This cycle of activities ensures students are understanding the novel and, perhaps more important, provides an opportunity to practice good reading processes. The parallel visual representation of the text allows students to practice visualizing, summarizing, predicting, and confirming even if they struggle with reading the text.

When we use movies at the end of a unit of study or a novel, different strategic purposes are at play. At the end of reading aloud *Night John* (Paulsen, 1993), we showed our seventh-grade students the movie of the same title (Hallmark Home Entertainment, 1996). In this case, we wanted students to compare and contrast the content of the book and movie. As part of this process, students created a Venn diagram plotting the similarities and differences between the book and the movie. Once students compared and contrasted the basic information included in each, the students were asked to write in their journals about whether they liked the book or movie better and why. The students overwhelmingly favored the movie, saying it provided more details and allowed them to see what was going on. Other students favored the movie due to affective reasons. Some students preferred the movie because Waller, the plantation owner, did

not seem as mean in the movie as he was in the book. Specific comments favoring the movie included, "I liked the *movie* more than the book because..."

- you can actly see whats going on and you can under-stand it better.

- you can get a better picture of things. I'n the movie it seems like Waller is nicer then in the book. Waller helps them pick cotton.... I'n the book Waller treats them with no respect what so ever.

- movies are really discriptive. It show you exactly whats happening. It's also more relaxing. I also like it better cause the ending isn't letting you hang there as much as the book does.

- the movie was more interesting. It had a lot more detels, and you could acealy see what was going on and you just couldn't amagin it.

It is interesting that some students who preferred the book also said they liked it better because it provided more details. Many of these students liked the fact that they could create their own images of the characters in their minds, rather than using the ones provided by the movie. Basically, they liked their images better. Examples of comments by students favoring the book version of the story included, "I liked the *book* better than the movie because..."

- the book has more detail you get to know the chariders a little better.

- it explind all the parts. I could see what I thought the book was about, and looked like. Not what someone else though.

- it had a lot more deatail and it longer. I also liked to imagine what it would be like being a slave.

- you get to pick what everything looks like in your head.

Our students have provided evidence that the use of movies as an instructional tool has supported their learning. However, we have found that students benefit most when we are strategic about the use of movies and are clear with students about why we are using movies and what they should attend to. This is consistent with the work of Solomon (1984) who found that setting a purpose for viewing a program increases the learning related to that purpose. Teachers need to decide whether movies would be useful in addressing the learning goals and the needs of the students and then be explicit with students about the desired outcomes.

Final Thoughts—A Summary of Important Issues

Research done on the role that imagery plays in reading comprehension has implications for teachers as they work with students of all abilities. Figure 6 presents a summary of the major points discussed throughout this article related to using external visual images to support reading comprehension. These are presented as "Primary Points for Practitioners" and are based on research and our experiences with middle school struggling readers.

A picture truly is worth a thousand words for students who struggle with reading comprehension. We have found that if students can create their own images on the television screens in their minds as they read, their potential for understanding the text is increased. If students are not able to develop images because they are using all their mental energy to decode the words or their personal experiences have limited their

---

Figure 6
Primary Points for Practitioners

1. Don't assume your students can use visual imagery to support reading comprehension. Check out their ability to create images with discussions of what they "see" or with student-generated drawings.
2. Students who have imagery skills may need to be prompted to use imagery to support comprehension. Those who don't have the skill will need to be taught.
3. Look for opportunities to model imagery strategies to your students. Discussing what you see on the television screen in your mind will help students better understand this process.
4. Support for comprehension with visuals tools does not need to be elaborate. A teacher-drawn sketch or picture can provide the necessary clarification for students who are confused or lack the knowledge necessary for understanding.
5. Lack of ability to create images or ineffective images may be due to lack of background knowledge or vocabulary rather than reading skill. If this is the case, background knowledge will need to be built. Providing the knowledge with picture books, movies, or other visual media also gives students a visual "memory peg" with which to connect new information from the text.
6. Student drawings can be used for multiple purposes, but must be used strategically. Provide students with a purpose for drawing. Help them see that their drawings are a representation of their understanding, that drawings can help them remember important information, and that earlier drawings can be used to make predictions about what might happen next.
7. Be mindful that lower ability readers tend to rely on text illustrations more than good readers. When the illustrations are accurate representations of the text, encourage students to use them to support comprehension. When the illustrations are not a good match, use this mismatch to provoke discussions that lead to deeper understanding of the text and build evaluation skills. Set students up for the mismatch beforehand so they won't be disappointed and possibly disengage from the text.
8. Use movies in ways that address students' learning needs. Carefully select movies based on the learning goals—to build general background knowledge about a topic addressed in text; to provide visual images of setting, characters, and relationships in the story; to teach comprehension skills such as summarizing, predicting, and confirming; or to promote evaluation skills by comparing and contrasting the movie with the text. Be explicit with students about the learning objective for watching the movie.

vocabulary and background knowledge, external visual images can be used to develop understanding. Strategic use of external visual images can provide the background knowledge and memory pegs to help students "see" what is happening and unlock confusing text (Levin, 1981). In our work with struggling readers we have found that the use of sketches, illustrations, picture books, and movies provides students with information on which to build their internal images. By supporting students with these tools, the teacher provides students with essential elements necessary for responding to the text. Don't be surprised that when you use these tools, comments like, "I don't know what happened, I was too busy reading the words" change to "Oh! Now I get it!"

References

Anderson, R.C. (1971). Encoding processes in the storage and retrieval of sentences. *Journal of Experimental Psychology, 91,* 338–341.

Bishop, S.R., & Hickman, J. (1992). Four or fourteen or forty: Picture books are for everyone. In S. Benedict & L. Carlisle (Eds.), *Beyond words: Picture books for older readers and writers* (pp. 1–10). Portsmouth, NH: Heinemann.

Clark, J.M., & Paivio, A. (1991). Dual coding theory and education. *Educational Psychology Review, 3,* 149–210.

Gambrell, L.B. (1981). Induced mental imagery and the text prediction performance of first and third graders. In J.A. Niles & L.A. Harris (Eds.), *New inquiries in reading research and instruction* (pp. 131–135). Rochester, NY: National Reading Conference.

Gambrell, L.B., & Bales, R. (1986). Mental imagery and the comprehension monitoring performance of fourth- and fifth-grade poor readers. *Reading Research Quarterly, 11,* 454–464.

Gambrell, L.B., & Jawitz, P.B. (1993). Mental imagery, text illustrations, and children's story comprehension and recall. *Reading Research Quarterly, 28,* 265–273.

Goldstein, R., & Underwood, G. (1981). The influence of pictures on the derivation of meaning from children's reading materials. *Journal of Research in Reading, 4,* 6–16.

Gombrich, E.H. (1982). *The image and the eye: Further studies in the psychology of pictorial representation.* Ithaca, NY: Cornell University Press.

Kozma, R.B. (1991). Learning with media. *Review of Educational Research, 61,* 179–211.

Levin, J.R. (1981). On functions of pictures in prose. In F.J. Pirozzolo & M.C. Wittrock (Eds.), *Neuropsychological and cognitive processes in reading* (pp. 203–228). New York: Academic Press.

Levin, J.R., Anglin, G.J., & Carney, R.N. (1987). On empirically validating functions of pictures in prose. In D.M. Willows & H.A. Houghton (Eds.), *The psychology of illustration: Vol. 1* (pp. 51–78). New York: Springer-Verlag.

McConnell, S. (1993). Talking drawings: A strategy for assisting learners. *Journal of Reading, 36,* 260–269.

Paivio, A. (1971). *Imagery and verbal processes.* New York: Holt, Rinehart & Winston.

Paivio, A. (1983). The empirical case for dual coding theory. In J.C. Yuille (Ed.), *Imagery, memory, and cognition: Essays in honor of Allan Paivio* (pp. 307–332). Hillsdale, NJ: Erlbaum.

Paivio, A. (1986). *Mental representations: A dual-coding approach.* New York: Oxford University Press.

Peeck, J. (1987). The role of illustrations in processing and remembering illustrated text. In D.M. Willows & H.A. Houghton (Eds.), *The psychology of illustration: Vol. 1* (pp. 145–155). New York: Springer-Verlag.

Pressley, G.M. (1976). Mental imagery helps eight-year-olds remember what they read. *Journal of Educational Psychology, 68,* 355–359.

Pressley, M., & McCormick, C. (1995). *Advanced educational psychology.* New York: HarperCollins.

Rusted, J., & Coltheart, V. (1979). The effect of pictures on the retention of novel words and prose passages. *Journal of Experimental Child Psychology, 28,* 516–524.

Sadoski, M. (1983). An exploratory study of the relationships between reported imagery and the comprehension and recall of a story. *Reading Research Quarterly, 19,* 110–123.

Sadoski, M. (1985). The natural use of imagery in story comprehension and recall: Replication and extension. *Reading Research Quarterly, 20,* 658–667.

Sadoski, M., Paivio, A., & Goetz, E.T. (1991). A critique of schema theory in reading and a dual coding alternative. *Reading Research Quarterly, 26,* 463–484.

Schallert, D.L. (1980). The role of illustrations in reading comprehension. In R.J. Spiro, B.C. Bruce, & W.F. Brewer (Eds.), *Theoretical issues in reading comprehension* (pp. 503–524). Hillsdale, NJ: Erlbaum.

Snowman, J., & Cunningham, D.J. (1975). A comparison of pictorial and written adjuncts in learning from text. *Journal of Educational Psychology, 67,* 307–311.

Solomon, G. (1984). Television is "easy" and print is "tough": The differential investment of mental effort in learning as a function of perceptions and attributions. *Journal of Educational Psychology, 76,* 647–658.

Stauffer, R.G. (1969). *Directing reading maturity as a cognitive process.* New York: Harper & Row.

Suzuki, N.S. (1985). Imagery research with children: Implications for education. In A.A. Sheikh & K.S. Sheikh (Eds.), *Imagery in education* (pp. 179–198). Farmingdale, NY: Baywood.

Swanson, H.L. (1989). Verbal coding deficits in learning-disabled readers: A multiple stage model. *Educational Psychology Review, 1,* 235–277.

Willows, D.M. (1978). A picture is not always worth a thousand words: Pictures as distractors in reading. *Journal of Educational Psychology, 70,* 255–262.

Young Adult Materials Cited

Ackerman, Karen. (1994). *The night crossing.* New York: Alfred A. Knopf.

Bunting, Eve. (1990). *Such nice kids.* New York: Clarion.

Bunting, Eve. (1996). *SOS Titanic.* New York: Scholastic.

Fox, Paula. (1991). *Monkey Island.* New York: Bantam Doubleday.

Hall, Lynn. (1988). *A killing freeze.* New York: Avon.

Hallmark Home Entertainment. (1996). *Night John* (videotape). Los Angeles, CA: Signboard Hill Productions.

Kehret, Peg. (1996). *Earthquake terror.* New York: Puffin.

Lee, Harper. (1960). *To kill a mockingbird.* Philadelphia: Lippincott.

Matas, Carol. (1993). *Daniel's story.* New York: Scholastic.

Myers, Walter Dean. (1996). *Slam.* New York: Scholastic.

Paulsen, Gary. (1993). *Night John.* New York: Bantam Doubleday Dell.

Scott, Jordan. (1999, January 8). A few dirty words. *Read, 48,* 20–29.

Wallace, Bill. (1995). *Watchdog and the coyotes.* New York: Simon & Schuster.

Yolen, Jane. (1988). *The devil's arithmetic.* New York: Trumpet.

Questions for Reflection

- In addition to engaging with the media types referred to here, today's students spend a great deal of time online. How might teachers harness students' interest in the Internet to promote development of abilities in visual image-making? What are the advantages and disadvantages of using online multimedia texts for this purpose?

- This article emphasizes the advantages of visual imagery for supporting the comprehension of struggling adolescent readers. How might these strategies assist students working at or above grade level? Is explicit attention to visualizing useful across grade and ability levels?

Getting the Big Idea: A Neglected Goal for Reading Comprehension

Sean A. Walmsley

American children, according to national surveys, seem to have well-developed basic literacy skills. But they falter when it comes to critical or "thoughtful" literacy (National Center for Education Statistics, 2004). Given the amount of time and attention paid to basic literacy—especially under the aegis of the No Child Left Behind Act of 2001 (2002)—perhaps we shouldn't be surprised by these findings. Indeed, a small study I recently undertook in a rural upstate New York school district suggested that engaging children in "big ideas" is not a common practice. Of 126 teaching or learning episodes observed in K–6 classrooms over a 3-day period, only 4 involved exposing children to or discussing big ideas with them. In most instances, I could not easily have imagined students being engaged in big ideas, either because the teaching or learning activity was focused on something quite specific, like decoding or writing mechanics (where big-idea discussions would not have been appropriate), or because the topic under discussion didn't easily lend itself to big ideas (e.g., having students talk about what they did over the weekend). In other words, I not only observed very few instances where students were engaged in big ideas but also very few in which they easily could have been. In this article, I suggest that it's time to focus again on big ideas.

What Exactly Are Big Ideas and Why Teach Them?

I define a big idea as the main point of a book, magazine article, argument, or film; the moral of a story or the underlying theme of a novel; what an author, poet, speaker, or artist is really trying to communicate; and, finally, the life lessons and deeper understandings a reader, listener, or viewer takes from a text, a work of art, or a performance. In reading, big ideas are associated with whole texts, not parts of them. They are not the same as the main idea of a sentence or paragraph.

One reason to teach U.S. students about big ideas is because they aren't strong in critical literacy. But there are more profound reasons: Understanding big ideas is critical to full participation in work, life, and democracy—especially in the era of the 30-second "in-depth" analysis. For example, the media seem to avoid complex topics. As I write this article, the United States is debating the future of Social Security—surely a big idea—but what do adults, let alone young workers who will be most affected by changes to it, actually know about the issue? As the media become more focused on the trivial, educators need to become more focused on the substantial.

Understanding big ideas also serves children well in many states' English language arts assessments, especially at the high school level. (In my state, New York, questions on the statewide

Reprinted from Walmsley, S.A. (2006, November). Getting the big idea: A neglected goal for reading comprehension. *The Reading Teacher, 60*(3), 281–285. doi: 10.1598/RT.60.3.9

English Regents assessment demand critical analysis and evaluation of big ideas.)

Finally, readers, listeners, and viewers can enter "text" at multiple levels (it is not necessary, as Bloom [1956] suggested, that text must be entered at literal levels before it can be engaged at higher levels). Encouraging children to focus on the big ideas of a text promotes understanding of not only big ideas but also smaller details. In fact, stronger readers routinely use their knowledge of the big ideas to work through and understand the text at sentence and paragraph levels.

Big ideas reveal themselves in different ways. In some cases, they stare the reader in the face. For example, in Cowcher's *Antarctica* (1991), a nonfiction book about the delicate balance between penguins, birds, seals, and humans in Antarctica, the big idea is explicit in the final pages:

> The penguins and the seals have always shared their world with ancient enemies, the skuas and the leopard seals. But these new arrivals [referring to humans] are more dangerous. The seals and penguins cannot tell yet whether they will share or destroy their beautiful Antarctica.... (unpaged)

Fables, especially, wear their big ideas on their sleeves. Some even repeat their big idea at the end of the fable:

The Crow and the Pitcher (Aesop)

A Crow, half-dead with thirst, came upon a pitcher that had once been full of water; but when the Crow put its beak into the mouth of the pitcher he found that only very little water was left in it and that he could not reach far enough down to get at it. He tried, and he tried, but at last had to give up in despair. Then a thought came to him, and he took a pebble and dropped it into the pitcher. Then he took another pebble and dropped it into the pitcher. Then he took another pebble and dropped that into the pitcher. Then he took another pebble and dropped that into the pitcher. Then he took another pebble and dropped that into the pitcher. Then he took another pebble and dropped that into the pitcher. At last, at last, he saw the water mount up near him, and after casting in a few more pebbles he was able to quench his thirst and save his life. Little by little does the trick.

In most good children's literature, big ideas lie under the surface of the text, revealing themselves indirectly. For example, Trapani's (1998) retelling of *The Itsy Bitsy Spider* recounts the four episodes in which Itsy Bitsy tries, in vain, to climb up the water spout, the kitchen wall, and the yellow pail, but finally climbs a maple tree where she successfully spins her web. Nowhere does Trapani explicitly state the big idea "if at first you don't succeed, try, try again," but that's the unmistakable big idea to which each episode inexorably contributes.

The big ideas of some books are even less transparent—perhaps their authors never really intended them to have big ideas. A good example is Morris's (1993) nonfiction book *Hats, Hats, Hats*, which presents photographs of hats with simple captions (e.g., "Work Hats," "Play Hats"). But as you read this book, you are drawn into big ideas about how different kinds of hats serve different purposes in different situations and especially in different cultures.

Further toward the more obscure end of this scale are texts that present big ideas in opaque ways. For me, despite repeated attempts (on my own, and with expert guidance) to understand Ritchie's exhibit "Proposition Player" (Massachusetts Museum of Modern Art, 2004), I am still hopelessly out of my depth. School children in the middle and upper grades struggle repeatedly with big-idea poems—many of the same ones (e.g., Keats, Wordsworth, Milton) with which I struggled as a child growing up in England.

How Should We Teach Big Ideas?

We need to engage children with big ideas in a variety of ways. We need to infuse big ideas into daily conversation. We need to read fiction, nonfiction, and poetry that express big ideas. We need to have children experience big ideas in a variety of media (art, sculpture, architecture, drama, film) both receptively and expressively. It's hard to understand or discuss big ideas in material that has precious few of them, or in the "content-less" confines of what Schmoker (2001) called the

"Crayola curriculum" in which students spend countless hours coloring worksheets. While they are valuable for other purposes, series books (e.g., Famous Five, Boxcar Children, Encyclopedia Brown) are not good sources for big ideas. Nor is "cutesy" poetry. Instead, we should select books and other materials that have what Peterson and Eeds (1990) called "multiple layers of meaning." Their favorite example of a multilayered book was *Tuck Everlasting* (Babbit, 1975). It wouldn't be difficult to select others from the hundreds published each year: the work of Betsy Byars, Cynthia Rylant, Jane Yolen, Gary Paulsen, Eloise Greenfield, and Eve Bunting come immediately to mind. To start with, we should choose fiction, nonfiction, and poetry in which the big ideas are fairly simple and easily accessible. These books need to be read to and with children, and they should be made available for children to read on their own.

We should model, teach, and have children practice strategies for accessing and understanding big ideas. To begin with, modeling might simply consist of telling children what the big idea of a book is before starting to read it aloud. Before reading Trapani's (1998) *The Itsy Bitsy Spider*, a teacher could say,

> Have you ever heard of the expression "If at first you don't succeed, try, try again?" Well, this is a story about a spider who at first didn't succeed, but she tried and tried again. Let's read and find out....

Later, a teacher could explain to children how he or she figured out the big idea of a story or poem. Later still, the teacher might teach children techniques like asking questions or making text-to-self, text-to-world, or text-to-text connections (Keene & Zimmerman, 1997) and show them how to use these techniques independently. Socratic seminars (Adler, 1982; Ball & Brewer, 1996) also provide excellent instructional strategies for teaching students to access, grapple with, and understand big ideas.

One interesting way to build children's understanding of big ideas is to use multiple texts and build understanding within and across them. Here's an example, using two of Kuskin's (1998)

poems from her anthology *The Sky Is Always in the Sky* (1998). A teacher might start by sharing "A Bug Sat in a Silver Flower" (p. 29). It's a poem about a little bug thinking "silver thoughts" who is suddenly eaten by a bigger bug. Asking the children what big ideas came to them as they heard or read the poem would probably elicit notions about the food chain: In nature, bigger bugs routinely eat smaller bugs, and smaller bugs in turn eat even smaller ones. They might also raise the point that in nature, not surviving is often a matter of chance—being in the wrong place at the wrong time. I see this daily in the summer at my pond, as the blue heron picks off the goldfish and small bass I so carefully stock. As with Kuskin's smaller bugs, the heron is simply doing to my fish what my fish are doing to smaller creatures like flies or larvae.

Next, the teacher might share another of Kuskin's poems from the same anthology, "Buggity-Buggity Bug" (p. 26). This particular bug was "wandering aimlessly" when all of a sudden, it too met its end, but this time under the shoe of a human being. The teacher can initiate a discussion about the big ideas of this poem. Children can come up with similar ideas as for the first discussion—the notion of being in the wrong place at the wrong time. Some children might latch onto the seemingly careless and thoughtless act of the shoes in relation to the unsuspecting bug underfoot.

Finally, the teacher can ask about the big ideas of the two poems combined. Children might see the difference between what happens to a small bug as part of the food chain as opposed to what happens to some of them as a result of human intervention (intentional or not). In this case, of course, it looks unintentional—careless at worst. But the discussion could easily lead to intentional acts of destruction of bugs by humans, as in the case of pesticides used around the home or garden. What's interesting is how there are big ideas associated with each of the poems individually, but additional ones emerge when the two poems are discussed together.

It always surprises and disappoints me that while so much really good literature is read to children in the early grades, the discussions that take place around this literature so frequently focus on trivial aspects of the books rather than their big ideas. A good example is *Chrysanthemum* (Henkes, 1991), a book about a mouse of the same name who gets teased mercilessly when she goes to school for the first time. The most frequent follow-up activity I see in early primary classrooms involves children doing projects on their names. But *Chrysanthemum* really isn't a book about names, it's a wonderful illustration of the proverb "Don't judge a book by its cover," or the need for children not to be swayed by the opinions of others. It isn't that researching children's names is a bad idea, it's missing the opportunity to broaden and deepen children's understanding of big ideas.

Without such opportunities for critical thought, many children will not develop these understandings, which may not hurt them much during the elementary grades, but will come back to haunt them in secondary school as the conceptual density of material across all subject areas increases.

As teachers, we should be able, by the middle of first grade, to simply pose the question, So, what's the big idea? and have children engage in a discussion of *Chrysanthemum* (Henkes, 1991), or a nonfiction book about recycling, or one of Karla Kuskin's poems about bugs, that engages the big ideas of these works. But we also, as Brown (1991) suggested, ought to be holding regular conversations in classrooms about big ideas in general—conversations about current events, history, science, art, music, politics, environment, and so on—so that children can build up knowledge about these topics, appreciate their importance, and use the knowledge to inform and strengthen their understanding of everything they read, hear, or view.

References

Adler, M. (1982). *The Paideia proposal: An educational manifesto.* New York: Macmillan.

Babbit, N. (1975). *Tuck everlasting.* New York: Farrar, Straus and Giroux.

Ball, W.H., & Brewer, P.F. (1996). Socratic questioning: Then and now. In R.L. Canady & M.D. Retting (Eds.), *Teaching in the block: Strategies for engaging active learners* (pp. 29–31). Larchmont, NY: Eye on Education Press.

Bloom, B.S. (1956). *Taxonomy of educational objectives: The classification of educational goals.* New York: Longman.

Brown, R.G. (1991). *Schools of thought: How the politics of literacy shape thinking in the classroom.* San Francisco: Jossey-Bass.

Cowcher, H. (1991). *Antarctica.* New York: Sunburst.

Henkes, K. (1991). *Chrysanthemum.* New York: Mulberry.

Keene, E.O., & Zimmerman, S. (1997). *Mosaic of thought: Teaching comprehension in a reader's workshop.* Portsmouth, NH: Heinemann.

Kuskin, K. (1998). *The sky is always in the sky.* New York: HarperCollins.

Massachusetts Museum of Modern Art. (2004). *The interventionists: Art in the social sphere.* Cambridge, MA: MIT Press.

Morris, A., & Heyman, K. (1993). *Hats, hats, hats.* New York: Trophy.

National Center for Education Statistics. (2004). Percentage of students, by reading achievement level, grade 4: 1992–2003. *The nation's report card: Reading.* Washington, DC: National Center for Education Statistics, Institute of Education Sciences, U.S. Department of Education. Retrieved March 9, 2005, from http://nces.ed.gov/nationsreportcard/reading/results2003/natachieve-g4.asp

No Child Left Behind Act of 2001, Pub. L. No. 107-110, 115 Stat. 1425 (2002).

Peterson, R., & Eeds, M. (1990). *Grand conversations: Literature groups in action.* New York: Scholastic.

Schmoker, M. (2001). The "Crayola curriculum." *Education Week, 21*(8), 42–44.

Trapani, I. (1998). *The itsy bitsy spider.* New York: Whispering Coyote Press.

Questions for Reflection

- Think about yourself as a reader. What books or magazines do you have on your bedside or coffee table at home right now? What big ideas do they contain? How do you identify the big ideas in your own reading? And what do you do with those ideas?

- Take stock of the books and other readings used in the language arts curriculum in your school. Have you considered the big ideas in each? How will you identify them and bring them to the attention of your students?

Teaching Summarization as a Content Area Reading Strategy

Rosalie Friend

Milli (pseudonym) proudly explained how she raised her score from 26% on the first psychology test to 79% on the second test. "It was that strategy you taught." The strategy, summarization, is very hard for students to pick up on their own, but it can be taught directly. Many students appreciate strategy instruction that makes summarization less mysterious. In this article I will describe a way to teach summarization that can be applied to all content areas, and I will explain the factors that make it effective.

A summary written for content area reading has four defining features: (a) It is short, (b) it tells what is most important *to the author*, (c) it is written "in your own words," and (d) it states the information "you need to study." We can make this powerful learning strategy available to high school and college students by teaching students to think about the passage and relate the ideas to one another to construct a summary rather than select sentences from the passage.

At the colleges and community colleges of our large U.S. urban university, diversity means that my classes have students of every race and religion along with immigrants from around the world. A class of 25 students may have people from 5 to 15 countries. Usually their ages range from 17 to mid 50s. Many of them need non-credit "developmental" reading or writing courses when they enter the university. Most of our students work and are responsible for children or older relatives while studying "full time." All my students know that the content area reading they do for school differs from reading for their own pleasure in two ways. One is that to study, they have to understand *and remember* new information. The other is that someone else has decided what should be learned.

Studying and Remembering

One of the most common strategies college students use to study is to underline parts of a text and read the text over and over (Ruddell & Boyle, 1989). Many students view learning as something mystical that will happen to them if they reread faithfully. They have a vague model of memory as a collection of discrete facts, probably neatly listed on separate file cards in their brains. Information processing research provides a more sophisticated model of memory and more effective ways to learn from text.

The best model of semantic memory, memory for school information, is a network (maybe hypertext) of related ideas, grouped into interlinked concepts (Reynolds, Sinatra, & Jetton, 1996). Each time you use an idea, that idea and the ideas associated with it are alerted, or primed. The more an idea is primed, the stronger the memory. Thus, the more connections or links between ideas and the better organized the connections are, the more readily an idea can be recalled and applied. This is the reason rehearsal study methods, like rereading a chapter or reviewing file cards, are limited in their effectiveness (Ruddell & Boyle, 1989). They will strengthen individual ideas, but will not be very effective at creating connections among ideas.

Reprinted from Friend, R. (2000/2001). Teaching summarization as a content area reading strategy. *Journal of Adolescent & Adult Literacy*, 44(4), 320-329.

The paucity of connections limits cues for recall of the ideas and also limits the ways the learner can retrieve the information to apply it in new situations.

The strongest study strategies are those using elaboration. To elaborate, the student explicitly creates associations for the information to be learned. A good example of elaboration is Ciardiello's (1998) method in which students are taught to construct high-level divergent questions so that they are actively thinking about the material they read. A simpler form of elaboration is found in Cornell notetaking (Pauk, 1997) in which students write an example of each concept they study. The major drawback of elaboration is that it requires additional thinking, time, and energy, sometimes distracting students from the concepts they set out to study. Many students have had little training in elaboration and find it difficult. They prefer rehearsal, which makes minimal demands on cognitive capacity. Unfortunately, they do not realize that rehearsal often leads to rote learning and limits transfer resulting in minimal recall of what was studied.

The third type of study strategy, organization, reaches a balance between effort and effectiveness (McCormick & Pressley, 1997). In order to organize new information, students must draw on prior knowledge and pay attention to the nature of relationships among ideas. As they organize information by constructing a summary, an outline, or a graphic organizer, students generate links among the new ideas they are studying. They must use prior knowledge of the topic in order to organize the new information, so connections are made among related concepts. New information that is linked with the network of prior ideas will be more easily recalled, and can be used in more adaptive ways. In particular, writing a summary requires evaluating the information that is read to determine what is important enough to include. It also requires transforming long detailed passages into terse statements of the gist of the information. This "deep" processing primes concepts related to the new information and improves recall.

Ineffective Student-Generated Strategies

Over the years students have told me that they have trouble writing summaries because it is hard to figure out what to put in and what to leave out. Like the students in earlier studies (Byrd, 1990; Winograd, 1984), my incoming students read the sentences in a passage and choose some sentences to copy or paraphrase while leaving out the other sentences. This "copy and delete" method is counterproductive. We discourage copying or close paraphrasing as plagiarism; it is against school rules and is illegal. In addition, while there are books and articles with paragraphs in which an explicit topic sentence states the main idea of the whole, many passages do not have explicit topic sentences. Most important, in order to enhance learning, summarization should be a process in which the ideas of a passage are related to one another, weighed, and condensed; a process of synthesis, not selection. What makes summarization a powerful study strategy are the connections formed as the reader groups ideas into associated concepts and the concepts into interrelated hierarchical networks or schemata. This grouping extends cognitive capacity.

A college student who has to read a 25- to 30-page chapter each week for each subject faces thousands of sentences of information. Remembering thousands of separate facts is a very difficult task. Summarization provides cognitive shopping bags: Students who group ideas into schemata and label the schemata and the relationships among them have a reasonable number of schemata to keep in mind instead of an unmanageably large aggregation of discrete ideas.

Novices often try to judge the importance of ideas for studying the way they would judge the importance of personal experiences. Personal experiences are stored in episodic memory. Novelty, emotion, and drama are cues to importance in episodic memory. In content area reading these elements may be used to add interest, but they are usually not important. In fact Garner (Garner & Gillingham, 1989) labeled them as seductive details, because they draw students' attention away from the important ideas, which are usually more abstract. How can students judge importance if personal experience and idiosyncratic personal values don't help them judge what is important to the author?

Cues to Text-Based Importance

In working with college and community college students on how to write summaries, I found two essential cues to text-based importance: repeated reference and generalization (Morton & Hosey, 1984). I was delighted to find that the research of van Dijk and Kintsch (1983) emphasized the same cues to provide a theoretical explanation of text-based importance. Van Dijk and Kintsch told us that expert readers learn the cognitive processes of summarization gradually through immersion. We can speed up the process for our students by presenting the essential cues to importance through direct instruction and guided practice. A discovery approach would leave students trying to apply personal criteria of importance or standards for episodic memory instead of standards for the semantic memory used for content area learning (Garner, 1987; Nordin, 1996). After students have learned the basic strategy, cooperative learning groups can be helpful in reinforcing the strategy as students practice applying it. They must practice the new strategy and learn to apply it so that the strategy becomes familiar. Otherwise applying the new strategy requires students' attention, reducing their concentration on the content they are trying to learn.

To exemplify students' own strategies for summarization and their responses to instruction, I shall present some summaries of "Native Americans," a passage I adapted from *News for You* (1990, December 12). (See Sidebar "Native Americans.") I have used this simple passage at different points in instruction with different classes over the years. I often begin teaching summarization by asking students to write a summary "the way you learned before." A student using personal criteria of importance or responding to the most dramatic ideas may even

miss the point of the passage. In this example a weak student wrote,

> Many years ago Native Americans were living on this continent. Their land was destroyed by Europeans when they had came to their homeland. The land was taken away from the Native Americans by Europeans. The United States government had set aside land for different tribes. They not only have land problems but job problems as well the unemployment rate was very high. Some tribes started their own business but were taken away from their customs and their way of life, especially language. Their way of life was changed by Europeans.

Students may identify with others who experienced discrimination, or they may have been so strongly influenced by the opening of the passage that they did not fully acknowledge the contrast the author set up (Sorrells & Britton, 1998). Other students ramble or include specific details that would enliven an essay, but should not be in a summary, for instance, "The Choctaw tribe built auto-parts factories." Strategy instruction will enable these students to determine what is most important to the author and to transform the information into a terse summary.

Repeated references. The first cue to importance found in all content area reading is what van Dijk and Kintsch (1983) called argument repetition. The more an idea is referred to by other ideas, the more important it is. It is primed most frequently, and it has more connections with other ideas than the less central ideas. Argument repetition is part of the surface structure of written material. In teaching I call it repeated references. Students find this cue easy to apply. Kintsch and van Dijk (1978) employed a research paradigm in which the number of references was counted, but our students do not have to count. They just have to ask themselves, "Is this idea central or on the edge?" or "Does the author keep talking about it?"

To introduce repeated references, I wrote a little exercise:

> Johnny Lee has a good imagination and loves playing tricks on people, so his mother tries to keep an eye on her little darling. Yesterday Ms. Lee had a

Native Americans

1. For thousands of years, Native Americans made their homes on this continent. Then, Europeans came and destroyed their way of life.

2. When Europeans arrived, they didn't share the same view of the land as Native Americans. Europeans believed land (and people) could be bought and sold. According to Native American tradition, land could not be owned. They thought human beings were part of nature, not above it.

3. The clash of views was settled by force. Europeans pushed Native Americans off their land. In the United States the government set aside land for each of the tribes. That land was called a reservation. Today, more than 330,000 Native Americans live on 260 reservations across the U.S.

4. Finding a job is a big problem for many Native Americans. The overall jobless rate for Native Americans is 40%. On the 10 largest reservations, 75% of the people don't have jobs. They can no longer live by hunting and fishing. Many Native Americans must leave their reservations to find work.

5. Some tribes have begun to build businesses on the reservations. The Choctaws in Mississippi run five auto-parts factories on their land. The Navajo nation grows mushrooms to sell to people in Asia. It also builds missiles for the army. The Seminoles in Florida own a 156-room hotel. The Cherokee Nation runs a plant and gardening business. These businesses provide many jobs.

6. The Passamaquoddy tribe of Maine bought a blueberry farm, two radio stations, and a failing cement plant. The tribe turned the cement plant into a successful business. Later, it sold the plant for a large profit.

7. The Choctaws started their factories as partnerships with car companies. The tribe's jobless rate dropped from 80% to 20%.

8. Education has changed. Once Native Americans were forced to assimilate (adjust to mainstream culture). Before 1934, many Native American children were sent to boarding schools. They weren't allowed to speak their native languages or wear native clothes.

9. Today, many reservation schools teach the tribe's language and customs. Native American students learn to compete in mainstream American culture. But, there is also an effort to teach ancient tribal religion and values.

10. Native Americans hold powwows each year to celebrate their culture. In the past, a powwow was mainly a religious event. The gathering was held when a tribe had a problem. Through prayers and dances, the tribe asked for help from the gods. Today, powwows are part religious ceremony, part dance festival, and part social event.

11. For Native Americans who have left reservations, powwows provide a link to old traditions. "When you move away to the city, you find out how important Indian identity is," said one woman.

12. Interest in powwows is growing. Seven years ago, 3,000 people attended the first "Gathering of Nations" powwow in New Mexico. This year 30,000 Native Americans came.

13. Many see powwows as key to their culture's future. "At one time we were a forgotten people, but I think we are getting stronger," said Linda Yardley, a Pueblo. "From the powwow we gain strength to go on into the 21st century."

Model Summary
Native Americans are adjusting to mainstream American practices and strengthening tribal economies and culture. When the Europeans came to America, they took over most of the land and forced the Native Americans onto reservations. Recently many Native American tribes have opened businesses on their reservations to reduce unemployment. Their schools now teach their traditions along with modern American ideas. Powwows have become a social and cultural force to hold Native American people together.

lot to do, so she left Johnny eating a snack while she started her work. Suddenly something cold and slimy slid down her back. She screamed. After a moment she realized that her son was up to more mischief.

I ask the students, "What does the author keep talking about all the way through? What other words or phrases does the author use to refer to Johnny?" It is important for students to recognize that the idea may be referred to in many different ways; it is an idea we are following, not a word or phrase.

Next I give each student a set of written guidelines to follow as the class learns how to write summaries (see Sidebar "Guidelines"). I also post or hand out the diagram shown in Figure 1. I have the students read a one-page passage, and I model the processes that I use to follow the guidelines to write a summary. Next I lead a whole-class session in which the class constructs the summary of a second short passage using the guidelines' *four steps to summarization.*

Step 1 in writing a summary is to think of the passage as a whole. We are learning to judge importance with respect to an entire essay or article or a section of a book chapter. Students must learn to read the entire passage and think about how the parts add up to a whole. They must find out how the authors resolve conflicting data or use straw men. Students must give the end of a chapter as much weight as the beginning.

Step 2 is to determine the thesis: What is the central idea (main idea) that the whole passage refers to? If students state only the topic, it is essential to teach them to tell what the author has to say about the topic. A content area summary must give information.

Step 3 involves determining the major supporting ideas. I have the students group consecutive paragraphs that refer to the same aspect of the topic and actually draw a bracket in the margin to identify each group of paragraphs. Then we write the central idea of each group of paragraphs as determined by repeated references. As students suggest major supporting ideas, we use repeated references for judging importance: Do the other ideas refer to this idea? Is it central or at the edge? Does the author keep talking about it?

Step 4 in writing a summary is checking your work. Students must be sure their thesis states the idea to which the rest of the article refers. A literary summary may refer to topics or discuss the author's craft, but a summary for content area study cannot. Every topic must have its comment: *what* does the author say about it? Do not refer to the author, and avoid the words *about, how,* or *the way.* Don't say "It is about Native Americans," but say "Native Americans are overcoming serious problems."

Following a whole-class construction of a summary, I ask each student to use repeated references to construct an individual summary. At this point a student summary of "Native Americans" usually includes the major supporting ideas, but many students still don't begin the summary with the thesis, and some may have trouble writing a single sentence to sum up several paragraphs. Typical summaries are as follows:

> Native Americans were stripped of their culture and when the Europeans arrived in the United States. Because of the two different views of life, the Native Americans were pushed off their land. They were then forced to live on reservations. Being used to living on natural instinct, Native Americans are having a hard time finding jobs. For those who are not, they have built many different businesses. There are many tribes of different names, and some have become well successful. They are now being educated the American way and the Native American way. Even though the Native Americans were treated badly, they still don't forget where they came from. Each year they hold gathering for all of their people. It is called powwows. With this gathering it shows the people that their culture will last a long time.

> Native Americans were forced to live on reservations across the U.S. The majority of them without jobs. Different tribes try and form jobs on the reservation. The children are deny the teaching of their culture. Celebration of religious ceremony are held each year which are called powwows.

Generalization. Repeated references are valuable as cues to importance, because they are part of the surface structure of the text. Frequently the gist of a text is not part of the surface structure, but is constructed by the reader. The second cue to importance that I teach, generalization, is a cognitive process that students have used in other contexts. Expository text is usually a hierarchical arrangement of ideas. Generalization enables students to identify the ideas at the top of the hierarchy.

Van Dijk and Kintsch (1983) found that while the reader is building a cognitive representation

Guidelines

Guidelines for using repeated references to write a summary

1. *Preview* the whole passage. *Think* about what you expect when you read it. Read the entire passage. Think about the passage as a whole. What does it all add up to? Be sure you understand the whole article.
2. Now figure out the *thesis*, the main idea of the whole article. Ask yourself two questions: What is the whole article about (the topic)? What is the message about the topic? Look the passage over until you have the one *central idea* that the rest of the passage refers to. Write this idea in a sentence in your own words. Be sure the thesis gives information for studying; avoid saying "how" or "about." Instead give the actual procedure, result, or other information.
3. To figure out the *central idea of each paragraph or group of paragraphs*, ask yourself two questions: What does the whole paragraph refer to (the topic)? What is the message about the topic? Reread the paragraph to be sure you have put together the idea that the author refers to the most. Write that idea in a complete sentence.

   Sometimes two or three paragraphs can be grouped together for your summary. Paragraphs should be grouped together if they refer to the same aspect of the topic or if one paragraph doesn't add new information. Then one sentence can sum up the group of paragraphs.

   To make the summary short, keep out the details that fill out the central idea. Keep out examples, illustrations, and little stories. Instead give the central principles they refer to.

   Don't repeat anything in a summary. Be sure to reduce each paragraph or group of paragraphs to a sentence that gives the central information and keeps out the details. Be sure to avoid saying "how," "the way," or "about," so the sentences give the information you need to study.
4. Check your summary against the passage. Look back over the rules to be sure you followed them. Make sure you have written sentences that tell the most important (most central) ideas referred to by the other ideas. Make sure your summary is written in complete sentences forming a paragraph (or paragraphs) you can use to study. Make sure your first sentence states the thesis (main idea of the whole passage). Make sure you wrote the information in your own words.

Guidelines for using generalization to write a summary

1. *Preview* the whole passage. *Think* about what you expect when you read it. *Read* the entire passage. Think about the passage as a whole. What does it all add up to? Be sure you understand the whole article.
2. To figure out the *thesis*, the main idea of the whole article, ask yourself two questions: What is the whole article about (the topic)? What is the message about the topic? Look the passage over until you have the one *general idea* that includes all the specifics of the article. Write this idea in a sentence in your own words. Be sure the thesis gives information for studying; avoid saying "how" or "about"; give the actual procedure, result, or other information. Be sure the thesis is general enough to cover the whole article but not more general (not vague).
3. Now figure out the *major supporting ideas*. They will be more specific than the thesis, but each one will be general enough to include all the details of a paragraph or a group of paragraphs. Paragraphs should be grouped together if they are on the same aspect of the topic or if one doesn't add new information. Write a sentence general enough to state the information from each paragraph or group of paragraphs.

   To make the summary short, *keep out the specific details*. Keep out examples, illustrations, and little stories. Instead give the general principles they illustrate.

   Don't repeat anything in a summary. Be sure to reduce each paragraph or group of paragraphs to a general sentence in your own words that covers the information. Be sure to avoid saying "how," "the way," or "about," so the sentences give the information you need to study.
4. Check your summary against the passage. Look back over the rules to be sure you followed them. Make sure you have written general sentences that sum up the specifics. Make sure your summary is written in complete sentences forming a paragraph (or paragraphs) you can use to study. Make sure your first sentence states the thesis (main idea of the whole passage). Make sure you wrote the information in your own words.

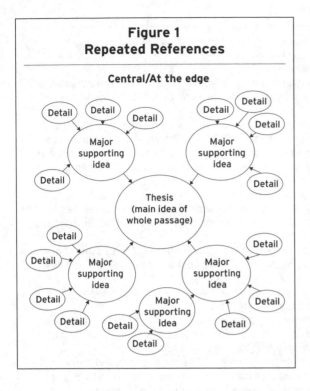

**Figure 1
Repeated References**

Central/At the edge

Detail, Detail, Detail

Major supporting idea

Detail

Detail, Detail, Detail

Major supporting idea

Detail

Thesis (main idea of whole passage)

Detail

Detail, Detail

Major supporting idea

Detail, Detail

Major supporting idea

Detail

Detail

Major supporting idea

Detail, Detail

Detail

of the surface structure of text, simultaneous processes construct a brief representation in long-term memory called "gist." They broke down the process into three rules that are applied recursively:

1. Deletion: Leave out specific details and background information unless an idea is necessary for interpreting the main ideas.

2. Generalization: For each group of ideas, paragraph, or group of paragraphs substitute a sentence that "pulls together" the specific ideas. It must be general enough to cover the details, but it must not go beyond the details to become vague.

3. Construction: In forming your generalization, include the inferences you drew from the ideas in the paragraph or group of paragraphs. (Adapted from van Dijk & Kintsch, 1983, p. 190)

These three rules can be taught as generalization. When a series of specific ideas are replaced by a general idea, deletion has occurred. The theorists distinguish between generalization and construction, but for the sake of teaching construction can be considered one way of making a generalization.

I introduce generalization after using repeated references to write summaries for a day or two. This cognitive process is very familiar from many other uses. When I introduce it, I recite a list like "carrots, spinach, tomatoes, string beans." Before I can finish the list, students are saying, "vegetables." I give them a second list, more abstract, but still familiar, "Washington, Lincoln, Roosevelt, and Bush." With weak students I have them compare pairs of ideas such as flavor/chocolate, poodle/dog, fingerprint/clue. Which is general and which is specific?

The little paragraph I made up to teach generalization says, "After work, I have to buy groceries and make dinner, and then wash the dishes. I'll have to do the laundry and then dust and vacuum. If I have time, I ought to wash the kitchen floor." I ask students to write the main idea in a sentence in their own words. If they write topics without comments, I use the cue "Who did what?" specifying that "who" may be an organization or an idea.

To teach generalization as a basis for summarization, I use the same procedure I used with repeated references: guidelines (see Sidebar "Guidelines"), a diagram (see Figure 2), modeling, and guided practice. The four steps are the same, but students now have a cue to importance, generalization, which also enables them to transform a list of detailed sentences into a single "higher level" sentence. In using repeated references students' attention is directed to the surface structure of the passage, but using generalization emphasizes that the thesis or major supporting idea may not be written on the page. The reader can put two and two together, make sense of the passage, and find the thesis and major supporting ideas "in your head."

When I have students write an individual summary after a couple of days of work with repeated references and a group lesson on using generalization, many more students can figure out the thesis and are able to group paragraphs

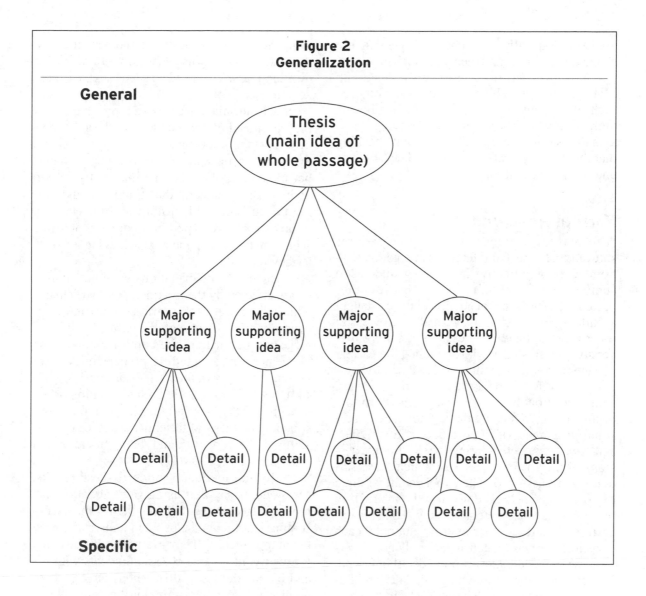

**Figure 2
Generalization**

General

Thesis
(main idea of
whole passage)

Major supporting idea

Major supporting idea

Major supporting idea

Major supporting idea

Detail

Specific

together. Typical summaries would be as follows:

In the early years Native Americans were faced with problems by the Europeans; nevertheless, they continued with their traditions. Finding a job is a big problem for Native Americans. In a way of finding a solution, Native Americans have started their own business. Education has become an important part of their lives. Their traditions have not changed throughout the years.

Native Americans were forced out of their land and culture but are finding a way to get back their traditions and to live. Europeans set them aside on reservation. Most of them are jobless and were forced to create their own businesses. Their children are learning their traditions. They use powwows for religious ceremonies and keep united.

By the end of the semester, everyone who has done the assignments conscientiously has learned to write an adequate summary.

To begin practicing summarization I use short passages in which it is easy to discern which paragraphs would be grouped together. Then I use longer passages and finally chapters from content area textbooks. In working with textbooks I usually recommend previewing the chapter as a whole, and then summarizing a section at a time, writing one sentence to sum up each subsection. While there are some courses such as anatomy in which every detail is important, in most courses determining the general idea that sums up each subsection and checking that the details all refer to that idea help students understand the material

Formal Research

A formal test of these classroom procedures showed that repeated references and generalization were both effective in assisting students to summarize (Friend, in press). In this study repeated references and generalization were taught separately to illustrate theoretical differences in processing. At three colleges of a large urban university, 149 freshmen who had failed the writing placement test were randomly assigned to summarization instruction using repeated references, summarization instruction using generalization, or instruction in relating the text to readers' personal judgments of importance (control). The study was conducted during two 90-minute sessions of the writing classes to which these students were assigned. The experimenters, three experienced teachers, delivered the instruction using scripts to assure consistency. To avoid experimenter effects, the condition taught by each experimenter was rotated at each college.

The procedure (discussed in detail in Friend, in press) used the definition, guidelines, and figures described earlier. The passages to be summarized, taken from Day (1980) or adapted from adult literacy materials, were comparable to "Native Americans," which was one of the passages used in the study. Experimenters modeled the strategy, led the class in developing a summary as a group, and then had students apply the strategy to construct a summary individually while the experimenter circulated and answered individual questions. Papers were collected, corrected, and returned in the next class section with a model summary for experimental conditions and a model self-response for the control group. The experimenter led the whole class in using the strategy to construct another summary, then each student was asked to write his or her own summary. This product served as the dependent measure.

Each summary was scored for inclusion of predetermined important ideas, exclusion of predetermined unimportant ideas, construction of a thesis statement, sentence transformation (number of sentences of the original text summed up by each sentence in the summary), and stating the full main idea, not the topic (how...). Summaries were typed and copied; each was scored by two experimenters achieving a .80 interrater reliability.

Sentence transformations were not significantly affected by the treatment, but participants who were taught to summarize using either generalization or repeated references did significantly better than the control group on the other measures: including predetermined important concepts in their final summaries, $F (2, 144) = 4.1032, p < .019$, excluding unimportant concepts, $F (2, 144) = 26.1525, p < .001$, constructing the thesis of the entire article $c2 (2, N = 129) = 10.04, p < .006$, and stating full ideas, not just topics $c2 (2, N = 147) = 26.64, p = .000$.

Informal feedback supports these results. My students say that using generalization and repeated references removes the mystery from summarization and helps them understand what the author means. They are using this strategy for their content area classes. Students with A's and B's in courses as different as biology, economics, music, and criminal justice say, "Now I know what to do!"

References

Byrd, M. (1990, May). *Summary writing strategies of junior college students*. Paper presented at the annual convention of the International Reading Association, Atlanta, GA.

Ciardiello, A.V. (1998). Did you ask a good question today? Alternative cognitive and metacognitive strategies. *Journal of Adolescent & Adult Literacy, 42*, 210–219.

Day, J.D. (1980). *Training summarization skills: A comparison of teaching methods*. Unpublished doctoral dissertation, University of Illinois, Urbana.

Friend, R. (in press). Effects of strategy instruction on summary writing of college students. *Contemporary Educational Psychology.*

Garner, R. (1987). Strategies for reading and studying expository text. *Educational Psychologist, 22,* 299–312.

Garner, R., & Gillingham, M.G. (1989). Effects of "seductive details" on macroprocessing and microprocessing in adults and children. *Cognition and Instruction, 6,* 41–57.

Kintsch, W., & van Dijk, T.A. (1978). Toward a model of text comprehension and production. *Psychological Review, 85,* 363–394.

McCormick, C.B., & Pressley, M. (1997). *Educational psychology: Learning, instruction, assessment.* New York: Addison Wesley Longman.

Morton, E.V., & Hosey, J.G. (1984). *Reading and studying for success.* Minneapolis, MN: Burgess International Group.

Nordin, M.S. (1996). Relative effectiveness of training in, or awareness of, the use of coded elaborative outline and question writing in learning from text. *Dissertation Abstracts International: Section A, Humanities and Social Sciences, 56,* 2615.

Pauk, W. (1997). *How to study in college.* Boston: Houghton Mifflin.

Reynolds, R.E., Sinatra, G.M., & Jetton, T.L. (1996). Views of knowledge acquisition and representation: A continuum from experience centered to mind centered. *Educational Psychologist, 31,* 93–104.

Ruddell, R.B., & Boyle, O.F. (1989). A study of cognitive mapping as a means to improve summarization and comprehension of expository text. *Reading Research & Instruction, 29,* 12–22.

Sorrells, R.C., & Britton, B.K. (1998). What is the point? Tests of a quick and clean method for improving instructional text. In C.R. Hynd (Ed.), *Learning from text across conceptual domains* (pp. 95–116). Mahwah, NJ: Erlbaum.

van Dijk, T.A., & Kintsch, W. (1983). *Strategies of discourse comprehension.* New York: Academic Press.

Winograd, P. (1984). Strategic difficulties in summarizing text. *Reading Research Quarterly, 19,* 404–425.

Questions for Reflection

• The author presents summarization as particularly helpful as a study strategy. Do you think it is equally helpful as a comprehension strategy? How could summarization be used in a classroom setting to help students understand text passages?

• What adaptations could be made to the strategies outlined here so that they could be used with students in upper elementary, middle, and secondary grades?

• The author suggests exercises for introducing generalization. What words, concepts, and paragraphs could you use to develop similar exercises for your students?

Teaching Expository Text Structure Awareness

Susan Dymock

It has been well established that skilled readers use a variety of strategies to comprehend written text (Calfee & Drum, 1986; Stanovich, 2000; Sweet & Snow, 2003). Many students will not develop these skills without the explicit teaching of comprehension strategies. Research shows, however, that the explicit teaching of comprehension is uncommon. Pressley, Wharton-McDonald, Mistretta-Hampston, and Echevarria (1998) reported a scarcity of comprehension instruction in grades 3–6. As put by Pressley et al., "We were struck by the almost complete absence of direct instruction about comprehension strategies" (p. 172). It is not surprising, then, that many students experience problems comprehending written text, especially the more complex expository text.

A summary of key findings from the research includes the following:

- Many students experience problems comprehending expository text. There are many reasons for this, one being that they can't see the basic structure of text. Some students get lost in the words and can't see the big picture (Dymock, 1998; Dymock & Nicholson, 1999).

- Some students require direct instruction in how to go about comprehending more complex expository text structures (Moore, Bean, Birdyshaw, & Rycik, 1999; Pressley, 2002; Vacca, 1998).

- Teachers play an important role in assisting students to develop reading comprehension strategies including expository text structure awareness (see Dymock, 1997, for a review of text structure research; Dymock & Nicholson, 1999; Pearson & Duke, 2002; Smolkin & Donovan, 2002).

- Students who have a good understanding of expository text structure have fewer problems with comprehension (Dymock & Nicholson, 1999).

- Teaching expository text structure awareness has a positive effect on reading comprehension (Dymock & Nicholson, 1999; Pearson & Duke, 2002).

- Expository text structure awareness is one reading comprehension strategy that should be explicitly and systematically taught (Sweet & Snow, 2003).

- The Literacy Experts Group's report (1999) to the New Zealand Secretary for Education recommended that, "Especially from year 3, more attention should be paid to the teaching of comprehension skills, across a range of text types, including *expository texts*" (p. 6; emphasis added). Some suggest that explicit teaching of comprehension strategies, to enhance comprehension of exposition, should begin during year 1 (Duke, 2000; Pearson & Duke, 2002).

Reprinted from Dymock, S. (2005). Teaching expository text structure awareness. *The Reading Teacher, 59*(2), 177–181. doi: 10.1598/RT.59.2.7

How to Go About Explicitly Teaching Expository Text Structure Awareness

Exposition can be written with many types of organizations or structures. These structures are used to organize discourse, and often they are very complex. Students should be taught explicitly how to recognize and use expository text structures to improve comprehension and recall. Knowledge about how expository text is structured, however, will not guarantee comprehension, but having a clear understanding of how the text is structured will help the reader build a coherent model of the text.

Expository text types can be divided into two groups, texts that describe and texts that are affected by time (Calfee & Patrick, 1995). Young readers encounter three descriptive text types and one sequential text during their first six years at school (Dymock & Nicholson, 1999). Teaching students the many expository text structures that writers use, and showing students how to organize the material graphically, can have a positive effect on comprehension. Demonstrating how to diagram the various expository text structures enables students to "see" how texts are constructed. These strategies enable the reader to make order out of the "sea of words." Creating a clear structure is critical for learning and thinking (Chambliss & Calfee, 1998).

The CORE model (*C*onnect, *O*rganize, *R*eflect, *E*xtend) provides a framework for lesson design when teaching the structure of expository text (Calfee, Chambliss, & Beretz, 1991; Calfee & Patrick, 1995; Chambliss & Calfee, 1998). An effective lesson *connects* students to the topic. Connectedness is the link between what the reader knows and what is being learned. Teachers should connect students to the content (e.g., native birds) and the text structure (e.g., matrix or compare/contrast). Calfee (1993) suggested that the teacher can build on the reader's knowledge base by focusing on what the reader knows, rather than on what the reader does not know. *Organize* includes the principle of keeping the lesson simple and the physical organization of the text. This includes the list, web, weave, and string text structure diagrams

that are discussed in this article. Teachers need to explicitly teach students that expository text has many structures. Diagramming (or organizing) the text enables students to "see" the structure and to understand and remember it better. These structures are critical in cognitive learning as the graphic organizers provide the reader with tools for creating order out of the text. *Reflect* is where students explain or critique content, structures, and strategies (e.g., What kind of text did we analyze today? How did we know it was a web? Why did we diagram the structure?). Finally, an opportunity is provided to transfer (or *extend*) learning to new topics. This extension offers a chance to reflect, as well as an opportunity for meaningful practice.

Sweet and Snow (2003) recommended that teachers model the strategy (e.g., teach children how to identify the text structure the writer has used and how to diagram its structure). Following this, the teacher should provide guided practice by working alongside the students as they diagram the text.

The following section describes common expository text structures students encounter in primary school (i.e., descriptive and sequential structures). The section forms the organize part of the lesson. After students are connected to the topic by well-developed questioning strategies that encourage them to think about what is being learned, the teacher then models how to diagram (i.e., organize) the text. The included figures demonstrate how four common expository text structures can be organized. Students then reflect on what they have learned (e.g., What have we done in this lesson today? Why have we done it?). Finally, an opportunity to extend their understanding to new material should be provided (e.g., "Today we created a web based on the descriptive article on the bald eagle. With your partner develop a web on the New Zealand kiwi, a flightless native bird.").

Common Expository Text Structures

Students encounter several common expository text structures during their first six years at school, and beyond. Diagrams of each enable students to "see" the structure the writer has used. It is recommended that only one text structure be taught at a time.

Descriptive Structures

Descriptive patterns focus on the attributes of something. Three common descriptive patterns found in school reading material for 6- to 12-year-olds include the *list*, *web*, and *matrix* (compare/contrast).

A basic descriptive pattern is the *list* (Calfee & Patrick, 1995). This may be as simple as the grocery list; a list of countries where English is the dominant language; or, in science, the attributes of penguins (e.g., black and white, eat fish, can't fly). With the list, it doesn't matter what goes first. The list pattern in Figure 1 is from the article, "Picking Up Rubbish." Gary Brackenbury (1996) listed the material found in a sparrow's nest.

The *web* is another descriptive pattern (Calfee & Patrick, 1995). In the web the attributes of an object are discussed. The attributes have a common link. For example, the article may be discussing the characteristics of snails or the features of San Francisco. The web diagram in Figure 2, completed by an 11-year-old, is based on an article on the kakapo, a New Zealand native bird (Bryant, 1990).

The *matrix* compares and contrasts two or more topics (Calfee & Patrick, 1995). For example, the author may be comparing the features of brown, polar, and black bears; native birds;

two Brazilian cities; or volcano types. Figure 3 is based on an article on mud, written at the 6-year-old level (Meharry, 2001).

Sequential Structures

Sequential structures present a series of events that progress over time. Normally, sequence texts are set out in a first-to-last pattern.

The *string* pattern (Calfee & Patrick, 1995) is a common pattern in beginning reading material and also in the material students encounter at the high school level. In the string pattern a chronological description of events is given (e.g., steps involved in baking bread or harvesting carrots). Or it could refer to the sequence to follow in working out a math problem. Or in science it could refer to the life cycle of the duck-billed platypus. The string pattern in Figure 4 is based on a section of *The Duckbilled Platypus: Nature's Experiment* (Bremer, 1984). The text is at the 10- to 12-year-old reading level.

Research shows that children who have a good understanding of the structure of expository text have fewer problems with comprehension. While some children are able to figure out the different textual patterns on their own, there are others who are not so lucky. Research shows that many students are unaware that exposition follows an organized pattern. These students require direct instruction in how to go about comprehending expository text structures (Dymock & Nicholson, 1999; Moore et al., 1999; Vacca, 1998). Explicit teaching of text structure awareness has a positive effect on comprehension

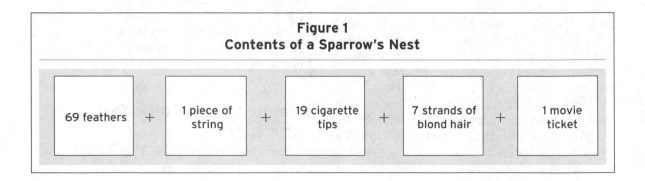

Figure 1
Contents of a Sparrow's Nest

69 feathers + 1 piece of string + 19 cigarette tips + 7 strands of blond hair + 1 movie ticket

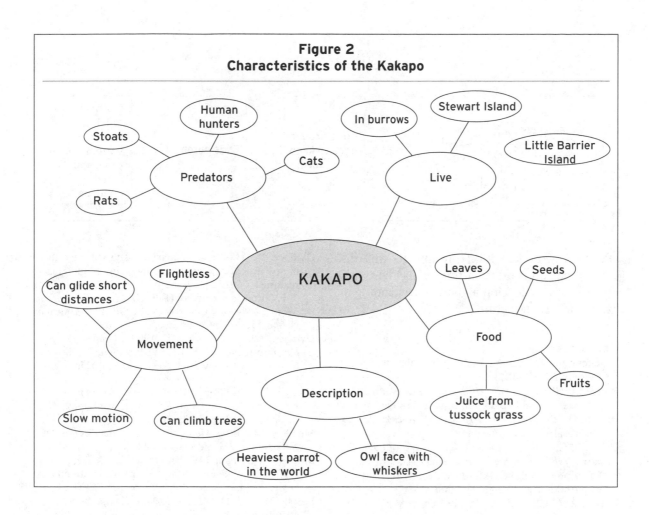

Figure 2
Characteristics of the Kakapo

- Human hunters
- Stoats
- Cats
- Rats
- Predators
- In burrows
- Stewart Island
- Little Barrier Island
- Live
- KAKAPO
- Can glide short distances
- Flightless
- Movement
- Slow motion
- Can climb trees
- Leaves
- Seeds
- Food
- Fruits
- Juice from tussock grass
- Description
- Heaviest parrot in the world
- Owl face with whiskers

Figure 3
Matrix for Animals and Mud

Animal	Does the animal like mud?	What animal does in the mud?	What mud does for the animal?	Size of animal
Pig	Yes	Rolls	Keeps it cool	Large
Frog	Yes	Sleeps	Helps it hide from enemies	Small
Water buffalo	Yes	Stands	Keeps bugs away	Very large
Rhinoceros	Yes	Bathes	Protects it from the sun	Very large

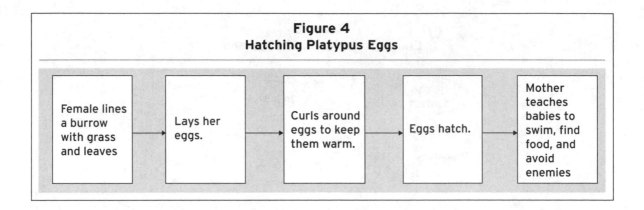

Figure 4
Hatching Platypus Eggs

Female lines a burrow with grass and leaves → Lays her eggs. → Curls around eggs to keep them warm. → Eggs hatch. → Mother teaches babies to swim, find food, and avoid enemies

(Pearson & Duke, 2002). It appears that the teacher has an important role to play in assisting children to develop a good understanding of expository text structure.

References

Brackenbury, G. (1996). Picking up rubbish. *School Journal, 1*(1), 16–18.

Bremer, P. (1984). *The duckbilled platypus: Nature's experiment.* Grand Rapids, MI: Instructional Fair.

Bryant, D. (1990). *The wildtrack book.* Auckland, New Zealand: Hodder & Stoughton.

Calfee, R.C. (1993, October). *Implications of cognitive psychology for authentic assessment and instruction.* Paper presented the Oxford Conference on Text Use with Children and Youth, Stanford, CA.

Calfee, R.C., Chambliss, M.J., & Beretz, M.M. (1991). Organizing for comprehension and composition. In R. Bowler & W. Ellis (Eds.), *All languages and the creation of literacy* (pp. 79–93). Baltimore: Orton Dyslexia Society.

Calfee, R.C., & Drum, P. (1986). Research on teaching reading. In M. Wittrock (Ed.), *Handbook of research on teaching* (pp. 804–849). New York: Macmillan.

Calfee, R.C., & Patrick, C.L. (1995). *Teach our children well: Bringing K–12 education into the 21st century.* Stanford, CA: Stanford Alumni.

Chambliss, M.J., & Calfee, R.C. (1998). *Textbooks for learning: Nurturing children's minds.* Malden, MA: Blackwell.

Duke, N.K. (2000). 3.6 minutes per day: The scarcity of informational texts in first grade. *Reading Research Quarterly, 35,* 202–224.

Dymock, S.J. (1997). *A comparison study of the effects of text structure training, reading practice, and guided reading on reading comprehension.* Unpublished doctoral dissertation, The University of Auckland, Auckland, New Zealand.

Dymock, S.J. (1998). A comparison study of the effects of text structure training, reading practice, and guided reading on reading comprehension. In T. Shanahan & F.V. Rodriguez-Brown (Eds.), *47th yearbook of the National Reading Conference* (pp. 90–102). Chicago: National Reading Conference.

Dymock, S.J., & Nicholson, T. (1999). *Reading comprehension: What is it? How do you teach it?* Wellington, New Zealand: New Zealand Council for Educational Research.

Literacy Experts Group. (1999). *Literacy Experts Group report to the Secretary for Education.* Wellington, New Zealand: Ministry of Education.

Meharry, D. (2001). *Mud, mud, mud.* Washington, DC: National Geographic School Publishing.

Moore, D.W., Bean, T.W., Birdyshaw, D., & Rycik, J.A. (1999). Adolescent literacy. A position statement. *Journal of Adolescent & Adult Literacy, 43,* 97–112.

Pearson, P.D., & Duke, N.K. (2002). Comprehension instruction in the primary grades. In C.C. Block & M. Pressley (Eds.)., (pp. 247–258) *Comprehension instruction: Research-based best practices.* New York: Guilford.

Pressley, M. (2002). *Reading instruction that works: The case for balanced teaching* (2nd ed.). New York: Guilford.

Pressley, M., Wharton-McDonald, R., Mistretta-Hampston, J., & Echevarria, M. (1998). Literacy instruction in 10 fourth- and fifth-grade classrooms in upstate New York. *Scientific Studies of Reading, 2,* 159–194.

Smolkin, L.B., & Donovan, C.A. (2002). "Oh excellent, excellent question!" Developmental differences and comprehension acquisition. In C.C. Block & M. Pressley (Eds.), *Comprehension instruction: Research-based best practices* (pp. 140–157). New York: Guilford.

Stanovich, K. (2000). *Progress in understanding reading.* New York: Guilford.

Sweet, A.P., & Snow, C.E. (Eds.). (2003). *Rethinking reading comprehension.* New York: Guilford.

Vacca, R. (1998). Let's not marginalize adolescent literacy. *Journal of Adolescent & Adult Literacy, 41,* 604–609.

Questions for Reflection

- Take stock of your classroom library and the texts used in your curriculum. Research has shown that children in the early grades get far more exposure to narrative than expository text structures. Do you have a balance of texts in your class? Do you have examples of expository texts that use the structures outlined in this article? Do you teach your students how to identify the text structure the writer has used? Do you feel your students are engaging with a sufficient variety of text structures?

- What writing activities could you design to help your students become more familiar with a variety of text structures?

Guidelines for Implementing a Graphic Organizer

Donna M. Merkley and Debra Jefferies

In 1985, the National Academy of Education's Commission on Education and Public Policy, along with the National Institute of Education, published *Becoming a Nation of Readers* (Anderson, Hiebert, Scott, & Wilkinson, 1985). The intent was to bring together panels of experts on reading instruction and leaders in the field of education to promote the policies and practices deemed necessary for academic achievement and school success. A special section within the research report was dedicated to extending the elementary literacy focus from "learning to read" to "reading to learn." That is, the experts acknowledged the importance of teaching students how to read narrative materials, but further emphasized the need to develop proficiency in content area reading as well. The National Council of Teachers of English and the International Reading Association (1996) have recommended within their standards that students develop an understanding of a wide variety of literature genres including expository material and, more important, that teachers equip students with a flexible set of skills and strategies to comprehend expository text.

Reading Expository Material

Although students are often avid readers of narrative materials and can comprehend and recall information from narrative texts, many students have difficulty effectively comprehending and recalling expository material (Griffin & Tulbert, 1995; Taylor, 1985; Winograd, 1984).

Expository text, written with the primary intent of communicating information, facts, and ideas, presents a challenge for elementary students because it includes text structures that are often different from those students have encountered in narrative material (May, 1990; McCormick, 1995). Text structure in expository material contains a complex organization of concepts arranged in a certain order so that relationships such as cause and effect, compare and contrast, problem and solution, and sequence classification are conveyed (McCormick, 1995). Expository materials often contain specialized vocabulary that is necessary in order to impart the intended meaning. The high density of concepts often makes expository passages difficult for readers to digest.

In addition, since expository text is written specifically to communicate information, facts, and ideas, students need to systematically activate background knowledge in order to make the necessary connections for learning to occur (Farnham-Diggory, 1992; Fry, 1989; Recht & Leslie, 1988; Rumelhart, 1980). Ausubel's premise (1968) that "the most important single factor influencing learning is what the learner already knows" (p. iv) is echoed by Novak (1991), who maintained that "new meanings must be constructed on the basis of knowledge students already possess" (p. 45). In response to the challenges posed by expository text, teachers plan prereading instructional techniques designed to activate students' schema, guide students' comprehension, and enhance students' retention

Reprinted from Merkley, D.M., & Jefferies, D. (2000/2001). Guidelines for implementing a graphic organizer. *The Reading Teacher, 54*(4), 350-357.

of new information (Carr & Thompson, 1996; Pearson, Hansen, & Gordon, 1979).

Research on Graphic Organizers

A number of authorities have addressed the impact of graphic organizers on students' reading comprehension and recall. Graphic organizers developed as a result of Ausubel's research (1960) into the benefits of using an *advance organizer* in the form of an introductory prose passage to enhance the reader's acquisition of new knowledge. Ausubel concluded that when used as a prereading tool, an advance organizer has the potential to link prereading information with a reader's existing schema.

Researchers such as Barron (1969), Earle (1969), and Baker (1977) continued investigating the use of advance organizers, but modified the prereading introduction to an outline format, called a *structured overview*, in place of Ausubel's prose passage. As practitioners and researchers expanded the application of structured overviews to include a hierarchically organized visual display of information, they adapted structured overview use for prereading, during-reading, and postreading tasks, and the term *structured overview* was replaced with the term *graphic organizer* (GO) (Dunston, 1992; Griffin, Simmons, & Kameenui, 1991). Novak and Gowin (1984) adapted the GO to develop concept mapping as a metacognitive tool for science learning, emphasizing the importance of labeled links between concepts in order to specify relationships.

Hawk's research (1986) favored the GO strategy because it provided (a) an overview of the material to be learned, (b) a reference point for putting new vocabulary and main ideas into orderly patterns, (c) a cue for important information, (d) a visual stimulus for written and verbal information, and (e) a concise review tool.

Research on GOs by Alvermann and Boothby (1986) suggested that the effects upon comprehension are increased when GOs are partially constructed by students as a during-reading or postreading activity. Novak (1991) indicated that learner-constructed concept maps (GOs with labeled links) reflected learners' understanding of

science concepts better than traditional forms of testing. Bean, Singer, Sorter, and Frasee (1986) reported enhanced results when GOs were combined with other metacognitive training such as summarizing and retelling. However, in a review of research relating to graphic organizers, Rice (1994) wrote that

> The findings suggest that currently there is no systematic approach to analyzing graphic organizer research resulting in a lack of explanations for why graphic organizers work or do not work.... Further, instructional implications are tenuous at best due to the lack of explanations of how graphic organizers work or do not work. (p. 39)

Constructing Graphic Organizers

Although instructional implications from the research are debatable, reading methodology textbooks typically include the GO strategy and provide directions for construction accompanied by examples from various content areas (Cooper & Flynt, 1996; Richardson & Morgan, 1997; Roe, Stoodt, & Burns, 1998; Ruddell, 1997). The suggestions for creating GOs usually include the following steps:

1. Analyze the learning task for words and concepts important for the student to understand.
2. Arrange them to illustrate the interrelationships and pattern(s) of organization.
3. Evaluate the clarity of relationships as well as the simplicity and effectiveness of the visual.
4. Substitute empty slots for certain words in order to promote students' active reading.

Implementing Graphic Organizers

There appears to be no source, however, that provides implementation guidelines for the teacher who is a novice GO user. We have observed that teachers inexperienced with GOs have a tendency to use the GO visual as a "worksheet" distributed to students, and to lecture from the GO visual with scant provision for student participation. The findings of Moore and Readence (1980, 1984) support the argument that the GO suffers from a lack of systematic operational procedures. Methodology textbooks typically offer fairly vague suggestions for GO implementation such as "Introduce students to the learning task by displaying the graphic and informing them why the terms are arranged in the given manner. Encourage students to contribute as much as possible." The next sections of this article suggest guidelines for GO implementation, provide a sample implementation, and identify and discuss attributes of effective GO implementation.

In formulating GO implementation guidelines, we turned to the literature on schema (Beers, 1987; Clark, 1991; Gordon & Rennie, 1987; Rumelhart, 1980; Sadoski, Pavio, & Goetz, 1991), classroom discussions (Clark, 1991; Darch, Carnine, & Kameenui, 1986; Nelson-Herber, 1986; Pearson et al., 1979; Stahl & Vancil, 1986), and concept development (Hawk, 1986; Kinnison & Pickens, 1984; Robinson & Schraw, 1994). After analyzing the research and the thinking in these three areas, we offer five attributes for effective GO implementation. When presenting the GO to students, the teacher should do the following:

- verbalize relationships (links) among concepts expressed by the visual,
- provide opportunity for student input,
- connect new information to past learning,
- make reference to the upcoming text, and
- seize opportunities to reinforce decoding and structural analysis.

The teacher should take care that the GO visual is detailed enough to present an overview of the material, yet not so detailed that reading the text is not required.

Sample Graphic Organizer Implementation

The example in the Table 1 is designed to illustrate GO implementation, highlighting the occurrence of the five guidelines in the left margin. A brief discussion of each guideline follows the example. Note that in this example the GO is presented to students on an overhead transparency sheet, removing sticky notes to uncover the GO elements as the prereading discussion proceeds. This enables the teacher to direct students' attention to the GO element under consideration. Figure 1 contains the text students used. Figure 2 is the actual graphic organizer.

Discussion of the Implementation Guidelines in the Example

Verbalize relationships (links) among concepts expressed by the visual. The teacher's verbal presentation of the GO elements attempted to reinforce the relationships and links between and among concepts, reminding students that the GO is an overview of material they will encounter during reading. ("Before you read the selection, let's look at the big ideas and how they fit together.") Main ideas were emphasized, and new vocabulary had a reference point. The teacher's verbal presentation, likewise, reinforced the cause and effect pattern of organization within the material. ("Because of the harsh environment....") This was especially important because a pattern of organization signal words was not present in the selection.

Provide opportunity for student input. With frequent pauses for student input, the teacher used the GO elements for brief, focused prereading discussion. The teacher encouraged student comments about GO elements to see what students already knew about the GO elements ("What do we know about the Arctic climate?") and to assess relationships that students understood. Note that the teacher's questions were open ended, avoiding yes or no responses and inviting hypotheses. ("What do you suppose the article will be about?" "How else do you suppose their appearance has been affected by the harsh Arctic environment?")

Table 1
Script for Graphic Organizer for "Deep Freeze Bees"

GO attribute(s)	Script
Student input and connecting old to new	Boys and girls, for the past 2 weeks, we have been studying various insects. Let's name these insects, listing their characteristics and their feeding habits. (Pause for student input.)
Verbalize relationships Student input; reference to upcoming text	One of the insects mentioned in our review was the bee. Today, you will be reading an article about bees, but before you read the selection let's look at the big ideas and how they fit together. The article is titled "Deep Freeze Bees." (Remove note to show the title.) What do you suppose this article will be about? (Pause for student input.)
Connecting old to new	The article will describe the Arctic bumble bee. (Remove note to show "Arctic.") Now think about our geography study this year. Who can come to the map to show us where the Arctic region is located? (Pause for student input.) What words can we use to describe the Arctic region? (Pause for student input.)
Reinforcing decoding	Compared with other regions, the Arctic could be described as...(remove note to show "harsh"). Look carefully at this word. What do we know about pronouncing a vowel that precedes an *r*? (Pause for student input.) Who can pronounce this word?
Reinforce structural analysis	What does *harsh* mean? So, the Arctic region can be said to have a harsh environment. (Remove note to show "environment.") What do we know about the Arctic climate? (Pause for student input.) The article will report an early summer temperature of 44° F. (Remove note to show 44°.) This is about 7° C. So the temperature reflects a harsh environment. The root of this word, *environ*, comes from French, meaning vicinity or surroundings. How could we define *environment*? (Pause for student input.) The dictionary defines *environment* as the conditions surrounding the development of an organism. What other words with this same root can you think of? (Pause and discuss *environmental, environmentalist*.)
Verbalize relationships Reinforce decoding	So, the harsh environment of the Arctic influences how the bumblebee can...(remove note to show "survive"). Who can pronounce this? How can we guess the sound *i* will have? (Student input to generate the generalization.)
Reference to upcoming text Student input	How the Arctic bumblebee survives in the harsh environment will be described in your reading. What conditions of the bumblebee's existence in the Arctic do you think will be different from bumblebees in Iowa or Florida? (Pause—students may anticipate how the bee looks, what it eats, or where it lives.)
Verbalize relationships: pattern of organization Vocabulary Student input Reference to upcoming text Student input	Because of the harsh environment the nests of the Arctic bumblebee are mportant. (Remove note to show "nest.") The article states that Arctic bees do not nest in burrows. (Remove note to show "burrows" and put an X through "burrows.") They build a nest above ground. (Remove note to show "top of ground.") Why do you suppose? (Remove note to show "?" and pause for student input.) The article will explain why. Look for that explanation as you read. The article will also describe other features of Arctic bees' nests. As you read, look for these features (remove note to show the two blank boxes) and we will discuss the difference these make. Who can guess what any of these might be? (Pause for student input.)

(continued)

Table 1
Script for Graphic Organizer for "Deep Freeze Bees" (*Continued*)

GO attribute(s)	Script
Connect old/new Relationships: 1. vocabulary 2. pattern of organization Reference to upcoming text	What else do you think that we will learn about Arctic bees? (Pause for student input.) In addition to their nests, the harsh Arctic environment influences the bees' feeding habits. (Remove note to show "feeding habits.") Think back to what we said about the feeding habits of bees. Arctic bees do gather pollen and nectar. (Remove note to show "pollen & nectar.") How might bees feed because of the very cold climate, the harsh environment of the Arctic? (Pause for student input.) As you read look for two additional details about the bees' feeding habits. We will come back to this after you read.
Student input Relationship: Vocabulary	So, we will discover in our reading how the nests and the feeding habits distinguish, or set apart, the Arctic bumble bee from other bees. What else do you suppose is different? (Pause for student input.) Yes. How they look is called their...(remove note to show "appearance") appearance. The article states that they are peanut size. (Remove note to show "peanut size.") How else do you suppose their appearance has been affected by the harsh Arctic environment? (Pause for student input.) As you read (remove note to show the two blank places), the article will explain how their appearance helps the bees in the harsh Arctic environment. (Remove note to show the two boxes with "?".) Look for these as you read.
Reference to upcoming text	Class, you will each receive a sheet just like the one I am showing on the overhead. Read the article, take your copy, and fill in information from the selection in these boxes. After you have filled in the boxes, write a two- or three-sentence summary of "Deep Freeze Bees" in the space provided. Remember this summarizing will be like the summaries we have been practicing. We will compare information and summaries in about 20 minutes. If you finish early, use the back of your sheet to sketch and label something you have learned about Arctic bees. What questions do you have?

Connect new information to past learning. The teacher's presentation of the GO elements was designed to guide students in activating stored experiences, in recalling previously encountered information ("For the past 2 weeks we have been studying insects. Let's name these insects, listing...."), and in making connections with previously encountered information. ("Now think about our geography study this year.") Depending on student responses, the teacher could correct errors in understanding or challenge students to read the upcoming information carefully to justify or to revise their thinking.

Make reference to the upcoming text. As suggested earlier, the teacher should be careful that the GO visual and discussion are detailed enough to present an overview of the material, yet not so detailed that reading the text is not required. In this example the teacher used the GO elements to raise students' expectations about meaning and provided students with frequent reminders that the upcoming reading would explain certain

---

Figure 1
Deep Freeze Bees

Rain or shine, wind or snow, an Arctic bee must eat!
Luckily, it's got neat ways to beat the bitter cold.

By Jack Kelley

It's early summer in the Arctic. But patches of snow still cover the ground and a cold wind is blowing. The temperature is only 44° F. Yet a black and yellow bee about the size of a peanut battles the cold and goes about its business.

To the Arctic bumble bee, the snow, cold and wind are no problem. Some flowers are in bloom and the bee does what it must—gather pollen and nectar for itself and the many other bees in its nest.

Of the 400 different kinds of bumble bees, only a few can survive in the Arctic. It is very hard to stay alive in their harsh environment, so Arctic bumble bees don't always behave just like ordinary bumble bees. And if you look at them very, very carefully, you can see that they don't look exactly the same either.

While many of their southern cousins nest in the underground burrows of other animals, Arctic bumble bees do not. Instead, they build nests on top of the ground. That's because underground nests in the Arctic are colder and wetter than nests above the ground. The floor, walls, and roof of an Arctic bumble bee nest are made of dried mosses, leaves, and grasses. The door of the nest faces the warm sun much of the day.

To get from their nests to their feeding grounds, Arctic bumble bees have to fly through the cold air. So to cut down on "commuting" time, they build nests close to clumps of flowers. They also choose the warmest, least windy route possible. That means they fly closer to the ground than ordinary bees.

Arctic bumble bees are also better "dressed" for cold weather than ordinary bumble bees. They have longer, thicker hair. These heavier "fur coats" are better at keeping their body heat from escaping. Their coats are darker too. And dark colors take in the sun's heat better than light colors do. So while the bees sip nectar, their dark coats soak up lots of warm sunshine. Neither cold nor wind can stop the amazing Arctic bumble bee. It survives in a harsh climate because it has its own special ways of keeping warm.

The End

Reprinted from the January 1983 issue of *Ranger Rick* magazine®, with the permission of the publisher, the National Wildlife Federation®.

concepts or provide additional details. ("The article will explain why." "Look for these as you read.") Tasks for students to complete after reading were clearly and carefully explained.

Seize opportunities to reinforce decoding and structural analysis. Because the GO elements contained technical vocabulary, the teacher capitalized on this context-relevant opportunity and used GO elements to remind students about relevant phonics generalizations ("What do we know about pronouncing a vowel that precedes an r?" "How can we guess the sound the i will take on?") and structural analysis applications ("environment"). It is important,

however, that this conversation not detract from the comprehension emphasis of the GO strategy.

A Step Beyond Worksheets

The GO strategy offers considerable potential to enhance students' comprehension of expository text. Thoughtful construction of the visual reflects how the teacher chooses to emphasize the important concepts in a selection, underscores the relationships between and among those concepts, and highlights the selection's explicit or inferred pattern of organization. In the sample lesson the GO visual had a top-to-bottom, left-to-right format. It is important to note that although this is a frequently occurring format, it is not a "standard" format. In

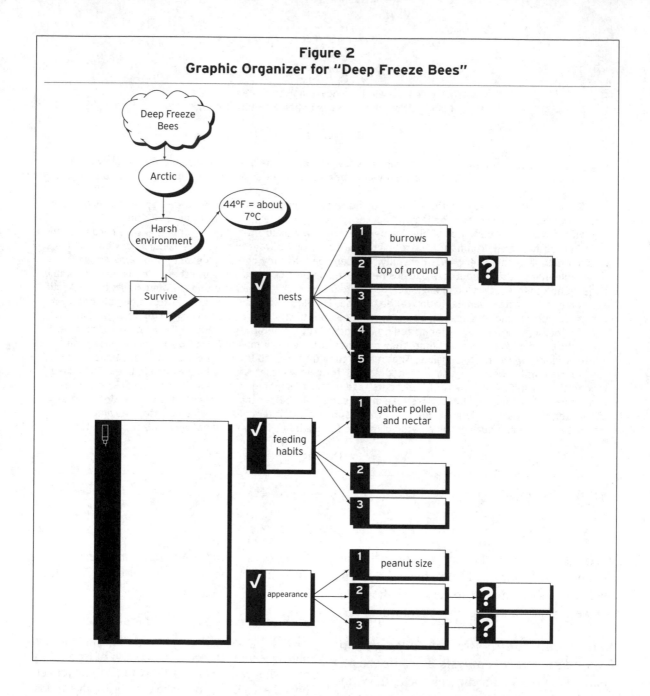

Figure 2
Graphic Organizer for "Deep Freeze Bees"

our experience a reading selection with a tight, obvious pattern of organization often results in a top-to-bottom, left-to-right, fairly symmetrical GO visual. For other reading selections, the GO visual may seem less "organized." In fact, one that is *not* well organized may be the reading for which students need the most guidance. Drawing from his work with GO-based concept mapping, Novak (1991) concluded, "My experience has been that whenever teachers (including university professors) constructed a concept map for a lecture, demonstration, book chapter, or laboratory experiment they wish to teach, they gain new insight into the meaning of that subject matter" (p. 48).

It is important, however, that GO planning extend beyond construction of the visual to the deliberate consideration of the teacher's strategies to elicit prereading dialogue to accompany the visual. It is this guided dialogue, stimulated by the visual, that elevates the GO strategy above the "worksheet" or the "lecture" level. The teacher-directed, prereading dialogue serves to stimulate students' prior knowledge, assist students' anticipation of upcoming text, and encourage students' active reading. These potential benefits depend on the teacher's carefully executed implementation of a skillfully crafted GO.

References

Alvermann, D.E., & Boothby, P.R. (1986). Children's transfer of graphic organizer instruction. *Reading Psychology: An International Quarterly, 7*, 87–100.

Anderson, R.C., Hiebert, E.H., Scott, J., & Wilkinson, I.A.G. (1985). *Becoming a nation of readers: The report of the commission on reading*. Washington, DC: National Institute of Education.

Ausubel, D.P. (1960). The use of advanced organizers in the learning and retention of meaningful behavior. *Journal of Educational Psychology, 51*, 267–272.

Ausubel, D.P. (1968). *Educational psychology: A cognitive view*. New York: Holt, Rinehart & Winston.

Baker, R.L. (1977). Meaningful reception learning. In H.L. Herber & R.T. Vacca (Eds.), *Research in reading in the content areas: The third report* (pp. 32–50). Syracuse, NY: Syracuse University, Reading and Language Arts Center.

Barron, R.F. (1969). The use of vocabulary as an advance organizer. In H.L. Herber & P.L. Sanders (Eds.), *Research in reading in the content areas: First year report* (pp. 29–39). Syracuse, NY: Syracuse University, Reading and Language Arts Center.

Bean, T.W., Singer, H., Sorter, J., & Frasee, C. (1986). The effect of metacognitive instruction in outlining and graphic organizer construction on students' comprehension in a tenth-grade world history class. *Journal of Reading Behavior, 18*, 153–169. (ERIC Document Reproduction Service No. 393 484)

Beers, T. (1987). Schema-theoretic models of reading: Humanizing the machine. *Reading Research Quarterly, 22*, 369–377. (ERIC Document Reproduction Service No. 355 395)

Carr, S.C., & Thompson, B. (1996). The effects of prior knowledge and schema activation strategies on the inferential reading comprehension of children with and without learning disabilities. *Learning Disability Quarterly, 19*(1), 48–61. (ERIC Document Reproduction Service No. 519 854)

Clark, S.R. (1990). *Schema theory and reading comprehension*. (ERIC Document Reproduction Service No. 325 802)

Cooper, R.B., & Flynt, E.S. (1996). *Teaching reading in the content areas*. Englewood Cliffs, NJ: Merrill.

Darch, C.B., Carnine, D.W., & Kameenui, E.J. (1986). The role of graphic organizers and social structure in content area instruction. *Journal of Reading Behavior, 18*, 275–295. (ERIC Document Reproduction Service No. 393 401)

Dunston, P.J. (1992). A critique of graphic organizer research. *Reading Research and Instruction, 31*(2), 57–65. (ERIC Document Reproduction Service No. 441 050)

Earle, R.A. (1969). Use of the structured overview in mathematics classes. In H.L. Herber & P.L. Sanders (Eds.), *Research in reading in the content areas: First year report* (pp. 49–58). Syracuse, NY: Syracuse University, Reading and Language Arts Center.

Farnham-Diggory, S. (1992). *Cognitive processes in education* (2nd ed.). New York: HarperCollins.

Fry, E.B. (1989). Reading formulas—maligned but valid. *Journal of Reading, 32*, 292–297.

Gordon, C.J., & Rennie, B.J. (1987). Restructuring content schemata: An intervention study. *Reading Research and Instruction, 26*, 126–188. (ERIC Document Reproduction Service No. 353 735)

Griffin, C.C., Simmons, D.C., & Kameenui, E.J. (1991). Investigating the effectiveness of graphic organizer instruction on the comprehension and recall of science content by students with learning disabilities. *Reading, Writing, and Learning Disabilities, 7*, 355–376. (ERIC Document Reproduction Service No. 441 315)

Griffin, C.C., & Tulbert, B.L. (1995). The effect of graphic organizers on students' comprehension and recall of expository text: A review of the research and implications for practice. *Reading and Writing Quarterly, 11*, 73–89. (ERIC Document Reproduction Service No. 496 028)

Hawk, P.P. (1986). Using graphic organizers to increase achievement in middle school life science. *Science Education, 70*, 81–87. (ERIC Document Reproduction Service No. 332 059)

Kinnison, R.L., & Pickens, I.R. (1984). *Teaching vocabulary to the L.D. student from an interactive view of reading comprehension*. Canyon, TX: West Texas State University. (ERIC Document Reproduction Service No. 276 222)

May, F.B. (1990). *Reading as communication: An interactive approach* (3rd ed., pp. 396–426). Columbus, OH: Merrill.

McCormick, S. (1995). *Instructing students who have literacy problems*. Englewood Cliffs, NJ: Prentice Hall.

Moore, D.W., & Readence, J.E. (1980). A meta-analysis of the effect of graphic organizers on learning from text. In M.L. Kamil & A.J. Moe (Eds.), *Perspectives in reading research and instruction*. 29th yearbook of the National Reading Conference (pp. 213–217). Chicago: National Reading Conference.

Moore, D.W., & Readence, J.E. (1984). A quantitative and qualitative review of graphic organizer research. *Journal of Educational Research, 78*, 11–17.

National Council of Teachers of English & International Reading Association. (1996). *Standards for the English language arts.* Urbana, IL: National Council of Teachers of English.

Nelson-Herber, J. (1986). Expanding and refining vocabulary in content areas. *Journal of Reading, 29*, 626–633.

Novak, J.D. (1991). Clarifying with concept maps. *The Science Teacher, 58*(7), 45–49.

Novak, J.D., & Gowin, D.B. (1984). *Learning how to learn.* Ithaca, NY: Cornell University Press.

Pearson, P.D., Hansen, J., & Gordon, C.J. (1979). The effect of background knowledge on young children's comprehension of explicit and implicit information. *Journal of Reading Behavior, 11*, 201–209.

Recht, D.R. & Leslie, L. (1988). Effect of prior knowledge on good and poor readers' memory of text. *Journal of Educational Psychology, 80*(1), 16–20. (ERIC Document Reproduction Service No. 384 774)

Rice, G.E. (1994). Need for explanations in graphic organizer research. *Reading Psychology, 15*, 39–67.

Richardson, J.S., & Morgan, R.F. (1997). *Reading to learn in the content areas.* Belmont, CA: Wadsworth.

Robinson, D.H., & Schraw, G. (1994). Computational efficiency through visual argument: Do graphic organizers communicate relations in text too effectively?

Contemporary Educational Psychology, 19, 399–415. (ERIC Document Reproduction Service No. 498 458)

Roe, B.D., Stoodt, B.D., & Burns, P.C. (1998). *The content areas.* Boston: Houghton Mifflin.

Ruddell, M.R. (1997). *Teaching content reading and writing.* Boston: Allyn & Bacon.

Rumelhart, D.E. (1980). Schemata: The building blocks of cognition. In R.J. Spiro, B.C. Bruce, & W.F. Brewer (Eds.), *Theoretical issues in reading comprehension* (pp. 33–58). Hillsdale, NJ: Erlbaum.

Sadoski, M., Pavio, A., & Goetz, E.T. (1991). A critique of schema theory in reading and a dual coding alternative. *Reading Research Quarterly, 26*, 463–484. (ERIC Document Reproduction Service No. 435 546)

Stahl, S.A., & Vancil, S.J. (1986). Discussion is what makes semantic maps work in vocabulary instruction. *The Reading Teacher, 40*, 62–69.

Taylor, B.M. (1985). Toward an understanding of factors contributing to children's difficulty summarizing textbook material. In J.A. Niles & R.V. Lalik (Eds.), *Issues in literacy: A research perspective* (pp. 125–131). Rochester, NY: National Reading Conference.

Winograd, P.N. (1984). Strategic difficulties in summarizing texts. *Reading Research Quarterly, 19*, 404–425.

Questions for Reflection

- This article acknowledges Rice (1994), whose review indicated that research is inconclusive about the efficacy of graphic organizers. If you have used them yourself, what has been your experience? Do other teachers in your school use them? If so, what have been their experiences? How have you and your colleagues determined the effect of graphic organizers on your students' comprehension?

- Based on your and your colleagues' experiences with graphic organizers, can you identify commonalities that have made them successful? If they have not been successful, what strategies for implementation suggested in this article might improve their usefulness for your students?

Shared Readings:
Modeling Comprehension, Vocabulary, Text Structures, and Text Features for Older Readers

Douglas Fisher, Nancy Frey, and Diane Lapp

Modeling is the primary way through which teachers can demonstrate for their students how readers can interact with texts (e.g., Taylor & Pearson, 2002). One of the most common forms of teacher modeling of text processing is shared reading. Beginning with the work of Holdaway (1979, 1983), who developed Big Books as a way for teachers to model while young students watched, the definition of *shared reading* has evolved from a focus on Big Books to a variety of classroom interactions in which the teacher and students share a text. Currently, *shared reading* is a generic term many teachers use to describe a range of classroom activities, including echo reading (students echoing the words aloud after the teacher reads), choral reading (students reading aloud while the teacher reads aloud), or cloze reading (teacher reads aloud and pauses periodically for students to fill in the missing word; e.g., Blachowicz & Ogle, 2001).

In their study of effective teachers in England, Topping and Ferguson (2005) noted, "Effective teachers were more likely to teach a range of literacy skills and knowledge at the word, sentence and text level through the context of a shared text" (p. 126). According to the Topping and Ferguson study, shared reading involved the teacher modeling reading by focusing on word- or sentence-level work.

Alternatively, Short, Kane, and Peeling (2000) described shared and guided reading as allowing the teacher to "model and support the use of cues and self-monitoring reading strategies, which may include the use of pictures to help construct meaning, making predictions, rereading, segmenting and blending phonemes, and finding familiar word chunks to decode words" (p. 287). As can be seen in these two definitions, specifically identifying what constitutes a shared reading is difficult. Both definitions indicate that shared readings have potential with older readers and should not be limited to use with emergent readers.

Manning (2006) is concerned that new guidelines and policies have forced teachers to eliminate practices such as shared reading. This is troubling, especially given the evidence that shared reading positively affects student achievement. For example, Coyne, Simmons, Kame'enui, and Stoolmiller (2004) demonstrated the positive impact that shared readings had on kindergarten students' vocabulary. Ukrainetz, Cooney, Dyer, Kysar, and Harris (2000) showed how shared readings could be used to improve students' phonemic awareness. Davie and Kemp (2002) studied the language opportunities provided during shared reading and concluded that this approach elicited "significantly more utterances and more intelligible utterances than the facilitated play

Reprinted from Fisher, D., Frey, N., & Lapp, D. (2008). Shared readings: Modeling comprehension, vocabulary, text structures, and text features for older readers. *The Reading Teacher, 61*(7), 548–556. doi: 10.1598/RT.61.7.4

condition" in their sample of young Australian children with intellectual disabilities (p. 456).

Despite the evidence related to the effectiveness of shared reading, in his study of teachers in England, Fisher (2002) noted that while there should be opportunities for metacognitive modeling, teachers find it difficult to use these opportunities. The fact that teachers found modeling difficult was also confirmed by Pressley and Afflerbach (1995). We were intrigued by this because many teachers with whom we work self-report the significance of their modeling during shared reading on the literacy development of their students. Because of this, we decided to investigate how teachers used shared reading and what patterns emerged in their application of this instructional strategy.

Methodology

Participants

The methodological design employed in this study mirrors our previous study on the practices of expert teachers in delivering interactive read-alouds (Fisher, Flood, Lapp, & Frey, 2004). Letters were sent to 100 site administrators and peer coaches who worked in urban schools in a large county in the western part of the United States. All teacher and school names are pseudonyms. The letter introduced the research project and asked for nominations of current classroom teachers in grades 3–8 who had developed a level of expertise in shared reading. The letter defined an expert as someone who was often asked to model for other teachers, a teacher who regularly presented his or her instructional strategies in professional development forums, or one who was generally recognized for excellence in teaching. Seventy-four individuals responded, and they identified 67 expert teachers.

From this group of 67 nominated expert teachers, 25 teachers representing 25 schools were randomly selected for participation. An invitation letter was then sent to each of the 25 teachers inviting their participation. Follow-up phone calls were made and all 25 agreed to participate. Prior to conducting the observations,

all of the researchers observed a teacher not selected for the research pool as she conducted a shared reading. We did so in order to establish interobserver reliability among the researchers.

After establishing reliability among the researchers (.92), each expert teacher was observed on three different occasions (a total of 75 lessons were observed) by two of the researchers to identify the procedures used to implement a shared reading and modeled think-aloud. Two researchers participated in each observation in an attempt to ensure the reliability of the coded components. The observers agreed most of the time, with an overall interobserver reliability score of .88 for the 75 lessons.

Instruments

Observations. Teachers were observed while they conducted a shared reading and think-aloud with their students. When observing teacher experts, observational field notes were collected by the researchers in order to identify the components of a shared reading and think-aloud. The field notes focused on the ways in which teachers shared their thinking as they read.

Interviews. Once the observations were completed, a random stratified sample of six teachers was invited to participate in either individual or group interviews that were conducted by the researchers in an attempt to better understand the teacher's planning and practice. This sample included one teacher from each of the 3–8 grades. Before the interview, teachers were asked to identify the components of their shared readings. They were also asked to report on the frequency of shared readings in their classrooms and to determine a sequence of a shared reading they conducted regularly in their classrooms. During the interviews, participants and interviewers discussed the shared reading and think-aloud components that had been observed by the researchers. Each interview was fairly unstructured but focused on the following key points:

- The components of a typical shared reading

- The frequency of shared readings
- The process used to determine the focus of a shared reading
- A reaction to the four themes identified by the researchers

All interviews were audiotaped and transcribed so the investigators could compare the responses from each participant.

Analysis

Data from the expert teacher observations were reviewed by the researchers for procedures that could be considered essential components of quality shared reading and think-alouds. Using a constant comparative method in which the researchers met weekly to review the components of shared readings that were observed, we identified four major areas of instruction (comprehension, vocabulary, text structures, and text features). We assumed that comprehension would be one category but did not identify specific categories before analyzing data. In addition to identifying the major areas of instruction, we coded the data for subtypes and highlighted examples of each. Each of the four major areas of instruction contained subtypes that became clear after multiple reviews of the data.

The interview data were used to extend the observational findings by providing teacher examples and rationales for specific behaviors. The interview data were coded using a recursive approach as we reread the transcripts and identified explanations and examples (LeCompte & Preissle, 1993). In addition, the interview was used as a member check. The researchers presented the findings from the observational data and asked the participants to assess whether the findings fit with their experiences. The member check served to confirm the major categories and to provide additional examples from the teachers.

Findings

The observational data clustered into four major categories. Each of these categories contained a number of elements. In order of frequency, teachers modeled their thinking using comprehension, vocabulary, text structures, and text features. Figure 1 contains a list of each of these. In addition to the content of the modeling, in each of the 75 lessons we observed a number of commonly used instructional practices. For example, in every case students could see the text as the teacher read it aloud. Some teachers used a class set of books, others had photocopies of specific texts, and still others projected the text on a screen using an overhead or document camera. The teachers also modeled fluent reading and had clearly practiced the selections before reading them aloud.

These 25 teachers also modeled their own thinking and did not ask students individual questions. The focus clearly was on modeling thinking and not on asking students comprehension questions about the texts being read. That's not to say that students were silent observers during the shared reading. Students were often encouraged to talk with a partner, write a reflection, indicate agreement through unison responses such as fist-to-five (in which students hold up a number of fingers depending on how strongly they agree with a statement), and ask questions.

Reading Comprehension

The most common modeling during a shared reading focused on reading comprehension strategies such as activating background, inferencing, summarizing, predicting, clarifying, questioning, visualizing, monitoring, synthesizing, evaluating, and connecting. For example, a third-grade teacher displayed *The Red Book* (Lehman, 2004) using a document camera and data projector. As she examined each of the wordless pages, she shared her thinking with students. When looking at the cover, she said,

> It seems to me that this boy is cold. I see his hat, scarf, jacket, and boots. But it's just all red on the cover so I don't have all of the clues I need to make a good inference or prediction. But I can tell that he's walking quickly, and when I add that to the clothing, I predict that it's cold where he is.

Figure 1
Shared Reading Components

Component	Definition	Subtypes
Comprehension	Strategic and active moves to understand the text	Activating background, inferencing, summarizing, predicting, clarifying, questioning, visualizing, monitoring, synthesizing, evaluating, and connecting
Vocabulary	Focus on solving an unknown word, not providing the definition of the word	1. Inside-the-word strategies: Word parts such as prefix, suffix, root, base, cognates, and word families 2. Outside-the-word strategies: Context clues 3. Use of resources: peers, dictionaries, Internet
Text structures	Structures used in presenting information that readers can use to predict the flow of information	1. Compare/contrast 2. Problem/solution 3. Cause/effect 4. Chronological/sequence/temporal 5. Descriptive 6. Story grammar (plot, setting, character, conflict, etc.)
Text features	Components of the text added to increase understanding or interest	Headings, captions, illustrations, bold or italic words, charts, tables, diagrams, glossary, index, or graphs

As she talked about each page, she described her thinking. Several pages into the book, she said,

> Oh, wow. Now that's a surprise. The boy on the island is looking through the book to the girl in the cold city *and* vice versa. I'm wondering if they'll ever get to meet, or if it will be like other books where the reader gets to meet people through books that you'll never really meet in person. I remember meeting Charlotte from *Charlotte's Web* (White, 1952), and I'll never forget her advice. Have you met someone in a book that you'll never forget? Let's take a minute and talk with a partner about who we've met in books.

In a similar manner, a sixth-grade teacher modeled his comprehension strategies with students during a shared reading of *I Am the Mummy Heb-Nefert* (Bunting, 1997). Also using a document camera and projector, students followed along as he read. He paused periodically to share his thinking, such as when the author discussed a snake that was tightly coiled and sleeping inside the kitchen basket. He paused and said,

> I don't know a lot of people personally who'd want a snake sleeping in their kitchen, but I do know from the books we've read so far about ancient Egypt that they had a different relationship with snakes than we do. For example, I remember reading about the snake god *Apophis*. I also know from the photos and illustrations we've examined that snakes are all often thought of as protection. Making these connections helps me put this in context. Yes, I guess that people might have had snakes in their houses for protection and to keep the rodents away.

We asked the teachers why they modeled multiple ways of thinking about texts instead of just focusing on one strategy in each of their lessons. For example, we didn't see questioning used throughout the entire period of shared reading. In response, one of the teachers noted,

> I used to do it that way—focus on one comprehension strategy at a time. But I think that's a problem. I don't really read that way, and if I don't read that

way it's not really an authentic shared reading and think-aloud, right?

In response, another teacher commented,

> I hope you're not suggesting that we should model one at a time. [We assured her we were not.] For me, the shared reading is about consolidation. We need to show students how to incorporate these things automatically and not artificially stop and summarize or question or whatever. I use my guided instructional time to focus on specific strategies with specific students who need attention in a specific area.

Another teacher added, "Yes, I agree. And it's also about metacognition—knowing that you're doing this but not paying a lot of attention to it."

In response to the discussion about which comprehension strategies to use, the teachers who participated in the interview suggested that the strategies outlined in *Strategies That Work* (Harvey & Goudvis, 2007) were effective in promoting comprehension. As one of them put it,

> If I could get all of my students to automatically use all of the strategies from *Strategies That Work*, I'd be a happy person. Of course, these strategies aren't everything we do in our modeling, or everything that a reader does to understand, but these will help students make sense when they really use them.

Vocabulary

In no case did the teachers in this study simply tell students what the words meant or call on students and ask them to define words. Instead, they modeled solving words using one of three systems: context clues, word parts, and resources. In the interviews they talked about the importance of teaching students to solve for unknown words. As one of them said, "I don't have time to tell students the meaning of every word they'll encounter. What we need to do, year after year, is help students develop ways to figure out words as they read."

Another teacher focused on the ways in which unknown words can be solved. In her words,

> I want students to have both "inside" and "outside" word strategies. I want them to be able to go outside of the word to context clues. I also want them to be able to go inside the word, using parts of words, to figure out or make educated guesses about the word's meaning.

Another teacher added, "And when these systems don't work, they need to know how to use resources to figure out the words."

Context Clues. Readers use a number of clues provided by the author to understand unknown words. Of course, most readers use context clues, or their "outside-the-word" strategies, automatically as they read (Nagy, Anderson, & Herman, 1985). The teachers in this study modeled the use of context clues to figure out unknown or confusing words by focusing on embedded definitions, synonyms, antonyms, comparisons, contrasts, descriptions, and examples.

During her shared reading of *Coming on Home Soon* (Woodson, 2004), a third-grade teacher read the line "When she put her dress into the satchel, I held my breath" (p. 1) and said, "I'm not sure what a *satchel* is. I'll read this page and check out the picture. If I can't figure it out from this information, I'll ask someone for some help." A few sentences later, she read the line "Mama folded another dress and put it in the bag" (p. 1) and said,

> Another dress in the bag? She already put a dress in the satchel. I bet that a satchel is a special kind of bag, but it looks like a suitcase in the picture. I'm going to reread this page with the word *suitcase* in place of both *bag* and *satchel* to see if this makes sense.... Yes, it does. So there's another word for a *suitcase*—a special kind of bag for traveling.

A seventh-grade teacher, while reading from the history textbook, noted that the author had provided a "right there" meaning for the word. He said,

> Let me read that again. "Romans also learned from Greek science. A Greek doctor named Galen brought many medical ideas to Rome. For example, he emphasized the importance of anatomy, the study of body structure." I know that anatomy is the study of the structure of the body because the definition was embedded right there in the text. I'm always on the lookout for help the author provides.

I'm also thinking about the connections between the Greeks and the Romans. To summarize what I've read so far in the chapter, the Romans benefited significantly from the learnings of the Greeks. On your interactive note pages, list a few things that the Romans learned from the Greeks and then talk with your group about these things.

Word Parts. In addition to context clues, there are a number of "inside-the-word" strategies students can use to figure out word meanings. These include prefixes, suffixes, roots, bases, word families, and cognates. Word part lessons are often quick and somewhat explanatory. For example, a fourth-grade teacher reading from a textbook noted, "*Carnivore* reminds me of *carne* in Spanish meaning *meat*. It also reminds me of *carne asada*, a kind of meat, but that just makes me hungry. So, I use *carne* to remind me that carnivores eat meat."

A third-grade science teacher paused on the word *evaporation* while reading about the water cycle and said,

> I know how to remember this word. It has *vapor* in it and that means steam—like to vaporize. I also know that *-tion* is a process. So, evaporation is a process that allows the water to disappear into the steam or air.

A sixth-grade teacher, reading from a magazine article about war wounds, came across the word *malodorous* and said,

> Now here's a great word: *malodorous*. Say this wonderful word with me: *malodorous*. I know that the prefix *mal-* is bad and that *odor* has to do with smell and the suffix *-ous* means full of or having the characteristic of. So, putting it together, *malodorous* is being full of bad smells. Isn't that a delicious word? Now, instead of saying it's stinky or foul, you can say malodorous. The malodorous locker room, the malodorous streets filled with refuse, plants with malodorous bouquets. You try it—you use the word. [She paused while students talked together.] Just beautiful!

Resources. When outside-the-word and inside-the-word strategies fail, teachers modeled the use of resources. Most commonly, this involved asking another person. For example, when she came across the word atmosphere on a page with no context clues, the fifth-grade teacher said,

> I'm not sure about this word. I can't really get it from context. I'll try some resources. Well, there's no glossary to help me out. I guess I'll call Ms. Johnson next door and ask her if she knows what this word really means.

While reading *Patrol: An American Soldier in Vietnam* (Myers, 2002), a seventh-grade teacher stopped on the page that read, "Two clicks away, there are flashes of gunfire. Two clicks is the distance of my enemy" (p. 15). She then paused and said,

> I've heard of clicks before but mostly about the Internet, you know—click on this page and stuff. I think I want to know what this is, and I don't have any context clues to use to figure it out. I'm going to look it up really quick.

Turning to the computer, the teacher types "measurement click" into the search engine while she says, "I know that it's a measurement because the author says distance, so I guess I did have a little bit of context help." The teacher selects a couple of websites that define *click*, including The History Channel, which notes that *click* has two common definitions: one click = one kilometer or the adjustments on the sight of a weapon for elevation and wind. She then says, "So the enemy is about two kilometers away. That's not too far, but far enough to feel a bit safer. I'll reread this page with my new understanding."

In the interview, we asked about the difference between vocabulary instruction and vocabulary modeling. One of the teachers noted,

> I know that students will learn a lot of words from reading, so I have them reading all of the time. I also know that they will learn to solve unknown words when they're taught how to do this. They need the mental models to figure out how to do this.

A fourth-grade teacher added,

> I do a lot of vocabulary instruction—direct instruction—during the day. I think it's critical for learning

specific words and the families of those words. But that's not getting them to figure out words while they're reading. That's what I have to do during the shared reading. I have to set an example and show them *how* to solve words in addition to knowing a lot of words.

We also asked about the strategy of "skip it," which has been printed on several commercially available classroom posters. We wanted to know why none of the teachers modeled this strategy despite the fact that it was listed on classroom posters. Shocked, one of the teachers said,

Are you kidding me? I would *never* model something that I didn't want students to use and use. I know that what I model will be overgeneralized by students. That's a good thing when they're learning about visualizing and predicting. It would be terrible if they overgeneralized skip it! I only use the skip it strategy when I'm working with students individually or in small groups. Then I can control their use of this, and I can talk with them about when this works and when it doesn't work.

Another teacher responded,

Can you imagine me giving permission to my struggling readers to just skip it? I'd rather make sure that they were reading books they can read so that they can periodically solve unknown words like I do. If they are spending too much time solving unknown words, the book is too hard and they need to get a new one.

Text Structures

One of the ways that readers organize information as they read is to pay attention to the text structures that authors use. Informational texts are commonly organized into compare/contrast, problem/solution, cause/effect, chronological/ sequence/temporal, and descriptive. Narrative texts also have a common structure. Narrative texts use a story grammar (setting, plot, characters, conflict, etc.). Teachers regularly commented on the text structures and explained to students why this information was helpful.

For example, during a shared reading of an excerpt of *The Prince* by Niccolo Machiavelli,

the seventh-grade teacher noted the text structure as a way to organize information. In his words,

I think that Machiavelli is comparing and contrasting here. I'm thinking that he wants me to understand the difference in the two types of fighting he discusses. I see here, where he says, "You should consider then, that there are two ways of fight, one with laws and the other with force." I think he's setting up to compare and contrast these two ways. This leads me to organize my thinking into categories that I can use to help me remember what Machiavelli believes.

A fifth-grade teacher also noted the author's use of text structure while reading about circulating blood. She said,

So I'm seeing this as a process that occurs in a specific sequence. It reminds me of the water cycle we learned about and how that is also a process. So the author tells me about this in order. I understand from the text structure that blood circulates through the heart chambers, lungs, body, and then back again. I see that he's going to describe how carbon dioxide (CO_2) and oxygen (O_2) are exchanged in the lungs and tissues, and I bet that will be a process as well. This whole section is about the processes used by living things. Now that I know it will be a process, I'll get my notes ready so that I can record the major steps of the process.

In her shared reading of a narrative text, a fourth-grade teacher reading *Shiloh* (Naylor, 1991) paused and said,

I see our character changing. Marty has lied before, and he's lying again. But the difference is he *knows* it. I think that when he realizes this, he's changing. Here's what he says, let me read it again. "Funny how one lie leads to another and before you know it, your whole life can be a lie" (p. 60). I think Marty realizes that his whole life could change and that he'll think about this before he lies again.

In a similar manner, a sixth-grade teacher noticed a plot twist in the book *Esperanza Rising* (Ryan, 2000) and shared her thinking with students. In her words,

Now here's a plot twist. Esperanza could see a body in the back of a wagon, and Miguel has his head down and he's crying. I think that this is a really important change in the plot. I think so because all of the main characters we've met are there and I notice that the mood has changed. The author isn't using such happy words any more. I'm thinking that there is something bad about to happen—worse than the death. I know that authors often provide readers hints—foreshadowing—about future events or twists in the plot.

In discussing text structures during the interviews, we were reminded of signal words that authors use. As one of the teachers said,

When there are signal words, I notice them and talk about them. However, as texts become more sophisticated, I see fewer and fewer signal words. Instead, they are implied and readers have to intuit the structure. I think it's even more important to model thinking when the signal words are absent because that's when the reader is more challenged.

Another teacher commented that her attention to text structures developed as a result of her frustration with graphic organizers:

I was trying to have students complete graphic organizers after they had read something. I realized that they didn't know what to record or which tool to use. I could have just copied the correct graphic organizer, but then they wouldn't learn about the text. I now explain the text structure and how I know which structure the author has used. Then I model a sample graphic organizer to collect my information. My students have learned to do this on their own—they determine which graphic organizers to use because they're looking for the implicit structure of the text.

Text Features

There are a number of text features that readers use to determine meaning and importance in texts, including headings, captions, illustrations, boldface words, graphs, diagrams, glossaries, and so on. Unfortunately, there are a number of students who do not understand how to use these text features (Barton, 1997). In discussing text features, one of the teachers noted, "In some cases, the text features may even confuse the reader." Another commented,

At a minimum, students need to know when to attend to the text features. For example, when should they read the graph? Before reading the text, while reading the text, or after reading the text? The answer is, It depends. And any time that's the answer—students need a lot of modeling and practice.

And another teacher said, "I used to skip all of the features included in the text, but then I realized those weren't just decorations. They were there to aid comprehension. I decided I better teach students how to use the features."

As part of an investigation of disasters, a fifth-grade teacher shared the book *Disaster! Catastrophes That Shook the World* (Bonson & Platt, 1997). In talking about the page on the *Titanic*, the teacher noted the figure that discussed the number of people lost versus saved and how this information was presented by class. He said,

This figure is very interesting to me. The author uses the term *lost* really to mean they died. I think that's a better word for a figure like this. *Lost* seems more respectful of the families. For the passengers in first class, 130 were lost and 199 were saved. So, about 60% of the first-class passengers were saved. I can compare that with the information for third class: 536 were lost and 174 were saved. That's about 25%. What a difference. But then I look at the information for the crew. They seem to have had it the worst because so many of them died. Of the crew, 685 were lost and 214 were saved. That's almost just about 25% so I guess that I was wrong: The crew didn't have it much worse than the third class, but there were just a lot more of them.

An eighth-grade teacher, reading from *We Rode the Orphan Trains* (Warren, 2001), read a passage and then paused and said,

I can tell from the change in the font and the indent that this is a quote—this is what the person was really saying. The author doesn't need to use quote marks because this is a very long quote and she's used the text feature to tell me. Wow! What a quote: "I had no desire to ever meet my birth mother.... My adoptive parents are the ones who wanted and loved me. If I go to heaven, my eyes will search only for them. They gave me life."

(p. 5). This quote is from Lorraine Williams—there I see a picture of her as a child. I also see that she got to meet First Lady Barbara Bush. I know that from the picture—I know what Barbara Bush looks like—and from the caption under the picture, which gives me more information. Mrs. Williams got to meet the First Lady because she worked to promote literacy. I know that literacy is very important to Mrs. Bush, so I'm not surprised by their meeting.

Text features were also noted in textbooks. A third-grade teacher, while reading from the social studies text, paused to discuss the highlighted words and what that told her. A fourth-grade teacher noted the way that the headings helped her understand what the author would describe next. She informed the class,

> When I see headings like these, I think about what I already know and what I expect the author to tell me. I also know that I can use the headings to find specific information when I need to later on. And I also know that the headings can help me arrange my notes. The headings are often the main point of the text, which I can use to organize my thinking.

In discussing text features during the interviews, we were reminded of the connection between reading and writing when one of the teachers said,

> I teach text features, in part, because I want my students to use them in their writing. If I'm really clear about how I use text features as a reader, my students will incorporate these into their own writing knowing that I'm going to read their papers. They begin to see the connections between reading like a writer and writing like a reader. It's very powerful.

Discussion

The teachers in this study were observed using a number of common approaches for modeling, or explaining, reading. As Duffy (2003) has noted, explaining reading is an important component of literacy instruction. The expert teachers in this study reported that modeling, as expressed through shared reading, was a daily occurrence. Of course the model must be followed by opportunities to practice and apply skills. What this study contributes is an analysis of the specific behaviors that expert teachers use during modeling. It is important to note that they did not use all four components in each of their shared reading lessons. Some lessons focused more on vocabulary, for example, while others focused more on comprehension. In analyzing the 75 observations, we realized that no shared reading lesson focused solely on one of the four factors and that each of the 25 teachers demonstrated each of the four factors at some point in the three observations. We find this confirming of the applicability of the findings from this study. In addition, based on the discussions with the teachers we interviewed, several cautions regarding teacher modeling with shared reading are in order.

First, teacher modeling through shared reading should be based on an identified purpose. Teachers clearly knew why they had selected a particular piece of text and what they could use it for. We regularly observed texts with sticky notes attached to them that teachers used for their modeling. When we asked about this, one of the teachers said,

> Purpose is everything. I know why I'm reading something and explaining it to my students, and I let them in on that. I also know that they'll have opportunities to use what I've modeled during guided reading, centers, and during their independent reading.

Second, teacher modeling through shared reading should not lengthen the amount of time that students spend in whole-class instruction. As one of the teachers noted,

> I tried to help another teacher improve her shared readings, but she didn't take anything away. She still had her students participate in the modeling phase, but then she felt the need to explain and question students. As a result, the amount of time students spent in whole class increased and the amount of time they spent in small-group instruction decreased. Overall, I'm not sure that did anything positive.

The experts we observed averaged 10–14 minutes of shared reading. As they finished the shared reading, they often provided students with a discussion or writing prompt and then the class made a transition into small-group or collaborative learning.

Third, shared readings should not be used to "curricularize comprehension." The expert teachers we observed did not focus on one aspect of modeling or one comprehension strategy. This is consistent with the recommendations of Pressley (2002) who expressed concerns about focusing on one comprehension strategy at a time. One of the teachers we interviewed explained that "the text will guide you" to determine what needs to be shared and explained. Another teacher said,

> When you look at a piece of text through the lens of shared reading, you notice different things. You notice things that jump out and beg to be talked about—an illustration that does not match the words on the page, a word that is a perfect example of multiple meanings, or some descriptive language that simply must be visualized.

Still another teacher noted that she matched the shared readings with the needs of the class and the grade-level content standards.

Finally, we were reminded that modeling thinking is critical and yet difficult. As one teacher said,

> I know that my principal nominated me, but I'm frustrated. Most everyone else doesn't do this. They ask kids a lot of questions, as if that will make them better readers. I wonder if some of my colleagues don't know what they think when they read because they're just good at it. It takes a lot to slow down enough to pay attention to what your brain is doing and then learn to explain it to children.

References

Barton, M.L. (1997). Addressing the literacy crisis: Teaching reading in the content areas. *NASSP Bulletin, 81*(587), 22–30.

Blachowicz, C.L.Z., & Ogle, D. (2001). *Reading comprehension: Strategies for independent learners.* New York: Guilford.

Coyne, M.D., Simmons, D.C., Kame'enui, E.J., & Stoolmiller, M. (2004). Teaching vocabulary during shared storybook readings: An examination of differential effects. *Exceptionality, 12*(3), 145–162.

Davie, J., & Kemp, C. (2002). A comparison of the expressive language opportunities provided by shared book reading and facilitated play for young children with mild to moderate intellectual disabilities. *Educational Psychology: An International Journal of Experimental Educational Psychology, 22*(4), 445–460.

Duffy, G.G. (2003). *Explaining reading: A resource for teaching concepts, skills, and strategies.* New York: Guilford.

Fisher, D., Flood, J., Lapp, D., & Frey, N. (2004). Interactive read-alouds: Is there a common set of implementation practices? *The Reading Teacher, 58*(1), 8–17.

Fisher, R. (2002). Shared thinking: Metacognitive modelling in the literacy hour. *Reading: Literacy and Language, 36*(2), 63–67.

Harvey, S., & Goudvis, A. (2007). *Strategies that work: Teaching comprehension for understanding and engagement* (2nd ed.). York, ME: Stenhouse.

Holdaway, D. (1979). *The foundations of literacy.* Sydney, NSW, Australia: Ashton Scholastic.

Holdaway, D. (1983). Shared book experience: Teaching reading using favorite books. *Theory Into Practice, 21*(4), 293–300.

LeCompte, M.D., & Preissle, J. (1993). *Ethnography and qualitative design in educational research* (2nd ed.). San Diego, CA: Academic Press.

Manning, M. (2006). Celebrations in reading and writing: Be true to yourself. *Teaching Pre K–8, 36*(4), 68–69.

Nagy, W.E., Anderson, R.C., & Herman, P.A. (1985). Learning words from context. *Reading Research Quarterly, 20*(2), 233–253.

Pressley, M. (2002). Comprehension strategies instruction: A turn-of-the-century status report. In C.C. Block, & M. Pressley (Eds.), *Comprehension instruction: Research-based best practices* (pp. 11–27). New York: Guilford.

Pressley, M., & Afflerbach, P. (1995). *Verbal protocols of reading: The nature of constructively responsive reading.* Hillsdale, NJ: Erlbaum.

Short, R.A., Kane, M., & Peeling, T. (2000). Retooling the reading lesson: Matching the right tools to the job. *The Reading Teacher, 54*(3), 284–295.

Taylor, B.M., & Pearson, P.D. (Eds.). (2002). *Teaching reading: Effective schools, accomplished teachers.* Mahwah, NJ: Erlbaum.

Topping, K., & Ferguson, N. (2005). Effective literacy teaching behaviours. *Journal of Research in Reading, 28*(2), 125–143.

Ukrainetz, T.A., Cooney, M.H., Dyer, S.K., Kysar, A.J., & Harris, T.J. (2000). An investigation into teaching phonemic awareness through shared reading and writing. *Early Childhood Research Quarterly, 15*(3), 331–355.

Literature Cited

Bonson, R., & Platt, R. (1997). *Disaster! Catastrophes that shook the world.* New York: Dorling Kindersley.

Bunting, E. (1997). *I am the mummy Heb-Nefert*. San Diego, CA: Harcourt Brace.

Lehman, B. (2004). *The red book*. Boston: Houghton Mifflin.

Naylor, P.R. (1991). *Shiloh*. New York: Bantam Doubleday Dell.

Myers, W.D. (2002). *Patrol: An American soldier in Vietnam*. New York: HarperCollins.

Ryan, P.M. (2000). *Esperanza rising*. New York: Scholastic.

Warren, A. (2001). *We rode the orphan trains*. Boston: Houghton Mifflin.

White, E.B. (1952). *Charlotte's web*. New York: HarperTrophy.

Woodson, J. (2004). *Coming on home soon*. New York: G.P. Putnam's Sons.

Questions for Reflection

• Select one of the four areas (vocabulary, comprehension, text features, text structure) discussed in the article. Design a think-aloud that shows your students how you think when you're figuring out a vocabulary word, applying a comprehension strategy, or using a text feature or structure to support your understanding. After your modeling, allow time for students to practice while you offer additional support. (You might decide to prepare these think-alouds with your grade-level colleagues so that you can observe and offer feedback to each other.)

• Think with your colleagues about the four areas discussed in this article. Which of these are the most difficult for you to teach? Work together to plan a think-aloud that will not only help your students to understand better but will help you and your colleagues gain from each other's strengths.

"You Can Read This Text— I'll Show You How": Interactive Comprehension Instruction

Diane Lapp, Douglas Fisher, and Maria Grant

"You can read this text—I'll show you how" is what we heard teacher Maria Grant say to her students as we entered her high school science classroom. She stood in front of a linguistically, academically, and culturally diverse group of students. They were seated at their desks in clusters of five, staring at her and the document camera as she engaged them in an interactive think-aloud in an attempt to model how to use one's existing knowledge as the basis for constructing new knowledge (Bruner, 1986; McCarthy, 2005).

This constructivist approach to learning that she was modeling was designed to illustrate for her students how to flexibly use a wide variety of thinking, language, and reading strategies to acquire a more extensive understanding of the information they were attempting to process (Harste, 1994; Wilhelm & Friedemann, 1998; Wu & Tsai, 2005). Maria and her students often shared an interactive think-aloud. She realized that in order for students to gain independence at monitoring their own comprehension she needed to share this guided modeling through a gradual release of responsibility plan (Duke & Pearson, 2002), which enabled her students to take control of their learning over time. Her ultimate goal was that her students be able to independently monitor their own comprehension as they read challenging text. Guided modeling provides the scaffolding that allows them to see and practice the monitoring skills.

This interactive thinking out-loud, which situated the instruction within the student's zone of proximal development (Vygotsky, 1934/1978), provides students with adequate time to supportively and interactively observe, recognize, emulate, adopt, practice, and self-regulate these metacognitive strategies (Mathan & Koedinger, 2005; Schunk & Zimmerman, 1994).

To better illustrate this instruction, we've presented the interactive, shared reading and thinking out-loud Maria modeled with a science text about chemical reactions in Tables 1 and 2. The original text is in the first column, followed by the commentary Maria provided in the second column, and the strategies she used in the final column.

Her instruction was designed to accomplish the very general U.S. standard that "As a result of their activities in grades 9–12, all students should develop an understanding of chemical reactions" and the California standard that "Students know chemical processes can either release (exothermic) or absorb (endothermic) thermal energy."

In an attempt to situate the instruction within the students' existing knowledge base (Anderson & Pearson, 1984; Rosenblatt, 1978) and also to gain an initial assessment of their understanding about what they might remember from a very general introduction of the topic in their eighth-grade physical science class, Maria began by bending a light stick (glow stick) in front of the class and explaining that this causes a small

Reprinted from Lapp, D., Fisher, D., & Grant, M. (2008). "You can read this text–I'll show you how": Interactive comprehension instruction. *Journal of Adolescent & Adult Literacy, 51*(5), 372-383. doi: 10.1598/JAAL.51.5.1

Table 1
Maria's Introduction

Text	Teacher commentary during the think-aloud	Strategies modeled/practiced
Going Through Changes (Photo of pancakes)	"As I look over this piece of text, I see a photo of pancakes cooking on a griddle. Some are golden brown and others are still a beige batter color. The title of this reading is *Going Through Changes*. I wonder if the pancakes, some uncooked and others fully done, represent changes at a chemical level. I'll read the first paragraph."	Predicting and using titles and graphics provides focus and motivation to read further.
At a dinner table, a cook is making pancakes. He mixes together an egg, milk, and flour into a batter. When the batter is placed on the griddle, it becomes solid and golden brown. The batter has had a chemical change. All the atoms of the original ingredients are still in the batter. But the griddle's heat has arranged those atoms in a different pattern. Like the pancake batter, many substances go through chemical changes. These changes can break down complex substances into simpler parts. Or they can join simple parts into complex substances.	"So the cooking batter does represent chemical changes. I see from reading these paragraphs that chemical changes involve substances breaking down and substances joining together. I think the next section will tell me about how this process of breaking down and building up occurs. Do you have any ideas?" (Maria listens as the students share a few possibilities.) Janette, a student in Maria's class, responds, "Maybe the next section will talk about molecules being broken down or atoms being joined together." Dave adds, "Yes, I remember when I was in 8th grade we talked about how salt molecules are broken down when salt is added to water." Maria then continues. "OK, let's read on to see if we're correct."	The prediction is confirmed by reading the text. Note that sometimes the prediction is refuted after reading the text. Afterward, the main ideas are identified by summarizing a few lines of the text, which is followed by another prediction based on the text just read.
It usually takes energy to combine substances in a chemical reaction. This kind of reaction is called an *endothermic* reaction.	"An *endothermic* reaction. Wow, I'm not sure what that means, but I do know that *thermic* sounds like a word part from *thermometer* or *thermal* and both of those terms relate to heat. Maybe *endothermic* also relates to heat in some way. I'll continue to read. Maybe I'll gain an understanding of the meaning of this word if I read on."	Segmenting words into word parts brings attention to root words or affixes that might offer clues to meaning. In addition, understanding that clarification might come from context or from continued reading.

(continued)

Table 1
Maria's Introduction (*Continued*)

Text	Teacher commentary during the think-aloud	Strategies modeled/practiced
For example, heat was needed to turn the batter into a pancake.	"I guess I was right—*endothermic* does relate to heat."	Again, confirmation of a prediction, in this case of a word's meaning, may be confirmed or refuted by reading upcoming text.
If iron and powdered sulfur were mixed together, nothing would happen. But apply heat to those combined substances and you would form iron sulfide. This is an entirely new substance.	"So heat added to a mixture can cause a new substance to form. Interesting. Maybe *endothermic* means that heat is added."	Synthesizes and restates—examples offered in the text can help the reader to infer word meaning.

Note. Quotes from TIME and Teacher Created Materials (1993).

vial of a substance to be released. As students observed the stick emit a brightly colored light due to a chemical reaction, she asked them to think-pair-share in response to the following question: What is causing light to be given off? After a lively discussion among the students and their teacher, Ms. Grant began thinking aloud to model how she gained additional meaning from the science text *Chemical Reactions—Going Through Changes* (TIME & Teacher Created Materials, 1993). Table 1 illustrates how Maria introduced the text.

After this initial introduction, Maria realized that it was time for the students to "try on" what they had observed her do. In order to coach them as they recognized, adopted, imitated, practiced, and self-regulated their metacognitive strategies, she continued with the interactive conversation illustrated in Table 2.

After the students shared what they learned, Maria invited them to read the next section of the text together and to model for a selected partner how they were making sense of their reading. As they read, she circulated among them to listen in and offer support as needed. If the text surpassed the independent reading level of a team of students, she offered them an alternate, less difficult text on the same topic (Garner, Alexander, Gillingham, Kulikowich, & Brown, 1991; Goldman & Varma, 1995). She did this because she believes that as the students' topical or subject-matter knowledge base and language grow so will their reading proficiency (Alexander, 1996; Anderson, 1977; Stanovich, 1986).

It was obvious from Maria's think-alouds about the unfamiliar language, concepts, and structures of this chemistry passage that the challenges students face as they attempt content area reading, even with the support of a diligent teacher, cannot be underestimated (Pressley & Afflerbach, 1995). Thinking out loud during a shared reading of a content area passage models for students how a proficient reader grapples with the problems of unfamiliar vocabulary, new concepts, text features, and text structures that can seem quite foreign—even after years of success with narrative reading. The instructional comments this teacher shared while thinking aloud were neither unplanned nor inconsequential. Instead, they were deliberately planned to provide commentary and conversational support for comprehension, word study, and engagement by noting where students might need explanation, elaboration, or connection. While

Table 2
Monitoring Student Practice

Text	Teacher commentary during the think-aloud	Strategies modeled/practiced
When a substance breaks down into smaller parts, it usually releases energy. This is called an *exothermic* reaction.	*"Exothermic* sounds a bit like *endothermic* but with a different prefix. (Turning to the students) What do you think *exothermic* means? Make a prediction. Write your prediction and then share it with your partner. (James, a student, tells his partner that if *endothermic* meant heat was added *exothermic* must mean that heat is taken away or given off.) Now read the next section with your partner to see if your predictions were correct. If not, look back in your own experiences or in the text to see if there were clues you missed."	Noting prefixes may help clarify vocabulary. After the teacher models a strategy, she or he may ask students to practice it later in the reading.
This happens in the flame of your gas stove. Oxygen from the air reacts with methane gas, giving off light and heat.	"Turn to your partner and decide if your predicted meaning of *exothermic* was correct or if you'd like to revise your ideas." (James turns to his partner and says, "I think I was right. Heat is given off or removed in an *exothermic* reaction.")	Allow students to practice verbalizing their thoughts so that they can consolidate their understanding of comprehension strategies.
At the same time, the methane breaks down into carbon and hydrogen atoms, which form carbon dioxide and water.	"We talked about atoms and compounds a few weeks ago in class. Methane must be a compound. It's broken down into atoms—smaller parts. Then the atoms form new compounds. I think I'm beginning to understand chemical changes. Compounds are broken down sometimes and other times they are formed from smaller parts like atoms."	Make explicit connections to previously learned content. Summarize what you know thus far and what you know based on prior or background knowledge.
There are signs that a substance had gone through a chemical change. These reactions might produce light,	"I see a photo of fireworks. I sat on the lawn watching fireworks last Fourth of July with my family. I remember the loud exploding sound and the	Use photos or other graphics to clarify novel ideas from the text. Graphics also provide information that may be used to make predictions.

(continued)

Table 2
Monitoring Student Practice (*Continued*)

Text	Teacher commentary during the think-aloud	Strategies modeled/practiced
sound, bubbles or smoke. (Photo of fireworks)	colored light that filled the sky. I bet those fireworks were produced by a chemical reaction. Turn to a partner and share an experience you've had with a chemical reaction." (Jose talks to his partner, Sofia, about the changes he saw on a camping trip when wood logs were burned for a campfire. "Eventually," Jose relays, "all the wood turned to a black, powdery substance—charcoal I think." Sofia describes how her mother placed a dime-sized tablet into a tall glass of water a few weeks ago. Sofia's sister was in need of a cure for her aching stomach and the antacid was supposed to do the trick. According to Sofia, "The tablet fizzled and bubbled away. The text we're reading says that bubbles are often produced during a chemical reaction."	Ask students to make connections between the text and their own experiences. Have them articulate these connections.
Often a new substance has a new color.	"The fireworks I saw had many colors. The colors were brilliant in the sky."	Make connections to the text and your experiences.
Remember that pancake batter? It went from white batter to golden flapjack. (Heading: Slow vs. Fast)	"The next heading says 'Slow vs. Fast.' This must be referring to the speed at which reactions occur. What does this make you think about? Turn to your partner and share your connection."	Connect headings to previous content to predict upcoming content.
Metals combine with oxygen. This can happen very slowly, as when iron rusts.	"Last summer when I was repairing my old fence, I left a few iron nails outside. After a few weeks, they were coated with reddish brown material— rust I think. They must have combined with oxygen from the air outside."	Use newly learned content to clarify real-world experiences.

(continued)

Table 2
Monitoring Student Practice (*Continued*)

Text	Teacher commentary during the think-aloud	Strategies modeled/practiced
Some metals tarnish. For example, when copper oxidizes it turns green, forming copper sulfate or copper chloride.	"Read the next section of the text with your partner and think out loud about a connection you can make between what you've read and what you've experienced in your life." After observing the students as they interact, Maria asks Angul to share her connection. (Angul: "That sounds just like that copper bowl I have on the corner table in my home. It has a greenish tinge to it."). The students confirm Angul's connection.	Again, connect content to personal experiences and background knowledge.
Fireworks are an example of very fast oxidation.	"*Oxidation*—this is a new word. Read on with your partner to see how I'm going to figure this term out."	Sometimes new or challenging vocabulary can be clarified by reading further in the text.
Inside a firework is gunpowder, a combination of potassium nitrate, sulfur, and charcoal. When gunpowder is heated, the nitrate releases oxygen, making the sulfur and carbon burn fast. The gases they produce send the fireworks high into the sky.	"Yes, *oxidation* must mean that oxygen is added to another substance. So it seems that fireworks are the result of chemical reactions that cause new substances to be produced. You've seen how I think through a reading that has new vocabulary and challenging text. After I finish reading I always try to summarize what I've learned. If I can't do this I know I need to read the text again and chunk it into smaller segments. After each chunk I ask myself, 'What did I learn?' Let's see how this worked for you. Ask yourself, 'What did I learn from this text?' Now, write about three concepts you learned from this shared reading with a think-aloud." (Alexandra writes about the difference between *exothermic* and *endothermic* reactions, characteristics of chemical reactions, and *oxidation*.)	Clarify vocabulary by deciphering meaning from examples in the text. Ask students to summarize the main ideas. This will promote rereading and will guide students to clarify content.

Note. Quotes from TIME and Teacher Created Materials (1993).

being implemented, the teacher drew students in during the think-aloud and then capitalized on points in the text where they naturally experienced anticipation. When engagement of this type occurs, we found that the teacher feels more fulfilled as a teacher and that the students will learn more subject-specific information (Lapp & Fisher, 2007). In addition, students are learning strategies for comprehending challenging text, which can be directly translated into a motivation to read.

As Deci (1975) explained, intrinsic motivation is founded in the human need to be competent and self-determining in relation to a person's surroundings. This explanation is illustrated in the work of Palmer, Codling, and Gambrell (1994); Gambrell (1996); and Guthrie (1996, 2004). Guthrie noted that students are motivated to read by rich literacy environments that offer choice and by supportive successful experiences in which they feel they can tackle an interesting albeit difficult text. Thus, specifically modeled and practiced comprehension strategies are a foundation to garner student interest through the development of reading competency. An interactive think-aloud provides a means for modeling, scaffolding, and practicing. It offers struggling readers the opportunity to see and hear how proficient readers approach a text, and it allows advanced students to engage in conversations that draw on their prior knowledge.

What's New?

While thinking aloud during shared reading may seem like old news to teachers in grades K–5, we found as we visited the classrooms of middle and secondary teachers in three large urban schools (one middle and two high schools) that we were unlikely to see this type of instruction (Lapp & Fisher, 2007). Perplexed as to why interactive comprehension modeling and instruction did not exist in this arena, we realized through our conversations with these dedicated teachers that they echoed the insights of Moje (1996) and Shearer and Ruddell (2007). These researchers noted that content area teachers, trained to be content specific specialists, define themselves by their specializations as scientists, historians, athletes, and musicians first and teachers second. This doesn't mean that they are not committed to their students; it just means that they are intrigued by a content specialty that through study grew into an area of expertise they want to share with others. To do so, they decided to become teachers.

Students in the classrooms of these content experts often do not exhibit the same love for the topic or natural interest in studying it that their teachers do. These are students who need to be motivated through effective instruction to learn and enjoy the pursuit of the complexities of a particular subject. This entry-level mismatch between student and content is often exacerbated as students are asked to read textbooks that are rich with topic specific concepts, language, and structures. These textbooks are simply too difficult for a significant number of students. When examining this disparity, it quickly becomes obvious that these content experts, like all teachers, must become the liaisons between their students and the texts. Realizing this need, a common dilemma among secondary teachers, school administrators, and policymakers is how best to connect the expertise of the teacher or specialist to the interests' of the students in a way that accommodates students' diversity and promotes students' learning about content topics.

What's Next?

For many decades books and articles (Herber, 1978; Strang, 1938; Vacca & Vacca, 2007) have swept the field of secondary education in an attempt to provide middle and high school teachers with instructional supports that can strengthen their teaching and, thus, student learning. In spite of efforts to expand teachers' knowledge about modeling for students how to apply comprehension strategies to support the learning of content specific information, O'Brien, Stewart, and Moje (1995) and Bintz (1997) found that many of these efforts were not completely successful. The secondary teachers they studied noted difficulties when attempting to do any more than assign strategies for student use during instruction. Now, over a decade later, we are having the same experience as we spend time in classrooms and are asked by secondary teachers how they can "fill up" the allotted minutes of class time. Our recent experiences with these teachers, as well as a review of this research, have inspired our belief that the instructional role of the content teacher needs continued study in order to better understand

1. How to provide content related interactive instructional experiences that engage students while at the same time teaches the language and concepts needed to understand a particular subject

2. How teachers can best model for a diverse population of students how to read, write, and think about issues and language related to a topic of study

The suggestions of Wood and Muth (1991) and Alvermann (2003) that drastic changes are needed in the types of teaching that currently exist in high school classrooms are supported by the percentage of students who are not succeeding in high school; the dropout rate now exceeds 30% for children of color. Increasing percentages of the students who do graduate and attend two- and four-year colleges are required to attend remedial classes (Sacchetti, 2005). Remedial writing courses also are becoming requirements for entry-level salaried and hourly employees (The National Commission on Writing, 2004).

What is causing this? Consider classrooms you've recently visited. Was lecture the primary mode of presenting new content? Were the lessons you viewed interactive with lots of student engagement and participation? If you can answer no and then yes to these two questions, it is highly probable that the students won't drop out of school and also won't be those in the remedial classes. If you answered yes and then no, you probably viewed the familiar arrangement of rows of desks with students facing front so as not to miss the lessons in which information is told, mentioned, and assigned. For example, a teacher might tell her or his class to read a chapter about momentum and then to write a paper about a particular topic by stating the required number of pages without emphasizing a purpose for writing, establishing an audience for the piece, or explaining how to go about the process of writing. The resulting paper would typically include the scientific definition of momentum, copied directly from teacher provided notes, and the regurgitation of information from the textbook in a dry, aimless manner. It would most likely lack personal input from the student and would probably be devoid of applications or extensions of concepts related to momentum.

In contrast, in a classroom to which you would give a positive nod you would expect to observe students learning through interactive conversations and teacher modeling—through engagement that motivated and supported their learning. In this type of classroom, you would witness interactive think-alouds during shared reading in which a teacher like Maria would explicitly demonstrate the transformation of energy from potential to kinetic, offering some choices to her student scientists about energy transformation projects they could construct. She would model through interactive think-alouds how to compose a series of text-explicit and text-implicit questions while guiding students to predict, clarify, and summarize the procedures of an upcoming lab experiment. This conversational engagement with students creates interactive thinking about the new language, topic, and strategies being explored.

Another example of the supported learning we witnessed in Maria's classroom involved her initiating a lesson by inviting students to participate in a writing-to-learn prompt. Students were asked to describe what they saw as they watched an object fall to the ground after being dropped by a classmate. The rich discussion that ensued from the writing helped Maria to understand what the students knew about acceleration due to gravity and changes in velocity. It also provided engaging information that motivated the students to better understand the work of Galileo Galilei, the scientist who first explored the ideas of freefall and gravity. This conversation was followed by an interactive shared reading of *Starry Messenger* that explored the life of Galileo Galilei and a think-pair-share activity in which the students discussed Galileo's work during a period of history when new ideas were being suppressed. At this point, students were motivated to tackle reading a text about Galileo's ideas regarding acceleration. They were given excerpts from *Galileo Galilei and the Science of Motion* to further explore the science behind falling bodies. With this preparation, students were ready to independently review the chapter on acceleration due to gravity in their textbook. To support their independence as readers, they were then introduced, as needed, to problem-solving strategies that have been designed through the years to make content area reading more accessible to students. A few of these strategies we have seen science, social science, and English teachers use are Survey, Question, Reread, Question, Compute, Question (SQRQCQ) by Fay (1965); Read, Encode, Annotate, Ponder (REAP) by Manzo (1994); and Student Symbolic Response (SSR) by Wilhelm (1997).

As illustrated, these examples acknowledge the diverse educational backgrounds and needs of students while providing planned opportunities to develop high-level oral, reading, and writing skills. As evidenced by Maria's teaching (Tables 1 & 2), the interactive think-aloud implemented during shared reading provides a venue for the classroom teacher to engage students in conversation about targeted information on which they are all visually focused. During the conversation, the teacher thinks out loud about the topic, the vocabulary, and the structure of the text while making connections to prior personal or subject-related experiences learned through other materials.

Dimensions of Interactive Comprehension Instruction

Having now observed 65 lessons in which teachers like Maria model their thinking of discipline-specific texts, we identified four dimensions of think-alouds: vocabulary, comprehension, text structures, and text features (Lapp & Fisher, 2007). Teachers use these dimensions differently based on the demands of understanding the text,

their purpose in reading the text, and the discipline in which they are engaged. In other words, a social studies teacher might focus on different dimensions of interactive comprehension modeling than an art teacher or science teacher. A summary of the four dimensions can be found in Table 3. We'll explore each of these here.

Vocabulary

Given the vocabulary demands of most content areas, it's not surprising that teachers commonly focus on understanding vocabulary as part of their think-alouds. Teachers do not simply define a word during their interactive comprehension instruction. Instead, they solve unknown words as they read by using context clues, their understanding of word parts or related words, or the resources available to them. Consider the following quote from an art teacher reading the biography of Vincent Van Gogh:

> An *asylum*. I wonder what that means? I understand from the paragraph that Van Gogh needed treatment for his psychiatric problems. It might be the place that they provide this treatment, but I can't be sure. I don't know any word parts that will help me. I guess I better look this one up.

Comprehension

Most teachers we observed provided comprehension strategy instruction during their think-alouds. They used common terms, such as *predicting* and *visualizing*, to help students incorporate these processes into their own habits (e.g., Harvey & Goudvis, 2000). The teachers we observed used comprehension strategy instruction purposefully and strategically. They often paused to model their use of a comprehension strategy and then asked students to discuss other comprehension strategies in pairs or small groups. They did not interrogate students about their thinking or focus on a single strategy at a time. Instead, they allowed the text and their purpose for reading the text to guide their selection of the comprehension strategy to be modeled.

In the same art class, this time for a shared reading of the song "Vincent (Starry, Starry

Table 3
Dimensions of Interactive Comprehension Modeling

Dimension	Definition	Components
Vocabulary	Focus on solving an unknown word, not providing the definition of the word	• Context clues • Word parts (prefix, suffix, root, base, related words) • Use of resources (peers, dictionary, Internet)
Comprehension	Strategic moves to support understanding the text	• Summarizing/synthesize • Predicting • Inferring • Visualizing • Questioning • Connecting • Monitoring • Activating background knowledge
Text structures	Structures used in presenting information that readers can use to predict the flow of information	• Cause/effect • Compare/contrast • Problem/solution • Temporal/sequence • Descriptive • Story grammar (plot, setting, character, conflict, etc.)
Text features	Components of the text added to increase understanding or interest	• Captions • Illustrations, diagrams • Headings, titles • Bold, italic words • Glossary, index

Night)" by Don McLean, the teacher paused a recording of it to share his thinking about a verse that the students saw on the document camera. He said,

> This line, "now I understand what you tried to say to me, how you suffered for your sanity" reminds me of the asylum from the biographical sketch [of Vincent Van Gogh]. I've made this connection between the song and the fact in the biography we read. Van Gogh had to live in an asylum for treatment.

Text Structure

In addition to vocabulary knowledge and comprehension strategies, readers use their understanding of text structures to understand what they read. While there are a number of text structures, five informational types and one narrative type are very common. Developing students understanding of text structures and how they aid understanding is another support teachers can provide through modeling. During his reading of the biographical profile of Vincent Van Gogh, for example, the art teacher paused and said,

> I think that this is going to compare and contrast the life of Van Gogh before and after his time in the asylum. I see that the author has provided us some information about Vincent and is starting to use some signal words that I know are used when comparing things. I see here in this paragraph that he used *in comparison*, *nevertheless*, and *in contrast*.

Text Features

Finally, authors and editors use specific text features to aid readers in understanding complex information and in maintaining interest in the reading. There are a number of text features that can be used, including table of contents, chapter or section headings, glossary, index, captions, and illustrations. While struggling readers often skip over these features, they can be critical to understanding. Text features can also be used to focus readers on key ideas or important points. As such, the teachers we observed regularly commented on their use of text features during their interactive comprehension instruction and modeling. For example, during his shared reading of a picture book about Vincent Van Gogh, the art teacher focused on the captions for each of the illustrations and how these captions reinforced and extended the main text. In his words,

> I see this caption and know that it's going to do a couple of things. First, it's going to tell me the name of this specific painting. That's helpful because the text describes a number of paintings. This caption also provides the date of the painting, which is critical. I know when Van Gogh was hospitalized in the asylum and what was happening to him before that. The date in the caption helps me know what was going on in Van Gogh's life around the time he completed each work.

Close the Reading Achievement Gap

If we are ever going to radically change the literacy achievement of the majority of adolescent youth, we must alter the significant amounts of time they spend doing independent work, reading from books that are too hard, and being asked questions based on things they have not read. We must ensure that students are not merely physically present, coasting from class to class in an unspoken agreement with adults to behave as long as the challenge remains low. We need to scaffold the experiences students have with texts so that they develop repertoires and habits for reading them. To do so requires significant teacher modeling as well as extensive class discussions. Interactive comprehension instruction, through think-alouds based on shared readings, can contribute to the success of students, providing them with tangible and authentic experiences for reading. Over time, across content areas, and with repeated practice, students will begin to incorporate these thinking processes into their interactions with texts. Only then will we see the achievement gap close and students engage in reading and writing.

References

Alexander, P.A. (1996). The past, present, and future of knowledge research: A reexamination of the role of knowledge in learning and instruction. *Educational Psychologist, 31*, 89–92.

Alvermann, D.E. (2003). Effective literacy instruction for adolescents. In R.D. Robinson, M.C. McKenna, & J.M. Wedman (Eds.), *Issues and trends in literacy education* (3rd ed., pp. 175–192). Boston: Allyn & Bacon.

Anderson, R.C. (1977). The notion of schemata and educational enterprise. In R.C. Anderson, R.J. Spiro, & W.E. Montague (Eds.), *Schooling and the acquisition of knowledge* (pp. 415–431). Hillsdale, NJ: Erlbaum.

Anderson, R.C., & Pearson, P.D. (1984). A schema-theoretic view of basic processes in reading comprehension. In P.D. Pearson, R. Barr, M.L. Kamil, & P. Mosenthal (Eds.), *Handbook of reading research* (pp. 255–291). New York: Longman.

Bintz, W.P. (1997). Exploring reading nightmares of middle and secondary school teachers. *Journal of Adolescent & Adult Literacy, 41*, 12–24.

Bruner, J. (1986). *Actual minds, possible worlds.* Cambridge, MA: Harvard University Press.

Deci, E.L. (1975). *Intrinsic motivation.* New York: Plenum Press.

Duke, N.K, & Pearson, P.D. (2002). Effective practices for developing reading comprehension. In A. Farstrup & J. Samuels (Eds.), *What research has to say about reading instruction* (3rd ed., pp. 205–242). Newark, DE: International Reading Association.

Fay, L. (1965). Reading study skills: Math and science. *Proceedings of the International Reading Association, 10*, 92–94.

Gambrell, L.B. (1996). Creating classroom cultures that foster reading motivation. *The Reading Teacher, 50*, 14–25.

Garner, R., Alexander, P.A., Gillingham, M.G., Kulikowich, J.M., & Brown, R. (1991). Interest and learning from text. *American Educational Research Journal, 28*, 643–659.

Goldman, S.R., & Varma, S. (1995). CAPing the construction-integration model of discourse comprehension. In C. Weaver, S. Mannes, & C. Fletcher (Eds.), *Discourse* comprehension: Essays in honor of Walter Kintsch (pp. 337–358). Hillsdale, NJ: Erlbaum.

Guthrie, J.T. (1996). Educational contexts for engagement in literacy. *The Reading Teacher, 49*, 432–445.

Guthrie, J.T. (2004). Teaching for literacy engagement. *Journal of Literacy Research, 36*, 1–30.

Harste, J.C. (1994). Literacy as curricular conversations about knowledge, inquiry and morality. In R. Ruddell, M. Ruddell, & H. Singer (Eds.), *Theoretical models and processes of reading* (4th ed., pp. 1220–1242). Newark, DE: International Reading Association.

Harvey, S., & Goudvis, A. (2000). *Strategies that work: Teaching comprehension to enhance understanding.* York, ME: Stenhouse.

Herber, H. (1978). *Teaching reading in the content areas.* Upper Saddle River, NJ: Prentice Hall.

Lapp, D., & Fisher, D. (2007). *Improving high school student achievement through teacher practices.* 41st annual California Reading Association Conference, Ontario, CA.

Manzo, A. (1994). *REAP Central.* Retrieved July 19, 2007, from members.aol.com/ReadShop/REAP1.html

Mathan, S.A., & Koedinger, K.R. (2005). Fostering the intelligent novice: Learning from errors with metacognitive tutoring. *Educational Psychologist, 40*, 257–265.

McCarthy, C.B. (2005). Effects of thematic-based, hands-on science teaching versus a textbook approach for students with disabilities. *Journal of Research in Science Teaching, 42*, 245–263.

Moje, E.B. (1996). "I teach subjects, not students": Teacher–student relationships as contexts for secondary literacy. *Reading Research Quarterly, 31*, 172–195.

O'Brien, D.G., Stewart, R.A., & Moje, E.B. (1995). Why content literacy is difficult to infuse into the secondary school: Complexities of curriculum, pedagogy, and school culture. *Reading Research Quarterly, 30*, 442–463.

Palmer, B.M., Codling, R.M., & Gambrell, L.B. (1994). In their own words: What elementary students have to say about motivation to read. *The Reading Teacher, 48*, 176–178.

Pressley, M., & Afflerbach, P. (1995). *Verbal protocols of reading: The nature of constructively responsive reading.* Hillsdale, NJ: Erlbaum.

Rosenblatt, L.M. (1978). *The reader, the text, the poem: The transactional theory of literacy work.* Carbondale: Southern Illinois University Press.

Sacchetti, M. (2005, June 26). Colleges question MCAS success: Many in the state schools still need remedial help.

The Boston Globe. Retrieved December 17, 2006, from www.boston.com/news/education/k_12/mcas/articles/2005/06/26/colleges_question_mcas_success

Schunk, D.H., & Zimmerman, B.J. (1994). *Self-regulation of learning and performance: Issues and educational applications.* Hillsdale, NJ: Erlbaum.

Shearer, B., & Ruddell, M.R. (2008). Engaging students' interest and participation in learning. In D. Lapp, J. Flood, & N. Farnan (Eds.), *Content area reading and learning: Instructional strategies* (3rd ed., pp. 115–132). Mahwah, NJ: Erlbaum.

Stanovich, K.E. (1986). Matthew effects in reading: Some consequences of individual differences in the acquisition of literacy. *Reading Research Quarterly, 21*, 360–407.

Strang, R.M. (1938). *Problems in the improvement of reading in high school and college* (2nd ed.). Lancaster, PA: Science Press.

The National Commission on Writing. (2004). *Writing: A ticket to work...or a ticket out: A survey of business leaders.* New York: College Entrance Examination Board. Retrieved July 19, 2007, from www.writingcommission.org/prod_downloads/writingcom/writing-ticket-to-work.pdf

TIME & Teacher Created Materials. (1993). *Science: Exploring nonfiction. Lesson 4: Chemical reactions—Going through changes.* New York: Authors.

Vacca, R., & Vacca, J. (2007). *Content area reading: Literacy and learning across the curriculum* (9th ed.). New York: HarperCollins.

Vygotsky, L.S. (1978). *Mind in society: The development of higher psychological processes* (M. Cole, V. John-Steiner, S. Scribner, & E. Souberman, Eds. & Trans.). Cambridge, MA: Harvard University Press. (Original work published 1934)

Wilhelm, J.D. (1997). *"You gotta BE the book": Teaching engaged and reflective reading with adolescents.* New York: Teachers College Press.

Wilhelm, J.D., & Friedemann, P.D. (1998). *Hyperlearning: Where projects, inquiry, and technology meet.* Portland, ME: Stenhouse.

Wood, K.D., & Muth, K.D. (1991). The case for improved instruction in the middle grades. *Journal of Reading, 35*, 84–90.

Wu, Y., & Tsai, C. (2005). Development of elementary school students' cognitive structures and information processing strategies under long-term constructivist-oriented science instruction. *Science Education, 89*, 822–846.

Questions for Reflection

• Modeling takes some practice, and it's often hard to learn to say "I" rather than simply asking students questions. Try working with a partner teacher to design a think-aloud for a small section of a lesson. Select the strategies you'll think aloud about (e.g., how you preview the text or how you stop to figure out vocabulary). Use Maria Grant, the teacher in the article, as an example. Once you have the think-aloud prepared, practice with each other. Each partner should help the other reflect on whether the thinking strategies modeled became transparent.

• Are there topics or strategies that keep reteaching because your students are just not comprehending? These may be the areas where a think-aloud that illustrates "how to" is all that is needed to provide added student support. Alone or together with your grade-level, identify students' most often asked questions. Then plan a think-aloud that models for students how you think through the target information in a way that will result in successful comprehension or task completion. Be sure to check that your think-aloud is transparent enough that the students can really see your thinking.

Interactive Teaching to Promote Independent Learning From Text

Annemarie Sullivan Palincsar and Ann L. Brown

Student 1: My question is, what does the aquanaut need when he goes under water?

Student 2: A watch.

Student 3: Flippers.

Student 4: A belt.

Student 1: Those are all good answers.

Teacher: Nice job! I have a question too. Why does the aquanaut wear a belt? What is so special about it?

Student 3: It's a heavy belt and keeps him from floating up to the top again.

Teacher: Good for you.

Student 1: For my summary now: This paragraph was about what aquanauts need to take when they go under the water.

Student 5: And also about why they need those things.

Student 3: I think we need to clarify gear.

Student 6: That's the special things they need.

Teacher: Another word for gear in this story might be equipment, the equipment that makes it easier for the aquanauts to do their job.

Student 1: I don't think I have a prediction to make.

Teacher: Well, in the story they tell us that there are "many strange and wonderful creatures" that the aquanauts see as they do their work. My prediction is that they'll describe some of these creatures. What are some of the strange creatures you already know about that live in the ocean?

Student 6: Octopuses.

Student 3: Whales?

Student 5: Sharks!

Teacher: Let's listen and find out.

Instructing Students to Read for Meaning

The dialogue presented above captures a bit of conversation a teacher and her group of first grade students recently had concerning a passage about aquanauts which the teacher was reading aloud. This article will suggest how a teacher might stimulate such discussion about text, what the purpose of such conversation is, and what the benefits of engaging in such dialogue are. Finally, we will address a number of questions teachers have asked about the instructional procedure we will describe.

The teacher and students above are engaged in an activity we call *reciprocal teaching*. In reciprocal teaching, the adult and students take turns assuming the role of the teacher. The "teacher" is responsible for leading a dialogue about a passage which the students are reading silently or with the assistance of the adult. Anyone who has struggled to make conversation will appreciate that dialogue flows more smoothly when the participants share similar goals. The

Reprinted from Palincsar, A.S., & Brown, A.L. (1986). Interactive teaching to promote independent learning from text. *The Reading Teacher*, 39(8), 771-777.

participants in reciprocal teaching share four goals: *predicting, question generating, summarizing, and clarifying.*

Teachers will recognize the each of these goals represents a strategy that promotes both comprehension of text and comprehension monitoring. When students make *predictions*, they hypothesize what the author will discuss next in the text. To do this successfully, they must activate the relevant background knowledge that they already possess. In the illustration above, the students have contemplated what they already know about creatures that live in the ocean and have anticipated some specific ocean life that they will read about. They now have a purpose for reading—to confirm or disprove their hypotheses. Furthermore, the opportunity has been created for the students to link the new knowledge they will encounter in the text with the knowledge they already possess. The predicting strategy also facilitates use of text structure. Students learn that headings, subheadings, and questions embedded in text are useful means of anticipating what might occur next.

Question generating gives the students an opportunity to identify the kind of information that provides the substance for a good question, to frame that question, and then engage in self-testing. The students become much more involved in the reading activity and in the text when they are posing and answering the questions and not merely responding to teacher or text questions.

Summarizing is an excellent tool for integrating the information presented in the text. In the example above, the students jointly identified the most important content of the paragraph. As they proceed through the passage, the teacher will guide them in integrating the content across paragraphs and sections of the passage.

Clarifying is particularly important with students who have a history of comprehension difficulty. Such students can be thought of as making a habit of not understanding what they read. These students very likely believe that the purpose of reading is saying the words correctly; they may not be particularly uncomfortable with the fact that the words and, in fact, the passage are not making much sense. When students are asked to clarify, their attention is called to the fact that there may be many reasons why text is difficult to understand, e.g., unfamiliar vocabulary, unclear referent words, new and perhaps complicated concepts. They are taught to be alert to the effects of such impediments on comprehension and to take the necessary measures to restore meaning, e.g., reread, ask for help.

Now, it is important to call the reader's attention to the fact that the dialogue above did not occur the first day that the teacher and students began reciprocal teaching. In fact, this dialogue occurred on the 10th day. What we wish to discuss is how the teacher went about working with her students so that by day 10 they are enjoying a spontaneous, informed, and informative discussion. The components might be described as the following: explanation, instruction, modeling, guided practice, praise, and teacher judgment.

When instruction first begins, the teacher explains what strategies the students will be learning, why they are learning these particular activities, in what situations such strategies will be helpful, and how they will go about learning the strategies (i.e., turn taking as the teacher). This explanation, which is reviewed regularly, is followed by instruction on the four strategies. This instruction is for the purpose of defining each of the strategies, teaching the students rules that will help them learn the strategies, and ensuring that the students have minimal competency with each of the strategies before they engage in the dialogue.

For the purpose of illustration, we will highlight the instruction students receive regarding questioning. After a brief discussion about the role that questions play in our lives, particularly our school lives, the students are asked to generate information seeking questions about everyday events, e.g., "If you are interested in knowing what time the afternoon movie begins, you call the theater and ask: _____." Such an activity allows the teacher to ascertain that her students do indeed know how to phrase a question. The students are then given simple sentences about which they are to ask a question and are supplied words they might use to begin their questions. The question words are then faded out and the sentences become longer.

Keep in mind that these activities are only for the purpose of exposing the students to the strategies; the teachers with whom we have worked spend but one day introducing each strategy. After this brief instruction, the group begins the dialogue and it is at this point that the major component becomes modeling. For the initial days of reciprocal teaching, the adult teacher leads the dialogue, modeling how she employs the four strategies while reading. At this point, the students are encouraged to comment on the teacher's summaries, add their own predictions and clarifications, and respond to the teacher generated questions.

As the days of instruction proceed, more responsibility for initiating and sustaining the dialogue is transferred to the students. It is this responsibility for leading the dialogue that we are describing when we speak of guided practice. The teacher is now monitoring the success with which the students are employing the strategies, praising their attempts, and providing further modeling and instruction as teacher judgment indicates.

To return to the dialogue above, while the students are playing the principal role in this discussion, the teacher maintains a critical role as well. After Student 1 asks his question, which requires the recall of specific pieces of information in the text, the teacher praises the group and models a question that requires the students to reason about the information; when the student teacher is unable to generate a predication, the adult teacher provides instruction about a clue the text has provided and then provides the opportunity for the students to do their own predicting.

The hallmark of this form of instruction is its interactive nature. There is ongoing interplay among the teacher and students as they work toward the goal of understanding the text. Such instruction has been called scaffolded instruction (Wood, Bruner, & Ross, 1976). The metaphor is quite appropriate, as a scaffold is a support that is adjustable and temporary. The teacher supports each student in the acquisition and mastery of the strategies through the use of explanation, instruction, and modeling, but the support is temporary and the student is challenged to use the strategy independently as he or she displays increased competence with comprehension.

Evaluating Reciprocal Teaching

For the past 5 years, we have been evaluating the effectiveness of reciprocal teaching. The research has been developmental in nature and has sprung not only from the questions that we have raised regarding reciprocal teaching but also from the questions that educators have posed. For this reason, perhaps the most effective manner in which we might present the research findings is by addressing the questions that motivated the research.

- What effect does reciprocal teaching have on the reading comprehension ability of poor comprehenders?

For the purpose of our research, poor comprehenders have been defined as students who are able to decode grade level material with a fair degree of fluency but whose comprehension of that text is not commensurate with their decoding ability. For example, the typical junior high student with whom we have worked was decoding seventh grade material at a rate of at least 100 words per minute correct, with fewer than 2 error words per minute; however, on standardized measures of comprehension, they were performing 2 years below grade level, and on criterion referenced measures of comprehension they averaged 45% accuracy.

Our initial investigations were conducted by adult tutors working with students in pairs and volunteer Chapter 1 teachers working with groups of about five students (Brown & Palincsar, 1982; Palincsar & Brown, 1984). These teachers engaged in reciprocal teaching for 20 consecutive school days using passages from basal readers. Several measures were taken to assess the effectiveness of the instruction:

(1) Quantitative and qualitative analyses of the transcripts showed substantial changes in the dialogue during the 20 instructional days. For example, students asked many more main

idea questions over the course of time and functioned more independently of the teacher as time passed.

(2) The changes in the dialogue were also reflected on other direct measures of comprehension. Daily, the students read independently a passage of about 450 words and answered 10 comprehension questions from recall. The students completed five of these assessments prior to the first day of instruction and one each day after the 30 minute reciprocal teaching session. All but one of the experimental students achieved criterion performance, which we had defined as 70% accuracy on the comprehension measures for 4 out of 5 consecutive days. This is in contrast to the control students, who completed an equivalent number of assessments but showed no improvement.

(3) The students were also given measures to evaluate their ability to write summaries of text, generate written questions about text, and detect incongruities in text. The experimental children were indeed able to transfer the skills they had learned to these similar but distinct activities.

(4) Finally, generalization probes administered in the social studies and science classes these students attended indicated they were able to apply independently the newly acquired skills, as their percentile rankings in these classes jumped from the 20th percentile and below to the 50th percentile and higher.

- Can reciprocal teaching be implemented in settings where there are larger and more heterogeneous groups of students?

To investigate this question, we implemented the reciprocal teaching procedure with six middle school remedial reading teachers in an inner-city district (Brown & Palincsar, in press; Palincsar, 1984; Palincsar & Brown, 1985a, 1985b). For each teacher we identified the two classes that come closest to the description of the students we described above, i.e., adequate decoders but poor comprehenders. One class served as the control group and received individualized basic skill instruction, while the second class received 20 days of reciprocal teaching. The number of students in the experimental groups ranged from 8 to 18.

In this study 71% of the experimental students achieved criterion performance, in contrast to 19% of the control students. Despite the larger number of students and the teachers' concerns that management of such large groups would be problematic, the students did extremely well and the teachers observed that they had fewer behavior problems than in their control groups, as the students involved in reciprocal teaching enjoyed it, particularly the opportunity to assume the role of the teacher.

As an alternative to whole group instruction, we investigated the use of peer tutoring in small group reciprocal teaching. Three seventh grade teachers trained four of their best students (who were averaging 72% on the daily assessments prior to instruction) in the reciprocal teaching procedure. After 10 days of instruction, the tutors were assigned two tutees who were achieving a mean of 49% on the assessments before instruction. After 20 days of instruction, the tutees were achieving 78% accuracy while the tutors were achieving 87% accuracy with the comprehension measures. It is important to note that the teachers in each of these classrooms monitored the performance of the tutors quite closely, dividing their time among the peer groups each day, providing the tutors evaluative information, suggesting how they might improve their instruction, and assisting when students were experiencing particular difficulty.

- How can reciprocal teaching be incorporated in content area instruction?

Our interest in teaching students how to learn from text across the curriculum motivated a further study with the students who had served as control children in the large group study reported above (Brown & Palincsar, in press). Reciprocal teaching, again for a 20 day period, was given with the following modifications.

The material with which the students worked were science texts that were not currently being used in the school but were available to all students. Each day the students were assigned segments of text to read. Given the heading of each segment, the students were to write two statements indicating what they thought they would learn in this portion of the text. In a discussion, the teacher elicited from the group and compared the predictions they had made. The students then read one segment (generally four paragraphs). They wrote two questions and a summary reflecting the information in that segment. Finally, they noted, in writing, any information which required clarification.

The classes then discussed their questions, summaries, and clarifications. To approximate the way in which students are tested in school, we assessed these students by giving weekly science tests which covered the material they had worked on during the week. When we had pretested them on their comprehension and recall of science text, they averaged 36% accuracy; by the 4th week, the students were generally scoring 20% higher on these weekly tests.

- What's the difference between reciprocal teaching and skill instruction?

There was a time not long ago in reading education when successful reading was thought to be the execution of a series of component subskills. This orientation suggested that our instruction be directed at the mastery of such skills as finding the main idea, identifying the sequence of events in a story, and using context clues.

We know now that it is possible for students to master such skills and still not be successful readers. In reciprocal teaching the acquisition of the strategies is not the ultimate goal of instruction. The strategies are but a means to an end; they provide the vehicle for teaching students to read for meaning and to monitor their reading to ensure that they are understanding.

- Can reciprocal teaching be used to teach narrative text?

In our research we have employed expository or informational text almost exclusively; yet the story structure found in narrative text lends itself quite well to reciprocal teaching. The discussion now becomes focused on the characters in the story; summaries can be attentive to the problem posed in the story; predictions can be directed at

speculating what the solutions might be. In short, the dialogue is guided by using the strategies as well as the structure of the text.

- Can reciprocal teaching be used with nonreaders?

Interest in exploring how very young children and students who are not yet decoding might engage in comprehension activities leads us to the series of studies we are presently conducting (Brown & Palincsar, in press; Palincsar, in press). First grade teachers are working with groups of six students. In each group there are two students of above average ability and four students who are experiencing academic difficulty as determined by teacher observation and performance on standardized measures of listening and reading comprehension.

The reciprocal teaching procedure is the same with the exception that the teachers read the text aloud. Our work to date suggests that this is a reasonable form of instruction. The first grade students become involved willingly in the dialogue and the more capable students serve as catalysts in the discussion. Assessments, which are being conducted orally as well, indicate that the students' ability to learn from text has improved and, very importantly, the classroom teachers report that their reciprocal teaching students are spontaneously engaging in discussion using the four strategies during their reading group instruction as well.

Summary

The purpose of this article was to describe one means by which teachers can provide instruction in learning from text. The procedure, reciprocal teaching, is best characterized as a dialogue in which the students and teacher work together to comprehend text. The dialogue is structured by the use of four comprehension fostering and comprehension monitoring strategies: predicting, questioning, summarizing, and clarifying. The teacher balances the use of explanation, instruction, and modeling with guided practice, so that there is a gradual transfer of responsibility for sustaining the dialogue, thus ensuring that the students can independently apply the strategies and independently learn from text.

Reciprocal teaching has been effectively implemented by teachers working in both small and large group settings, in a peer tutoring situation, in content area instruction, and most recently in listening comprehension instruction.

References

Brown, A.L., & Palincsar, A.S. (1982, April). Inducing strategic learning from texts by means of informed, self-control training. *Topics in Learning and Learning Disabilities, 2,* 1–17.

Brown, A.L., & Palincsar, A.S. (in press). Reciprocal teaching of comprehension strategies: A natural history of one program for enhancing learning. In J. Borkowski & J.D. Day (Eds.), *Intelligence and cognition in special children: Comparing studies of giftedness, mental retardation, and learning disabilities.* New York: Ablex.

Palincsar, A.S. (1984). The quest for meaning from expository text: A teacher guided journey. In G. Duffy, L. Roehler, & J. Mason (Eds.), *Comprehension instruction: Perspectives and suggestions.* New York: Longman.

Palincsar, A.S. (in press). The role of dialogue in scaffolded instruction. *Educational Psychologist.*

Palincsar, A.S., & Brown, A.L. (1984, Spring). Reciprocal teaching of comprehension-fostering and comprehension-monitoring activities. *Cognition and Instruction, 2,* 117–175.

Palincsar, A.S., & Brown, A.L. (1985a). A means to a meaningful end. In R. Anderson, J. Osborne, & P. Wilson (Eds.), *Research foundations for a literate America.* New York: D.C. Heath.

Palincsar, A.S., & Brown, A.L. (1985b). Reciprocal teaching: Activities to promote "read(ing) with your mind." In E.J. Cooper (Ed.), *Reading, thinking, and concept development: Interactive strategies for the class.* New York: The College Board.

Wood, D., Bruner, J., & Ross, G. (1976, September). The role of tutoring in problem solving. *Journal of Child Psychology and Psychiatry, 17,* 89–100.

Questions for Reflection

• The authors note that clarifying is a particularly important component of reciprocal teaching for students who experience difficulty with comprehension. How might this step be tailored to meet the needs of students in your class who struggle for different reasons? For example, are there particular ways to support clarifying for English learners?

• The article mentions reciprocal teaching taking place in pairs, in small groups of five or six students, and for whole-class instruction. Think about your students and your classroom organization. What do you think would be the optimal group size and composition for reciprocal teaching in your class? Why? What are the implications for implementation?

Using Writing to Enhance Content Area Learning in the Primary Grades

Evelyn T. Cudd and Leslie Roberts

Students who in the primary grades comprehend narrative texts quite well often have difficulty understanding and remembering content area material when they reach the intermediate grades. The reasons for this difficulty vary from student to student, but usually include the following:

- The text topics are not within the child's life experiences; thus background knowledge is limited.

- The text is written to inform, rather than to affect, so interest is not always inherent.

- The organizational structure of expository writing is unfamiliar (Winograd & Bridge, 1986).

- Logical connectives and transition words which are necessary for understanding the relationships among ideas are often implied rather than stated explicitly in elementary texts (Irwin, 1986).

- When transition words and phrases are included to show the relationship of one idea to another, they are often not explained adequately by the teacher (Marshall, 1984).

- Most elementary content area texts are written in a descriptive manner, an organizational structure that appears less useful for understanding and retaining material than are other structures such as sequential order, enumeration, or comparison/contrast (Englert & Hiebert, 1984).

Using paragraph frames can help children overcome these problems through writing about what they have read. These frames provide a bridge which helps to ease the transition from narrative to content area reading and writing.

A Cloze Approach

Paragraph frames employ a cloze procedure. Sentence starters which include specific signal words or phrases are provided for the student. When these starters are completed, a paragraph is formed which follows one of the organizational patterns commonly used in content area writing. Example 1 illustrates a sequentially organized paragraph frame.

Just as primary students can be taught to complete narrative story frames (Cudd & Roberts, 1987), so can they learn to complete expository paragraph frames. These can be used to review and reinforce specific content and to familiarize students with the different ways in which authors organize material in order to inform.

Most primary grade content area curriculum is based on a unit approach that requires pulling from a variety of sources, hands-on activities, and resource people rather than sole use of a textbook. Therefore, to involve students in writing about what they have learned either from textbooks or other sources, the teacher needs to begin by writing simple paragraphs organized in whatever patterns are appropriate to the content.

Reprinted from Cudd, E.T., & Roberts, L. (1989). Using writing to enhance content area learning in the primary grades. *The Reading Teacher*, 42(6), 392-404. doi: 10.1598/RT.42.6.8

Example 1
Elena, Grade 2

Before a frog is grown, it goes through many changes. First, the mother frog _____

_____

Next, _____

Then, _____

Finally, _____

Now they _____

_____

Before a frog is grown, it goes through many stages. First, the mother frog lays the eggs. Next, the eggs hatch and turn into tapoles. Then slowly the tadpoles legs begin to grow. Finally, the tadpole turns into a frog. Now and then they have to go into the water to keep their skin moist.

Stage No. 1.   Stage No. 2.

Stage No. 3.   Stage No. 4.

Extrordinary!

Start With Example

By the second semester of 1st grade, most children can begin working with paragraphs that are organized sequentially. We begin with the sequential pattern because it appears to be one of the easiest structures for children to recognize and use in their own writing (Englert & Hiebert, 1984). One possible reason for this is that sequence is a skill taught in basals; therefore, children are already familiar with the signal words such as *first*, *next*, *then*, and *finally* that are used as transition devices.

To ensure success in completing paragraph frames, the teacher begins instruction with a sample paragraph rather than a frame, as follows:

1. Write a simple paragraph about a topic that lends itself to sequential ordering, using the clue words *first*, *next*, *then*, *finally*.

2. Copy the sentences on sentence strips or transparency strips.

3. With the whole group, review the topic and the logical sequence of events.

4. In a pocket chart or on the overhead projector, have students arrange the sentences in correct order.

5. Read the completed paragraph together.

6. Have students re-order the paragraph on their own and copy it in paragraph form (Example 2).

7. Ask students to illustrate the details or some important aspect of the paragraph.

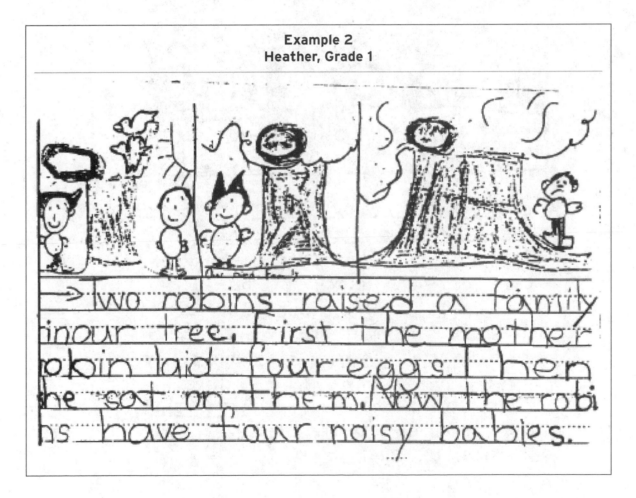

Example 2
Heather, Grade 1

Two robins raised a family in our tree. First the mother robin laid four eggs. Then she sat on them. Now the robins have four noisy babies.

Because research suggests that information presented with pictorial support is recalled more completely (Marshall, 1984), the final step of illustrating is important. Furthermore, it has been our experience that when children are encouraged to add details to their drawings to convey specific meaning, they are better able to understand the importance of adding details to convey a specific idea in writing.

By beginning with the prewritten sequential paragraph, the teacher can work on the concepts topic sentence, clue words, paragraph form, and organization before asking the child to be more creative.

Add a Frame

After practicing sequential organization with a full paragraph, as described above, the teacher gradually begins letting children fill in their own supporting information within the context of a framed paragraph (Example 3).

When working with a paragraph frame, the teacher should always model the paragraph first, either on the chalkboard or on an overhead. During the modeling process, blanks within the frame should be completed using responses elicited from the students. Most of the transitions or signal words within the paragraph frames are

Example 3
Rob, Grade 1

Mother box turtles prepare for their babies in a very interesting way. First, she looks for a safe place to burry her eggs. Next, she digs a hole so it will be moist for her eggs. Finally, she lays her eggs, burrys the hole, and then tamps it down. After this, the mother turtle leaves her babies on their own.

new to the children. This is the time to help them learn what these signals mean and how to use them effectively in writing.

After this prewriting phase of instruction, children use the frame as a guide for writing their own paragraphs by copying the frame on a separate sheet of paper and completing it with their own responses.

Enumeration Frames

Another organizational structure that is easily understood by young children is enumeration (Englert & Hiebert, 1984). Typical of this structure is a main idea followed by supporting details that do not necessitate a definite sequence.

Characteristic signal words are *first*, second, third, *in addition to*, *for example*, *another*, *also*. As with the sequential structure, we begin to teach children new transition words in the context of the paragraph frame (Example 4).

Reaction Frames

One offshoot of the enumeration frame that we have found particularly successful with primary students is the reaction frame, which allows children to "react" to what they have learned about a particular topic. Completing a reaction frame helps them understand that they have, indeed,

learned something about a topic, that ideas often need to be discarded or revised after reading new information, and that context learned or deemed important often varies from individual to individual (Example 5). Examples 6a and 6b illustrate the difference in student response to the same content.

Two types of reaction frames have proven particularly useful. One is structured so that prior knowledge is tied in with new information gained from reading a selection (Examples 7a and 7b). This type of frame is a positive means of reinforcing prereading activities in which the child's prior knowledge of a subject has been tapped. Completing this frame also helps children realize that although they may have already known something about a topic, new information was gained from the reading.

The second type of reaction frame focuses the child's attention on how his/her ideas were revised due to the acquisition of new information. This type of frame is important because children often have difficulty revising their preconceived ideas about a topic even after being presented with contradictory information (Example 8).

Comparison and Contrast

Having worked with sequential, enumerative, and reaction frames, children are usually ready

---

Example 4

Bats are unusual animals for several reasons.

First,_____ .

Second, _____ .

Third, _____ .

Finally, _____ .

As you can see, bats are unique in the animal world.

Illustrate with a picture of what you
consider to be the most unusual thing
about the bat.

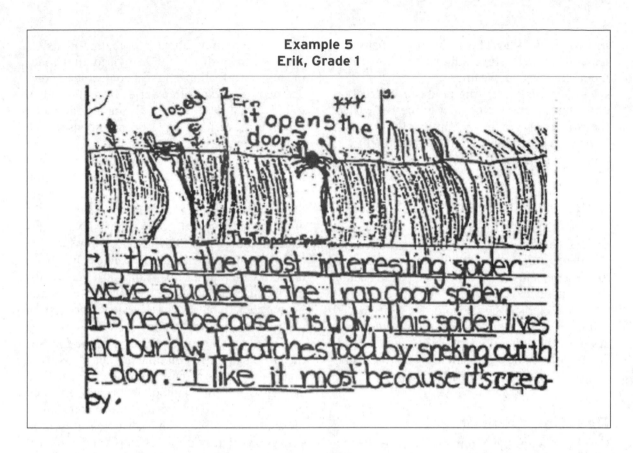

Example 5
Erik, Grade 1

closed *it opens the door*

→ I think the most interesting spider we've studied is the Trapdoor spider. It is neat because it is ugly. This spider lives in a burrow. It catches food by sneaking out the door. I like it most because it's creepy.

for comparison/contrast frames. Although comparison/contrast is considered a difficult structure for children to understand and use, it appears that this type of organization facilitates retention in adults (Meyer & Freedle, 1984). It has been our experience that comparison/contrast is a strong facilitator of retention in children, also.

Comparison and contrast are usually presented together, but we have found that young children grasp the concepts more readily when they are introduced separately. We begin with comparisons and link the frame together with signal words such as *alike, similarly, same as, resembles*, and other words that are useful for comparing (Example 9).

After work with comparison frames, contrast frames can be introduced. Specific transitions that are helpful in telling about differences (*different from, on the other hand, however*) can be included in the frame (Example 10).

When teaching children to work with comparison and contrast frames, it is essential to list

likenesses or differences on the board during the prewriting stage. A grid is helpful and can serve as a word bank when the students begin writing (Example 11).

Illustrations are especially useful with comparison and contrast paragraph frames. Children must visualize the likenesses or differences as well as write about them, a process which enhances their understanding of the concepts of comparison and contrast.

Bridging the Gap

In conclusion, we feel that having primary grade students use paragraph frames to help them write about what they are learning in the content areas is an effective means of bridging the gap between narrative and expository reading and writing. Expository paragraph frames provide children with a structured way of using writing as a learning tool. Writing facilitates understanding and retention of material and introduces students to

This morning our class visited the Georgetown College Planetariam. I learned some new things about our Solar System. For Instance, I learned that other planets have moons and not just us. I also learned that Jupiter has sort of a hurricane. Another fascinating thing was Pluto is such a small planet. It is a outer planet and doesn't get crushed. Besides this, I learned that stars and planets are different things. One thing about space I would like to learn more about is why other planets doen't have gravity.

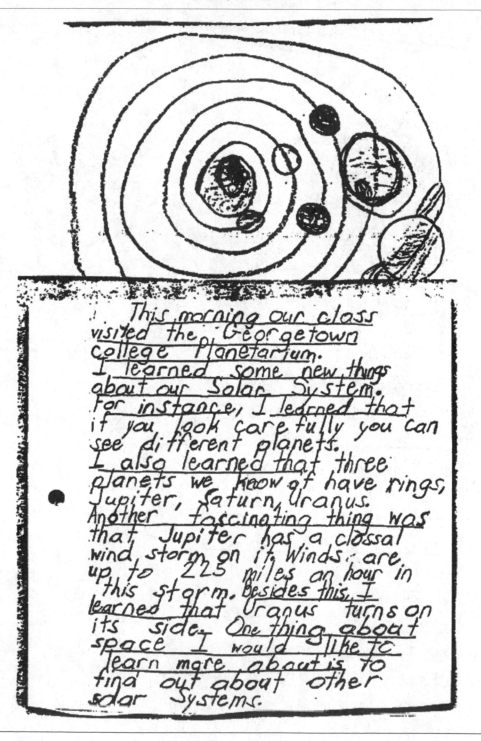

This morning our class visited the Georgetown college Planetarium.

I learned some new things about our Solar System.

For instance, I learned that if you look carefully you can see different planets.

I also learned that three planets we know of have rings, Jupiter, Saturn, Uranus.

Another fascinating thing was that Jupiter has a clossal wind storm on it. Winds are up to 225 miles an hour in this storm. Besides this, I learned that Uranus turns on its side. One thing about space I would like to learn more about is to find out about other solar Systems.

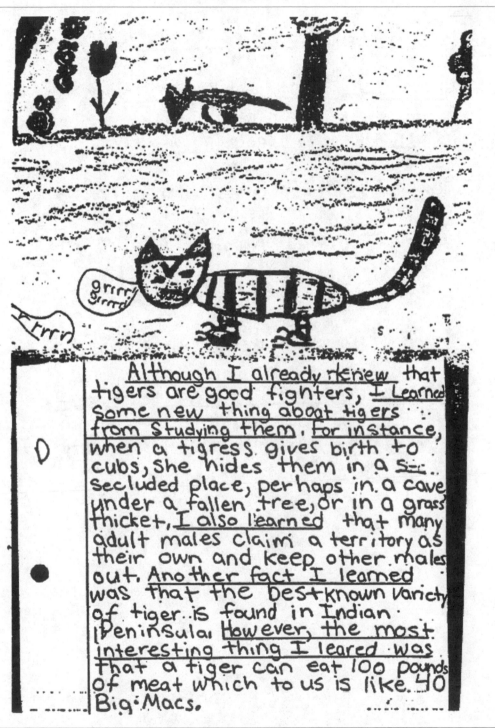

Although I already rknew that tigers are good fighters, I Learned some new thing about tigers from studying them. for instance, when a tigress gives birth to cubs, she hides them in a s— secluded place, perhaps in a cave, under a fallen tree, or in a grass thicket, I also learned that many adult males claim a territory as their own and keep other males out. Another fact I learned was that the best known variety of tiger is found in Indian Peninsula. However, the most interesting thing I leared was that a tiger can eat 100 pounds of meat which to us is like 40 Big Macs.

Although I already knew that stars are hot, I learned some new things about stars by reading this story. I learned that the coolest star is red, the warmest star is yellow, and the very, very hot stars are blue. I also learned that seven stars make a shape of a dipper. However the most interesting thing I learned was that the north star stays in it's place.

Example 8
Alison, Grade 3

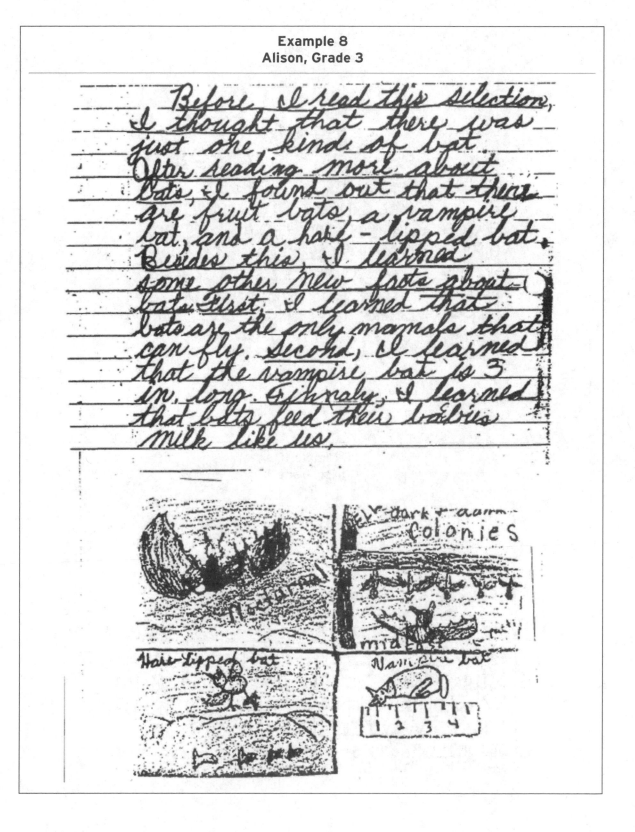

Before I read this selection, I thought that there was just one kind of bat. After reading more about bats, I found out that there are fruit bats, a vampire bat, and a hare-lipped bat. Besides this, I learned some other new facts about bats. First, I learned that bats are the only mamals that can fly. Second, I learned that the vampire bat is 3 in. long. Finaly, I learned that bats feed their babies milk like us.

Example 9
Erin, Grade 1

Although whales are mammals and sea turtles are reptiles, they are alike in some interesting ways. First, both whales and sea turtles used to have feet but after many years they developed flippers. Second, they cant get out of the water because of their body whiet. Finally, they both swim in water.

Example 10
Chris, Grade 1

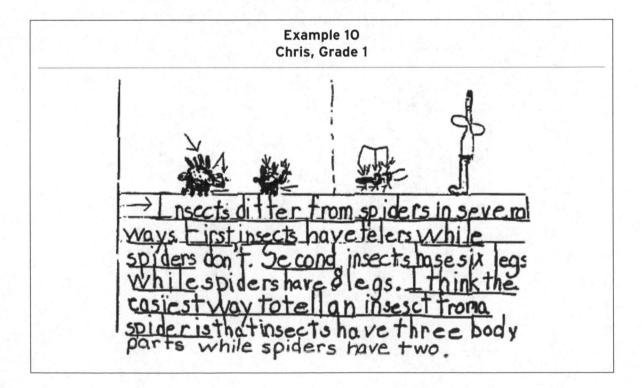

Insects differ from spiders in several ways. First insects have telers while spiders don't. Second, insects hase six legs while spiders have 8 legs. I think the easiest way to tell an insect from a spider is that insects have three body parts while spiders have two.

Example 11
Difference

	Sea turtles	Land turtles
Size		
Habitat		
Food		
Appearance		
Habits		
Other		

some of the organizational structures authors use to convey information.

Working in the context of paragraph frames, students are taught to use and understand the transitional devices often omitted in elementary content area texts. Thus, they will be better prepared to understand and use such transitions when reading and writing in the more heavily content oriented intermediate grades.

References

Cudd, E.T., & Roberts, L.L. (1987, October). Using story frames to develop comprehension in a first grade classroom. *The Reading Teacher*, *41*, 74–79.

Englert, C.S., & Hiebert, E.H. (1984, February). Children's developing awareness of text structures in expository materials. *Journal of Educational Psychology*, *76*, 65–74.

Irwin, J. (Ed.). (1986). *Understanding and teaching cohesion comprehension*. Newark, DE: International Reading Association.

Marshall, N. (1984). Discourse analysis as a guide for informal assessment of comprehension. In J. Flood (Ed.), *Promoting reading comprehension*. Newark, DE: International Reading Association.

Meyer, B.J., & Freedle, R.O. (1984, Spring). Effects of discourse type on recall. *American Educational Research Journal*, *21*, 121–143.

Winograd, P.N., & Bridge, C.A. (1986). The comprehension of important information in written prose. In J.F. Baumann (Ed.), *Teaching main idea comprehension*. Newark, DE: International Reading Association.

Questions for Reflection

• It is well established that comprehension demands are different for expository and for narrative text. We also know that very young children generally are exposed to considerably more narrative than expository writing, despite the fact that, as they move up through the grades, exposition becomes the dominant form of academic text. If you teach children in the upper elementary grades or beyond, what advice do you have for your colleagues working at the primary level that might help them prepare learners for the demands ahead?

We Learn What We Do: Developing a Repertoire of Writing Practices in an Instant Messaging World

Gloria E. Jacobs

Instant messaging (IM) and its cell-phone sibling, texting, are much used and beloved by young people but sometimes are ridiculed or even reviled by adults. Periodically, newspaper articles recount how teachers are finding non-standard spelling and writing forms common to IM in students' writing (see, for example, Cobb, 2002; Helderman, 2003; Lee, 2003). Despite the reassurances of educators such as William Kist (cited in Martineau, 2007) and Leila Christenbury (cited in National Council of Teachers of English [NCTE], 2003) and a number of teachers' creative lessons that use IM to teach audience and purpose (NCTE, 2003), there remains an undercurrent of fear and distrust among teachers and parents toward these new literacy practices.

In response to these concerns, and drawing on my experience as a high school English teacher in the late 1990s when IM became popular, I spent two years with a 15-year-old white girl whom I call Lisa (a pseudonym) who lived in an urban area in western New York state. I wanted to learn more about adolescent use of IM and its implications for literacy learning. I found that part of the distrust comes from not understanding what IM practices entail (Thurlow, 2006) and the meanings youths apply to the practice (Jacobs, 2006; Lewis & Fabos, 2005).

Beginning with the assumption that we learn what we do within a community where a particular practice is valued (Rogoff, 1995, 2003; Vygotsky, 1978), I discuss how Lisa developed skills in school-based writing even as she engaged in what she called "hardcore" IM. I argue that Lisa was able to develop proficiency in IM, as well as in the writing expected in school, because for her IM was part of a repertoire of literacy practices. I also draw on what we know about writing instruction to suggest ways to help students build a repertoire of writing practices in an IM world.

The Relationship Between IM and Formal Writing

In this section, I turn to existing research to explore the relationship between IM and formal writing. I begin with the research into computer-mediated communication (CMC) and IM in particular. I then explore the relationship between the new, or posttypographic, literacies and the old, or typographic, literacies (Reinking, 1998). I argue that CMC is not poor writing but is a response to social needs as mediated by technological constraints. I suggest that IM is caught within the tensions between the new literacies and the traditional literacies.

Baron (1984) questioned whether CMC was a possible agent of language change, and subsequent research documented the development and use of short, fragmented sentences; emoticons, such as smileys; abbreviations; and initialisms, such as "lol" for "laugh out loud" (Walther,

Reprinted from Jacobs, G.E. (2008). We learn what we do: Developing a repertoire of writing practices in an instant messaging world. *Journal of Adolescent & Adult Literacy*, 52(3), 203-211. doi: 10.1598/JAAL.52.3.3

1996). The research suggested that these forms served to approximate the rhythms and prosody of speech in a "lean medium" (Walther, 1996, p. 3) that lacked the feedback cycle possible in face-to-face interactions. With the advent of IM in the late 1990s and its rapid adoption by adolescents, CMC conventions became part of public consciousness. Despite the lack of empirical evidence, a "moral panic" (Thurlow, 2006, p. 667) arose that IM and texting would damage people's ability to write sustained, cohesive texts in standard edited English.

There are only a few published studies that look specifically at the relationship between IM and literacy development. Lewis and Fabos (2005) indicated that IM supports the use of text for social purposes and provides an opportunity for youth to explore identity. Similarly, Jacobs (2006) argued that IM can create opportunities for adolescents to build the skills, attributes, and achievements that position them for participation in a fast capitalist, information economy. In a review of research across a range of disciplines, Jacobs (2008) found no empirical evidence to indicate that IM contributes to the deterioration of writing skills. Instead, she found that context of use, which includes consideration of the reader's needs as well as the social purposes for which the text was being used, was the most important aspect of how language was used in IM—not the technology itself.

IM, however, is only one of the nontypographic literacies in which youth are engaged. As expanded definitions of literacy led researchers and teachers to look beyond traditional and school-based literacy practices, it became apparent that many adolescents engage in a wide variety of literate activities outside of school such as e-mail and IM (Alvermann, 2006), zines (Gustavson, 2007), e-zines (Guzzetti & Gamboa, 2004), and website creation (Davies, 2006).

In an effort to engage with and meet the needs of students, some teachers and researchers attempt to integrate students' in- and out-of-school literacies (Millard, 2006). Accomplishing this is difficult, however, given the complex relationship between the traditional, typographic literacies and the new, posttypographic or digital literacies. Dressman et al. (2006) suggested that the new literacies and traditional literacies can be complementary, oppositional, or mutually exclusive. A complementary view is that the new technologies have the potential to open up a wide range of opportunities for youths to engage in literacy practices beyond what traditionally has been available in schools (Dressman et al., 2006). An oppositional view holds that youths may lose the motivation to learn traditional literacies if the new literacies gain in value (Dressman et al., 2006), and a mutually exclusive view is concerned that new literacy practices will be appropriated as we attempt to transfer them into the classroom (Knobel & Lankshear, 2006).

The literature demonstrates that literacy practices such as IM are part of the unsettled relationships between in- and out-of-school literacies as well as between typographic literacies and the digital literacies. Specifically, it is unclear whether to ignore IM as being exclusive of school, to see it as damaging to schooled literacy, or to see it as a way to engage students in writing. However, if we resist the tendency to dichotomize literacy practices as old/new, in/out-of-school, or traditional/nontraditional and instead see them as part of a repertoire, then we can move toward understanding how engagement in *any* literacy practice can provide insight on an individual's literate development.

Theoretical Considerations

The National Commission on Writing in America's Schools and Colleges (2003) and the Carnegie Corporation (Graham & Perin, 2007) raise the specter of declining writing skills among young people. These reports claim that large numbers of adolescents are unable to write coherent, meaningful texts using standard conventions. It is beyond the purpose of this article to contest the findings of these reports, but the evidence does point to changes in people's skill in particular textual forms.

What we need to remember is that definitions of *coherent* and *meaningful* are determined by the context of the writing. What is good essay writing for a high school social studies class is not good writing for IM. Writing an effective memo for work is different from writing a letter of complaint, which is different from writing a real estate advertisement. In this article, the definition of "good writing" is based on The New Literacy Studies (NLS) definition of literacy as a social practice situated in the immediate context of use (Hull & Schultz, 2001; Street, 1995). Being literate means using text for culturally meaningful purposes within culturally meaningful activities (Barton, Hamilton, & Ivanič, 2000), and text is defined as being part of a meaning-making system within localized sociocultural, historical, and political contexts (Hull & Schultz, 2001; Lankshear & Knobel, 2003; Street, 1995). Good writing, then, is writing that meets the purposes of the author and fulfills the requirements of the audience as defined by the social and cultural expectations of the community in which the writing is used.

Conducting the Study

I spent two years observing and videotaping Lisa as she used IM in her home. I interviewed her and several of her friends with whom she regularly conversed online and attended after-school events such as soccer games and her pre-prom party. The interviews, observations, and videotaping sessions were supported by field notes, and interviews and videotaped sessions were transcribed. I collected 12 samples of Lisa's school-based writing from a variety of courses and amassed over 100 online status postings (away messages) and 7 biographical sketches (profiles).

I used the constant comparative method (Bogdan & Biklen, 1998; Strauss & Corbin, 1990) to code data and the tools of discourse analysis (Fairclough, 1995; Gee, 1996; Ochs, 1992) to develop an understanding of how Lisa and her friends constructed meaning in their IMs. I transcribed IMs from video data and included pauses, self-corrections, and the ways Lisa negotiated multitasking (see Jacobs, 2004, for a detailed explanation of data collection and analysis methods). I transcribed each utterance as closely as possible to the spoken and did not edit it to remove extraneous words. My purpose was to capture a sense of who Lisa was as a teen and how she used language. I also drew on my background as an English teacher and writing instructor to analyze her writing for organization, tone, voice, diction, grammar, and mechanics.

Discovering Lisa's World: Life as a Hardcore IM User and Award-Winning Writer

Early in the research, Lisa told me she couldn't live without IM:

> Like here's the scenario. I hadn't cleaned my room in like six months, and my parents were like—well it was probably, it was a long time—and my parents were like, if you don't clean your room by the end of this weekend we're going to ground you. And I'm like that would suck. But then they were like or we'll take away IM. And I'm like ground me, just ground me, OK I'll clean it. And if I don't, ground me, don't take away IM.

Lisa called herself a hardcore user of IM and that was the primary reason I selected her for my study. She was part of the 75% of online Americans between the ages of 12 and 17 who use IM (Lenhart, Madden, & Hitlin, 2005). As I came to know her, I discovered that she was a high-achieving student and award-winning teen writer. Her ability to write across these two different worlds contradicted what I had experienced as a teacher, what I read in the news, and what other teachers told me. How was Lisa able to successfully negotiate the demands of school-based writing and those of IM? How did Lisa gain facility in different genres when other students seemed unable to do so?

Some answers can be found in the context of Lisa's home and school life. At the beginning of the study, Lisa was a sophomore at Arts High School, a magnet school run by the City School District (CSD) in a midsized city in western New York state. Students at Arts High select a major from a choice of vocal music, instrumental music, dance, drama, visual arts, theater technology, or creative writing. Lisa, a creative writing major, took courses such as poetry writing, play-writing, creative nonfiction, and journalism as well as core courses in English literature, Latin, social studies, math, earth science, biology, and chemistry. All courses were at either the honors or advanced placement level.

As a creative writing major, and as a student in a school where writing across the curriculum is part of the school culture, Lisa had multiple opportunities to write in a variety of genres. These genres included creative fiction, nonfiction, poetry, plays, literary response essays, article summaries, book reports, and responses to document-based questions. Lisa consistently received positive feedback on her writing in the form of high grades. She also submitted her creative pieces to locally and nationally adjudicated writing competitions and won several awards.

Lisa's family also supported her writing development. Both parents are professionals with advanced degrees. The room where the computer was located and where Lisa did her homework was filled with a variety of texts. A full bookshelf covered one wall, a desk overflowing with household paperwork sat against another, and the family television, movie library, and video game collection were against a third wall. A desktop computer sat in one corner of the room, and the house had wireless broadband Internet, which could be accessed from almost anywhere in the house.

While online, Lisa was surrounded by traditional typographic texts and nontraditional, post-typographic, multimodal texts. However, Lisa said she did not read or write for pleasure, which she defined as reading novels or writing for her own enjoyment. All Lisa's traditional typographic reading and writing was devoted to school assignments—even her summers were dedicated to reading for advanced placement courses. It was within the new literacies that Lisa engaged in reading and writing for fun.

During the first year of the study, Lisa spent several hours a day sending and receiving IMs. Because both parents worked, Lisa came home to an empty house and used IM to meet her need for socializing. She said she hated to be alone and messaging kept her from feeling lonely. Most conversations were playful and included word

play, inside jokes, and the discussion of television programs. She and her friends also used IM to rehash events of the day, discuss homework assignments, and make plans for the weekend. She said that people who did not have access to IM were often inadvertently left out of social events because plans and announcements were made using IM. As such, rather than being a time waster, as it is sometimes construed, IM served as an important literacy practice for Lisa. Like most literacy practices, it served to connect her to her community.

Furthermore, Lisa developed skill at multitasking. Because she had a broadband connection, Lisa was able to use the telephone while messaging and would often be on the telephone while sending messages online. At one point during the study, Lisa was simultaneously on the telephone, messaging, and studying for an exam. Although this may appear to be detrimental to effective studying, analysis revealed that Lisa's activities were all used for the purpose of preparing for the exam. Her IMs were short, her telephone conversation was focused, and her written notes and textbook were used to support the conversations.

During the second year of the study, Lisa learned to drive and took an SAT Reasoning–test preparation course. As such, she spent less time online because she was home less. She did not, however, abandon IM. Instead, she began to use the "away message" function more to notify her friends of her whereabouts. Similar to Nardi's (2005) study of workplace use of IM, Lisa said away messages kept her company during late study sessions, and she found it comforting to know her friends were engaged in the same activities as she and that she could contact them should the need arise.

If grades and public accolades are used to measure achievement, Lisa was a successful writer of school-based texts. If participation is used as a measure, Lisa used IM to be successful socially. It is also clear that Lisa learned that text and text use vary across different contexts. I have yet to understand how she gained facility in each of these worlds. In the next section, I explore possible explanations for her success.

Finding Success by Creating Separate Worlds

Lisa may have developed facility in IM and school-based writing by keeping the conventions of the two worlds separate. Interviews revealed that for Lisa, IM was not considered writing; it was simply "talking." Although literacy theory proposes that IM and note writing are literacy practices, for Lisa they were not. Lisa defined writing as lengthy and involving some level of thought, and IM did not fit that definition. Lisa's attitude is consistent with the findings of a large-scale survey study that found that adolescents do not view their online communications as writing (Lenhart, Arafeh, Smith, & Macgill, 2008).

Lisa also used her understanding of genre to guide her. In IM, if a message followed rules of academic writing, Lisa saw the writer as an outsider. For instance, she said it was annoying to watch adults IM because their responses were too lengthy, too labored, and overly correct. Furthermore, Lisa said that IMs that attended to conventions such as punctuation and capitalization were breaches of online etiquette; short entries, abbreviations, lack of punctuation, minor spelling errors, and typographic errors all connoted spontaneity and speed of response. Her reaction to adult efforts at IM reveals that Lisa recognized IM as having a set of conventions that differed from the writing she did for school.

Despite her avowed inattention to spelling, punctuation, and capitalization, analysis of Lisa's IMs showed that she did attend to writing style when messaging. For instance, Lisa told me that she could tell a serious IM by the length and amount of thought that was put into it. She commented, "They think out what they're saying more, so you can almost tell, and like people write like longer things and stuff." A close examination of various IM exchanges revealed that serious conversations had fewer spelling mistakes and lengthier entries than playful exchanges. Observations showed that when Lisa shifted into a serious conversation, she took longer to respond and corrected misspellings as they occurred. Her sentences tended to be longer than average and more grammatically complex. This indicates that Lisa drew on her writing skills when engaged in serious online conversations.

Lisa was also aware of the requirements of school writing differences between classes. Lisa said she would carefully craft her creative writing pieces but would not craft papers for content area classes such as English and biology. She said first drafts for English papers were generally good enough to earn an A and writing a biology paper was simply typing.

Lisa: Like they um, the bio essays are just, they aren't good writing. Like I mean, they're, they're just things that I sit down and like I'm typing and I don't know what I'm talking about.

Gloria: So you don't do the crafting on them like you do for creative writing.

Lisa: I do like no crafting on them. I just write them.

An analysis of her biology essays revealed her writing to be straightforward summaries of science articles. These essays contained a few minor grammatical and mechanical errors, but for the most part, the writing matched the depersonalized style typically associated with science writing. None of the conventions of IM appeared in any of the writing she gave me. When asked whether IM conventions crept into her school-based writing, Lisa answered that they did on occasion, but only when she was rushed or pressured.

When given time to write, Lisa demonstrated facility with not only the mechanics of writing but also with rhetorical structure, diction, tone, and voice. For example, in an English essay, Lisa analyzed a quote from Henry David Thoreau's *Walden*. She began her essay by explaining the quote and then illustrated the quote by describing an incident in her life. Her description, however, was not simply a narrative of an event; it included explicit explanations of how the event connected to the quote. She wrote,

> When Thoreau says, "Things do not change; we change," I am reminded of things in nature that remain completely unchanged by humans, but that humans still experience throughout their lives as they change.

Lisa then described three hiking trips and how she had changed against the seemingly never-changing face of Mt. Katahdin in Maine. In the essay, Lisa demonstrated an understanding of Thoreau's argument, and she did so by using an example consistent with the transcendentalist's view of the world. Furthermore, she showed an awareness of Thoreau's writing style by using a two-part sentence structure that attempted to echo the rhythms and patterns of Thoreau.

I propose that Lisa gained facility in IM and in school-based writing because she was aware of the differences between writing for school and writing for friends and made the effort to match her writing to her audience and purpose except when pressured by time constraints. I suggest that working with students to develop this meta-cognitive awareness of how they switch language and literacy practices according to context may contribute to a decrease in the crossover of IM conventions in school-based writing.

Finding Success Through Engagement in Communities of Writers

Lisa's development as a writer was explicitly supported by the culture of Arts High, where writing activities connected Lisa to a larger community of writers. At her school, writing was not limited to classroom exercises, test preparation, or assessments. As a creative writing major, she took writing classes where she experimented with a range of genres. The school also embraced writing across the curriculum, and Lisa was required to write in every class including biology, Latin, and social studies.

At Arts High, writing extended beyond the walls of the school; students were encouraged to submit their writing to competitions and to participate in the local arts community. Furthermore, the English language arts teachers modeled membership in the arts community. For example, three were practicing writers as well as certified teachers. Lisa's playwriting teacher published a book of fiction, her poetry and creative writing teacher was an award-winning haiku poet who gave workshops around the region, and her journalism and English teacher was a former actor who directed school plays and regional theater productions. Two of her teachers were National Writing Project fellows.

If we want students to develop as writers, teachers should be active writers as well (Atwell, 1998). It is one thing to critique student writing; it is another to actively model what it means to be a writer. By being active members of the arts community, Lisa's teachers modeled how writing extends beyond the walls of the classroom. Moreover, because her teachers were connected to the professional writing community, they had an insider's knowledge of the art and acted as artistic mentors. Although not all teachers can and should be expected to have such a second professional life outside of teaching, asking teachers to engage in writing as writers to better understand writing instruction is consistent with the recommendations of the National Writing Project (2007).

Implications for Teaching and Final Thoughts

I suggest that Lisa's development as a writer was influenced by the following three primary factors:

1. She was surrounded by text at home.
2. Her school helped her develop writing skills in a variety of genres and for a variety of authentic purposes.
3. Her awareness of differences between genres helped her understand the need to adapt her writing to different situations.

These aspects provide us with insight into ways we can support students who struggle with school-based writing forms. Next, I discuss instructional implications in relation to points two and three.

Lisa's success in school-based writing and the ways she shifted language use as she used IM demonstrate that, for her, IM has not gotten in the way of developing writing skills. She was able to select words, make stylistic choices, and attend to grammar, spelling, and mechanics according to the needs of her audience, her purposes, and the requirements of genre and mode of communication. IM was one of a repertoire of literacy practices Lisa used depending on her needs. Although Lisa may not be representative of most student writers, her successes as a writer demonstrate that IM does not have to be a negative influence on writing development.

Forces larger than CMC carry more weight in the development of adolescent literacy. Although I have not explored issues of identity in this article, we must remember that a person's literacy development is tied to identity and membership in Discourse communities (see for example Edwards, 2005; Gustavson, 2007; Knobel, 1999; Lam, 2000; Lewis & Fabos, 2005; Warschauer, 2000). Research indicates that when taking up particular literate identities, especially those tied to school, youths may experience tensions between their different Discourse communities and their roles within each community (Gee, 1999, 2004). Lisa's development as a writer is strongly related to her identity as a white, middle class, college-bound youth. The literacy practices she takes up in school are congruent with those of her home, her friends, and her vision of her future as a member of professional and middle class society.

Given that literacy and identity are linked, for other students, particularly those from historically marginalized groups, taking up schooled literacies brings risks such as a loss of voice, distanced connections to home cultures, and a changed identity. For example, Hartman (2006) showed how working class girls in an English class silenced themselves to be seen as good students, and Rodriguez's (1982) memoir captured the personal loss that occurs as a person takes up a new language, new literacies, and new identities. The work of Fordham (1996) and Ogbu (2003) explored the negotiations, compromises, and costs students of color experience as they struggle to find their way in an educational environment that is often hostile to their home cultures, languages, and literacies.

There are no easy answers; however, providing student choice and multiple opportunities to write for a variety of authentic purposes across a variety of genres may help students make connections between their lives inside and outside of school. These opportunities can include, but should not be limited to, activities such as contests, online publications, and writing for social action.

I also call for renewed efforts to integrate writing with content area classes and across the curriculum to help young people experience a variety of writing practices. When young people are engaged in one type of writing without being able to experience other forms, either through school or elsewhere, the conventions of that one genre tend to dominate. Using writing in the content areas allows students to see how writing changes depending upon context and thus strengthens metacognitive awareness of genre.

When working with students, I urge teachers to refrain from treating the appearance of CMC conventions as errors, but instead to use those "miscues" (Goodman, 1973) as opportunities to raise students' metacognitive awareness of their writing decisions. Simple questions such as, Why did you choose this word? or Why did you choose this spelling? provide the teacher with insight on the student's writing process as well as increase student recognition of the authorial decision-making process.

Additionally, I encourage teachers to become active writers within traditional forms and to explore different aspects of CMC. By engaging in writing and in online communities, teachers can model the behaviors and thinking processes of writers and demonstrate that writing is something that reaches beyond the walls of the classroom and can be used to connect to the community.

Granted, Lisa's text-rich home life, which contributed to her development as a writer, is different from that of many students. This fact, however, does not negate my argument. Instead, I suggest that the need for the above-mentioned instructional actions, while not new, is more salient than ever. Rather than passing the blame for weak writing on to parents or popular CMC forms, teachers need to create spaces for their students to experience authentic and powerful uses of texts within communities that are meaningful to them. It is time to stop complaining and worrying and turn instead to developing opportunities for students to write.

References

Alvermann, D. (2006). Ned and Kevin: An online discussion that challenges the 'not-yet adult' cultural model. In K. Pahl & J. Rowsell (Eds.), *Travel notes from the new literacy studies: Instances of practice* (pp. 39–56). Clevedon, England: Multilingual Matters.

Atwell, N. (1998). *In the middle: New understandings about writing, reading, and learning* (2nd ed.). Portsmouth, NH: Heinemann.

Baron, N.S. (1984). Computer mediated communication as a force in language change. *Visible Language, 18*(2), 118–141.

Barton, D., Hamilton, M., & Ivanič, R. (Eds.). (2000). *Situated literacies: Reading and writing in context*. London: Routledge.

Bogdan, R.C., & Biklen, S.K. (1998). *Qualitative research for education: An introduction to theory and methods*. Boston: Allyn & Bacon.

Cobb, C. (2002, October 12). Kewl or 2 much. *Orlando Sentinel*, p. E1.

Davies, J. (2006). Escaping to the borderlands: An exploration of the Internet as a cultural space for teenaged Wiccan girls. In K. Pahl & J. Rowsell (Eds.), *Travel notes from the New Literacy Studies: Instances of practice* (pp. 57–71). Clevedon, England: Multilingual Matters.

Dressman, M., O'Brien, D., Rogers, T., Ivey, G., Wilder, P., Alvermann, D., et al. (2006). Problematizing adolescent literacies: Four instances, multiple perspectives. In J.V. Hoffman, D.L. Schallert, C.M. Fairbanks, J. Worthy, & B. Maloch (Eds.), *Fifty-fifth yearbook of the National Reading Conference* (pp. 141–154). Oak Creek, WI: National Reading Conference.

Edwards, L.Y. (2005). Victims, villains, and vixens. In S.R. Mazzarella (Ed.), *Girl wide web: Girls, the Internet, and the negotiation of identity* (pp. 13–30). New York: Lang.

Fairclough, N. (1995). *Critical discourse analysis: The critical study of language*. London: Longman.

Fordham, S. (1996). *Blacked out: Dilemmas of race, identity, and success at Capital High*. Chicago: University of Chicago Press.

Gee, J.P. (1996). *Social linguistics and literacies: Ideologies in discourses* (2nd ed.). London: Taylor & Francis.

Gee, J.P. (1999). *An introduction to discourse analysis: Theory and method*. New York: Routledge.

Gee, J.P. (2004). *Situated language and learning: A critique of traditional schooling*. New York: Routledge.

Goodman, K. (1973). *Miscue analysis: Applications to reading instruction*. Urbana, IL: National Council of Teachers of English.

Graham, S., & Perin, D. (2007). *Writing next: Effective strategies to improve writing of adolescents in middle and high schools: A report to the Carnegie Corporation of New York*. Washington, DC: Alliance for Excellent Education.

Gustavson, L. (2007). *Youth learning on their own terms: Creative practices and classroom teaching*. New York: Routledge.

Guzzetti, B.J., & Gamboa, M. (2004). Zines for social justice: Adolescent girls writing on their own. *Reading Research Quarterly, 39*(4), 408–436. doi:10.1598/RRQ.39.4.4

Hartman, P. (2006). "Loud on the inside": Working-class girls, gender, and literacy. *Research in the Teaching of English, 41*(1), 82–117.

Helderman, R. (2003, May 20). Click by click, teens polish writing. *The Washington Post*, p. B1.

Hull, G., & Schultz, K. (2001). Literacy and learning out of school: A review of theory and research. *Review of Educational Research, 71*(4), 575–611. doi:10.3102/00346543071004575

Jacobs, G. (2004). Complicating contexts: Issues of methodology in researching the language and literacies of instant messaging. *Reading Research Quarterly, 39*(4), 394–406. doi:10.1598/RRQ.39.4.3

Jacobs, G. (2006). Fast times and digital literacy: Participation roles and portfolio construction within instant messaging. *Journal of Literacy Research, 38*(2), 171–196. doi:10.1207/s15548430jlr3802_3

Jacobs, G. (2008). People, purposes, and practices: Insights from cross-disciplinary research into instant messaging. In J. Coiro, M. Knobel, C. Lankshear, & D.J. Leu (Eds.), *Handbook of research on new literacies* (pp. 469–493). New York: Routledge.

Knobel, M. (1999). *Everyday literacies: Students, discourse, and social practice*. New York: Lang.

Knobel, M., & Lankshear, C. (2006). Weblog worlds and constructions of effective and powerful writing: Cross with care, and only where signs permit. In K. Pahl & J. Rowsell (Eds.), *Travel notes from the New Literacy Studies: Instances of practice* (pp. 72–94). Clevedon, England: Multilingual Matters.

Lam, W.S.E. (2000). Literacy and the design of the self: A case study of a teenage writing on the internet. *TESOL Quarterly, 34*(3), 457–482. doi:10.2307/3587739

Lankshear, C., & Knobel, M. (2003). *New literacies: Changing knowledge and classroom learning*. Buckingham, England: Open University Press.

Lee, C. (2003). *How does instant messaging affect interaction between the genders?* Retrieved May 12, 2005, from www.stanford.edu/class/pwr3-25/group2/projects.html

Lenhart, A., Arafeh, S., Smith, A., & Macgill, A. (2008). *Writing, technology and teens.* Washington, DC: Pew Internet & American Life Project.

Lenhart, A., Madden, M., & Hitlin, P. (2005). *Teens and technology: Youth are leading the transition to a fully wired and mobile nation.* Washington, DC: Pew Internet & American Life Project. Retrieved August 4, 2005, from www.pewinternet.org

Lewis, C., & Fabos, B. (2005). Instant messaging, literacies, and social identities. *Reading Research Quarterly, 40*(4), 470–501. doi:10.1598/RRQ.40.4.5

Martineau, P. (2007, September 12). Tapping instant messaging. *Education Week, 1,* 10.

Millard, E. (2006). Transformative pedagogy: Teachers creating a literacy of fusion. In K. Pahl & J. Rowsell (Eds.), *Travel notes from the new literacy studies: Instances of practice* (pp. 234–253). Clevedon, England: Multilingual Matters.

Nardi, B. (2005). Beyond bandwidth: Dimensions of connection in interpersonal communication. *Computer Supported Collaborative Work, 14*(2), 91–130. doi:10.1007/s10606-004-8127-9

National Commission on Writing in America's Schools and Colleges. (2003). *The neglected "R": The need for a writing revolution* (No. 997548). New York: College Board.

National Council of Teachers of English. (2003). *Rest assured—Students, teachers, and language are "alive and kickn."* Retrieved August 18, 2006, from www.ncte.org/pubs/chron/highlights/117019.htm

National Writing Project. (2007). *About NWP.* Retrieved December 17, 2007, from www.nwp.org/cs/public/print/doc/about.csp

Ochs, E. (1992). Indexing gender. In A. Duranti & C. Goodwin (Eds.), *Rethinking context: Language as an interactive phenomenon* (pp. 335–358). Cambridge, England: Cambridge University Press.

Ogbu, J. (2003). *Black American students in an affluent suburb: A study of academic disengagement.* Mahwah, NJ: Erlbaum.

Reinking, D. (1998). Introduction: Synthesizing technological transformations of literacy in a post-typographic world. In D. Reinking, M. McKenna, L. Labbo, & R. Kieffer (Eds.), *Handbook of literacy and technology: Transformations in a post-typographic world* (pp. xi–xxx). Mahwah, NJ: Erlbaum.

Rodriguez, R. (1982). *Hunger of memory: The education of Richard Rodriguez.* Boston: David R. Godine.

Rogoff, B. (1995). Observing sociocultural activity on three planes: participatory appropriation, guided participation, and apprenticeship. In J.V. Wertsch, P. del Rio, & A. Alvarez (Eds.), *Sociocultural studies of mind* (pp. 139–164). Cambridge, England: Cambridge University Press.

Rogoff, B. (2003). *The cultural nature of human development.* New York: Oxford University Press.

Strauss, A., & Corbin, J. (1990). *Basics of qualitative research: Techniques and procedures for developing grounded theory.* Newbury Park, CA: Sage.

Street, B.V. (1995). *Social literacies: Critical approaches to literacy development, ethnography, and education.* New York: Addison Wesley.

Thurlow, C. (2006). From statistical panic to moral panic: The metadiscursive construction and popular exaggeration of new media language in the print media. *Journal of Computer-Mediated Communication, 11*(3), 667–701. doi:10.1111/j.1083-6101.2006.00031.x

Vygotsky, L.S. (1978). *Mind in society: The development of higher psychological processes.* (M. Cole, V. John-Steiner, S. Scribner, & E. Souberman, Eds. & Trans.). Cambridge, MA: Harvard University Press.

Walther, J.B. (1996). Computer-mediated communication: Impersonal, interpersonal, and hyperpersonal interaction. *Communication Research, 23*(1), 3–43. doi:10.1177/009365096023001001

Warschauer, M. (2000). Language, identity, and the Internet. In B. Kolko, L. Nakamura, & G.B. Rodman (Eds.), *Race in cyberspace* (pp. 151–170). New York: Routledge.

Questions for Reflection

- The reading–writing connection means that activities in one area can support development of skills in the other. How can you establish a "community of writers" in your school such that writing activities will support comprehension of text as well as development of writing ability?

- This article describes Lisa as she texts, talks on the telephone, and simultaneously studies for a test and indicates that these activities all supported her school learning. What do you know about how your students use literacy and literate practices outside of school? Can you think of ways to harness their enthusiasm for out-of-school writing and speaking to support their learning from text?

Recentering the Middle School Classroom as a Vibrant Learning Community: Students, Literacy, and Technology Intersect

Dana L. Grisham and Thomas D. Wolsey

Community is the soul of learning. Anything worth learning is situated in our consciousness as an artifact of who wrote, who said, who demonstrated, and who mediated that understanding. In the same way, what we learn is defined by those with whom we are able to share and build that learning (Borko, 2004). These tandem ideas delineate the world of the teacher. When the give and take of community becomes too lopsided, genuine learning becomes a meaningless rite, rather than a rich opportunity to learn, to share, and to grow. Human beings don't need to possess information only; they need to belong to a community. In this article, we examine a way in which community can be constructed in the middle school classroom using online electronic discussions of literature.

Goodlad (1984) wrote that much of classroom discourse is disconnected from students and is teacher driven. Hillocks (2002) reiterated that impassioned discussion revolves around complex, even intractable, issues that students feel are of value. Our experience in U.S. classrooms and through research demonstrates that when students are given the opportunity and appropriate structures, they are competent and willing to think critically about complex situations and

to work together to construct an understanding. The transcripts from asynchronous electronic discussions included in this article illustrate how students may construct communities of learning that transcend the traditional teacher-driven discourse in classrooms.

The Breadwinner (Ellis, 2001) is a novel about Parvana, a girl living in Afghanistan under the rule of the Taliban. Students in one eighth-grade humanities class grudgingly agreed to read the story with prompting from their teacher. They read the book, talked about it with their group members, and wrote about it to one another in electronic threaded discussions using First Class Client software (a program similar to Microsoft Outlook). The following exchange emerged (student names are pseudonyms; otherwise it is excerpted exactly as written):

> Jenny:
> Dear Group,
> I think the book is alright so far. What do you kids think. I think it suck to live in Afganistan because girls can't get an education and have to stay covered up. Well talk to you guys later. Bye.
>
> Leslie:
> So far the book is pretty good. Pervana is becoming a boy. The family is struggling and the Taliban took her father away.

Reprinted from Grisham, D.L., & Wolsey, T.D. (2006). Recentering the middle school classroom as a vibrant learning community: Students, literacy, and technology intersect. *Journal of Adolescent & Adult Literacy, 49*(8), 648–660. doi: 10.1598/JAAL.49.8.2

Elsa:
Dear group,
I just want to tell you what I think about Parvana. Ok I think that Parvana is pretty brave to go out & disguise hereself as a boy & take the chance of getting in trouble & getting put in jail. And her sister Noorie I dont think that Parvana & her sister Noorie get along as well as other brother's and sister's. And her mother must be really woried about letting her young daughter go out and do something outragious like that. Ok group I'll see you guys later

Eliza:
dear group,
This book is getting SSSSOOOOOOOOOO much better, i am at the part well way past it, but im at around the part where parvana is going to be a boy and stuff and yeah i cant wait to find out what happens next. and mr wolsey i guess you were right about this book, it is pretty good. the lady in the window is kewl. i want to know who she is, that would be so kewl if peaople could like read like super duper fast! like just look at a page and know what it is about. ok blonde moment!!! hehe, im gunna go reply to your guyses psts now!

Eliza again:
REPLY!!!!!!!!!!!!!!!!!!!!
ok the reply to about what you guys were talking about, yes that would suck to have to cut your hair, but its not like it wont grow back! but she did it for a good reason! yes and i would do that if i was in that situation!!! she did a good thing and i think parvana should get something good for doing that! yes and jenny, i dont think the window lady is a stalker, i think it might be someone she knows!! and i think that is so kewl how she ran into her friend from school who is in the same situation as parvana, if any of you guys read that part, it is really kewl!.

As students continued to read and write, their engagement level increased as well. They were writing to and for one another about a topic that was timely but also of interest to this group of adolescent girls. They struggle every day, as adolescents in middle school, to define themselves. In reading the book, these girls identified with the character Parvana, who was forced to assume the identity of someone she was not—a boy—just to survive.

The mediating tool students used was threaded discussion, a technological innovation that allows students to communicate by combining the best of written journals and face-to-face discussion (Wolsey, 2004). During their electronic, or threaded, discussions and in face-to-face interactions, they were able to create a community through which they had control of the conversation, the meanings they jointly constructed, and the connections they wanted to make to their own lives and worlds. These students had found an electronic home.

A Home in Cyberspace

A community of practice has been defined by Wenger (2003) as "a group of people who share an interest in a domain of human endeavor and engage in a process of collective learning that creates bonds between them: a tribe, a garage band, a group of engineers working on similar problems" (p. 1). Wenger described three components of a community of practice: (1) a "domain" wherein members share a minimum level of competence; (2) "community" that involves joint activities and sharing information; and (3) the "practice," or the development of shared resources, experiences, and tools. Engagement of the members of the community with the activities that take place determines whether the community of practice is a rich one. Members of a community of practice value their membership, work hard to become more competent at the practice involved, and share important social relationships with other members. In terms of what "communities of practice" mean for the middle school classroom, we must examine current conditions in the classroom in middle schools to see if they fit the construct.

To promote community, students should exchange ideas, but the concept of "discussion" in school is somewhat misunderstood. In 1979, Mehan identified the recitation or I-R-E discourse format that many teachers use in the mistaken notion that they are holding "discussions." The *I* stands for "initiating the question." The teacher thus asks almost all the questions (for a discussion of questioning research, refer to Dillon, 1990). The *R* is for "response." Students respond to the questions that the teacher asks.

E represents "evaluation," which is done by the authority figure and repository of knowledge—the teacher. Did the student answer the question appropriately? Whether the student did, the teacher is now positioned to ask the next question. Thus the "discussion" is really not a discussion at all but a teacher-centered discourse pattern. Over 20 years ago, John Goodlad wrote, "Students in the classes we observed made scarcely any decisions about their learning, even though many perceived themselves as doing so" (1984, p. 229). Goodlad went on to emphasize that teachers dominate the classroom discourse, out-talking students nearly three to one. This one-sided discourse structure silences students for most of the instructional time. And this condition was confirmed more recently by Hillocks (2002), who noted, "the classroom discourse is largely disconnected and serves mainly to let teachers know if students know bits and pieces of isolated information about whatever is being studied" (p. 7). Thus, one area that teachers may need to spend time reflecting upon is the tone and structure of discourse in the middle school classroom.

Our observations in classrooms document the persistence of this lopsided ratio. In the middle school classrooms of today students are even more tightly constrained. The pressures of the accountability movement often dictate the curriculum and its pacing. Recently a teacher in one of our graduate classes complained that her new administrator, after his first observation of her classroom, asked her to justify why she was 20 minutes "off her lesson plan." The expectation that teachers will adhere to rigidly structured lessons promotes the teacher-centered discourse pattern even more strongly.

Smith and Wilhelm (2002), in their study of boys and literacy, made a point about school discourse that is undoubtedly true of many girls as well. That is, the boys in their study envisioned school as "functional" and therefore valuable in a generalized way. Boys regarded school as necessary to an often vague future. They saved their real interest and energies for the areas outside of school where they belonged to more vital communities of practice. "They were willing to do what needed to be done. But we can't help wondering how different they would have sounded if they had regarded school and reading as healthy work" (Smith & Wilhelm, 2002, p. 91). We would argue that the discourse patterns at work in middle schools are harmful to the intent of most teachers, that of empowering students to become more competent at academic literacies and more engaged with this particular community of practice. The community of practice we envision is often not realized in middle school classrooms.

Another aspect of community building concerns the social aspects of learning. Many researchers have presented compelling arguments about the centrality of the social aspect of learning. From Vygotsky (1934/1978) to Wertsch (1985), to more recent works on the value and essential nature of social interactions to learning (e.g., Gee, 2003; Street, 1995), the message is that all knowledge is socially constructed. Thus, the social nature of humans makes the social milieu in which they find themselves integral to their engagement with learning. The unintended curriculum—that *bête noir* of education—can act to make a school experience the very antithesis of the learning intended (Apple, 1975). Bintz and Shelton (2004) suggested an antidote, a written conversation as a mediating tool inducing social and instructional engagement. The written conversation incorporates students' love of passing notes with instructional purposes. Bintz and Shelton found that the social interaction produced student writing that reflected the true written voices of the students, increased responsibility for the task, and attained a deeper perspective. The use of an earlier, non-Internet version of "threaded discussions" evoked a sense of community in students in that study as it did in ours.

Why Technology?

Technology is pervasive, especially for young people, and definitions of literacy are swiftly evolving. McEneaney (2000) argued that the hypertext environment will transform the way in which we read and write. As Reinking (1998, p. xi) noted, "we are heading into a post-typographic world; that is, one in which printed texts are no longer dominant." And media sources invariably employ both text and visuals that were unheard of even 10 years ago, such that today's students are swimming in a sea of media. Many authors call this a "media-saturated" world. More important for middle school education, technology is motivating to students, providing for three essential components long believed important to learning.

Choice, power, and belonging, according to Glasser (1986), are necessary for students to become engaged in learning. Csikszentmihalyi (1990) offered similar suggestions for social learning experiences that are critical to vital communities of practice and to total absorption in learning—what he termed "flow." Technology magnifies the power of popular culture. Students either are already competent at some forms of technology (e.g., electronic gaming) or they *want* to be. In either case, we wanted to harness it in service to motivation and academic engagement (Guthrie & Wigfield, 2000). As with Ivey and Broaddus (2001), we believe that we can use reading to capitalize on middle school students' motivation to learn.

The Project—Recentering the Focus of Student Learning

Over the past three years we (Thomas Wolsey is a teacher and teacher educator, and Dana Grisham is a professor at a large university) have worked together to create a vibrant learning community in eighth-grade English classes. We sought to do this through the integration of technology and literacy in a number of ways. Most germane to this discussion is the use of threaded discussion groups. An *electronic threaded discussion group* is a group of people who exchange messages about topics of common interest. A thread is a chain of postings on a single topic. Produced in several ways and known by several names, such as bulletin boards, online conversations, and eDiscussions, they involve a student sitting down at a computer station and typing in a response, in this case, to what he or she has read. This provides an online forum, an electronic learning space, for students to participate in discussion.

Students are assigned or choose their own groups to read a particular text and then to discuss a common topic. In our example of *The Breadwinner*, students chose their group and were then persuaded to try reading this young adult novel. Over the course of the year students in the class had the opportunity to read many novels. A total of 24 novels were used, but each student read and responded to at least 7 different books over the year, and for 4 of these, the students participated in online discussion. Representative titles include *The Old Man and the Sea* (Hemingway, 1952), *Romiette and Julio* (Draper, 1999), *She Said Yes* (Bernall, 1999), *A Child Called It* (Pelzer, 1995), *Esperanza Rising* (Ryan, 1995), *The Watsons Go to Birmingham-1963* (Curtis, 1995), and *The Fellowship of the Ring* (Tolkien, 1965).

Threaded Discussion Groups (TDGs) are asynchronous. Unlike "chat rooms" where posts are done in real time, in an asynchronous format the threads accumulate over time. Thus one student might post a response to the novel on Monday, and another student respond to that post on Tuesday. As Burniske (2000, p. 60) noted, asynchronous communication "allows the writer/speaker to compose statements in the absence of an audience. The 'turn-taking' here does not allow for interruptions, which means each participant has an opportunity to speak without pause, inspiring declamations as well as dialogues." Asynchronous communications are interactive, like discussion, but thoughtful, like written discourse.

Like Sherry (2000), we had several goals for the Threaded Discussion Groups. We wanted to build group coherence among students. We wanted to share information about the readings with them and have them share information with one another. We wanted students to process ideas about the reading. We envisioned that we might do some tutoring online, refine students' communication skills, and also provide feedback to students.

Fortunately, the district in which Wolsey worked used First Class software for all students, teachers, and parents. This software allowed us to set up the Threaded Discussion Groups for the various book groups and permitted access to all the transcripts. Grisham could participate in the Threaded Discussion Groups from her university office. Students were able to post responses from their homes, provided they had Internet access and could navigate the web browser as opposed to the First Class interface that was loaded on the computers at school.

The school is part of a large unified district in southern California with a mostly working class population and the diversity that one sees in California, including many English-language learners. Three classes of students participated in the Threaded Discussion Groups. Students had prior experience with literature circles (Daniels, 2002), and continued to participate in face-to-face discussions during the academic year.

We spent time at the beginning of the year acquainting students with the First Class software on library computers. There were three Macintosh computers in Wolsey's classroom that worked reliably and three others that worked sporadically. Students used the teacher's desk computer as well. Occasionally there was time during the language arts class for online responses. Students also responded during their advisement or library periods and, sometimes, from home.

We were surprised to find that 92% of all students had access to a computer at home. We learned that students spent an average of 5.14 hours per week on their computers, with some students spending far more than that. Seventy-three percent of the students preferred to type on the computer rather than write with pencil and paper, citing that writing made their hands hurt. Boys spent more time on the computer than girls (except in one very unusual class).

A recent U.S. Census Bureau report (Newburger, 2001) detailed that 68.1% of students aged 3–17 with Internet access reported using it for school research at home. During the first year of our study we surveyed our students to find out how they spent their time online. What we found is summarized in Table 1.

Playing games on the computer accounted for the largest number of activities in all three classes surveyed. Top activities on the computer were (a) playing games (and downloading them); (b) surfing the Internet; (c) e-mail and chat—primarily through America Online's "buddy lists"; and (d) homework and reports. Thus, it is obvious that students were fairly avid users of technology, but little of what they were doing was related to academic learning.

Daniels (1994, 202) reported that literature circles can provide valued outcomes for students as they engage with literature through group discussion. For example, they can understand themselves and others better, see themselves as readers, become aware of different approaches to reading instruction, and obtain (and prefer) choice and control of their reading activities. Wolsey had been using literature circles with some success but observed that the discussions tended to be fairly superficial unless he was in close proximity to the groups. Threaded discussion groups appeared to offer the benefits of face-to-face discussion without any of the drawbacks, plus it provided for thinking time to consider responses.

We wondered if students could talk about some of the themes or "Big Ideas" they discovered in the books. Could they discuss and reflect intelligently upon their own personal response to the book in question? We hoped that the

---

Table 1
Amount of Time Spent Online
by Eighth-Grade Students by Gender

Class A (N = 33)	144 hours per week
19 males	87 hours
14 females	57 hours
Class B (N = 33)	156 hours per week
17 males	96 hours
16 females	60 hours
Class C (N = 29)	178 hours per week
9 males	29 hours
20 females	149 hours

Threaded Discussion Groups would allow us to work with students individually, in each student's zone of proximal development, and that we could encourage more "academic" uses of technology, bridging the "kid culture" and the school culture more effectively.

We learned that we needed to structure the experience carefully and that we had to plan, just as for any other learning activity. For example, students created a rubric for grading their responses to ensure that assessment would be fair and to provide for accountability (Grisham & Wolsey, 2005). An example of a simple rubric appears in Table 2. Students also received points for their postings that counted toward their academic grades.

Another thing we needed to do was to provide an instructional model, so that students new to the instructional strategy could envision some of the types of responses that they might make. Examples of the quantity and quality of responses that were desired were shown. Students were taught Netiquette (www.albion.com/netiquette) and finally the teacher discussed with students the need to use academic language in their posts, stating, "This isn't a chat room." Later, we realized that most students weren't using academic language as we had anticipated (more on that later).

In determining the teacher's role, we saw the following as important tasks. Most important was to monitor conversations. Despite impressing upon students the responsibility to keep messages proactive and academic, a few students did things that lost them their First Class privileges for a while. The teacher acted as a model, replying to student messages, encouraging student responses, modeling good netiquette, and instructing and modeling the use of computers and software. Wolsey had a data projector that was invaluable in doing the modeling in class.

Most students enjoyed the Threaded Discussion Groups. We gave students several surveys about Threaded Discussion Groups and interviewed selected students, who provided us with the following feedback:

> "I type faster than I write and when I do it on the computer I think more." "I liked it—it was interesting!" "It was cool." "You get to write more, and people can read your writing." "When Mr. Wolsey writes back to us, because in class he talks to all of us, but on the computer, it's like he hears what you say."

Of course, some students disliked the Threaded Discussion Groups. The primary reasons had little to do with the books or the discussions:

> "I kept forgetting my password." "Not enough time on the computers." "I didn't get a chance on the computer." "I type too slow."

At first, Wolsey was dismayed by the use of colored and fancy fonts, smileys, and other emoticons that students used in their electronic responses. It appeared that students spent as much time on formatting their messages as on composing them. Leu, Kinzer, Coiro, and Cammack (2004) and Norton-Meier (2004) suggested that literacy in the electronic environment includes decoding the strategic use of color, icons, and selection and placement of images. It turned out that the students were ahead of the authors' learning curve in their use of these symbols to help communicate their messages.

During many of the book groups, Wolsey asked students to participate in threaded discussion and keep a paper journal. At the inception of the project, we suspected that the students would write more when they wrote in the electronic

---

Table 2
Rubric for Threaded Discussion Group Participation

Each of the indicators is to be ranked on a scale of 1 (absence of indicator) to 5 (presence of indicator, high quality).

- references to other students' literary responses and to the book itself
- quotes
- paragraphs
- descriptive words
- humor

---

environment than they would in their paper journals. We were surprised again to find that students did not write more. A word count analysis (between 70 and 80 words per entry) showed that the number of words for journals written on paper and responses in threaded discussion were not significantly different. (See Table 3.) In addition, because students needed access to a limited number of computers, there are fewer electronic entries. What was different was the quality of what students wrote. Analysis of a typical student's two types of responses helps to establish this point. Ronald's paper journals, where the only other audience was the teacher, are acceptable but lifeless. (See Figure 1.) Compare this with his electronic threaded discussion entries written for his classmates reading the same book

(*I Heard the Owl Call My Name*, Craven, 1973) in March of 2002, as shown in Table 4. Note that his paper journals consisted largely of summaries of the reading, but in his threaded discussion entries he made inferences, predictions, connections to experiences outside of class (an extracurricular field trip to the Maritime Museum of San Diego), and descriptions of literary elements.

Students writing in isolation on paper with the teacher as sole audience wrote perfunctorily, recounting the story and making occasional attempts at prediction. But in the social environment created in the electronic learning space of threaded discussion, students found a voice, developed perspectives, made meaningful predictions, connected the literature with other media, and established the motivation to read as only

Table 3
Word Count and Quality Indicators—Ronald

March 2002 entry	Paper journal sentences	Statement
1	5	prompt—vocabulary
2	11	discussion summary
3	3	reading summary
4	4	reading summary, response to prompt—setting descriptive
5	7	reading summary
6	6	reading summary
7	5	role preparation—questions
8	7	discussion summary
9	6	reading summary
10	6	reading summary
11	6	reading summary
12	5	reading summary
13	4	role preparation—quotes and connections
14	6	discussion summary
Average	5.79	

Entry	Threaded discussion sentences	Statement
1	5	response to prompt—setting description
2	6	reading summary, prediction, inference, note, and agree with another student
3	9	reading summary, inference
4	5	inference—connection to field trip
5	4	reading summary
Average	5.8	

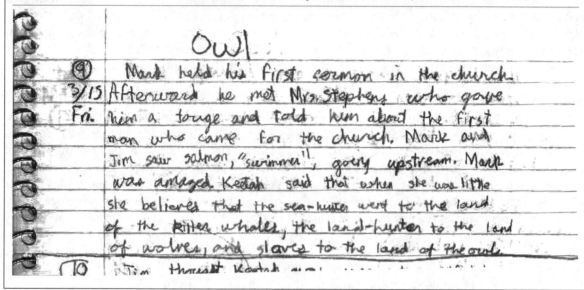

Figure 1
An Example of Ronald's Paper Journal Entries
for *I Heard the Owl Call My Name* (Craven, 1973)

Table 4
Ronald's Discussion Group Postings

Wednesday, March 20, 2002 10:40:19 PM
WolseyTDG5_IHeardOwl
From: Ronald
Subject: 4th
To: WolseyTDG5_IHeardOwl
Cc:
While I was reading this book I was wondering how their life was so hard. But then after I went onto that boat (for the field trip) and had to sleep on the wooden floor and had no modern everyday thigs with me (i.e., pillows, mattress, hot water). I realized how much tougher it must have been, because that was only a little bit of their lifestyle. Ecspecialy Mark, because he had to patroll the islands at night sometimes. After I got a little taste of it I got into this book.

Wednesday, March 20, 2002 10:29:59 PM
WolseyTDG5_IHeardOwl
From: Ronald
Subject: 3rd
To: WolseyTDG5_IHeardOwl
Cc:
So far, Mark has been working with his hands and is living like the Indians are, which has gained their respect. They have offered to help build the new vicarage. It is also August, which is when the Indians can buy alcohol. Sam, the poor guy, somehow ran into a lot of fish. Sam got very rich, but lost most of it gambling. With the rest of it he bought a washermachine. While getting it up the river he tipped the canoe and the washermachine sunk right to the bottom. His wife got really mad at him. He's got it pretty bad.

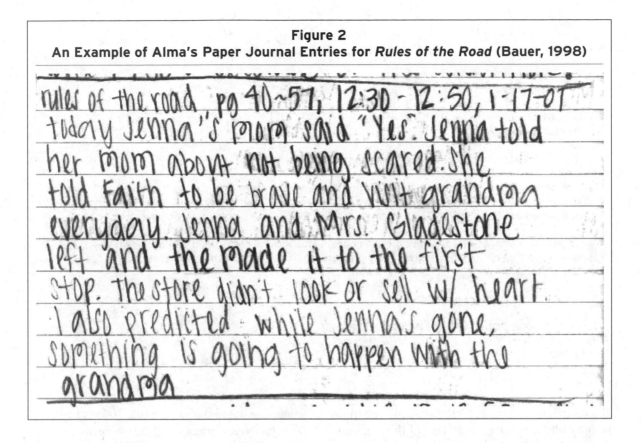

Figure 2
An Example of Alma's Paper Journal Entries for *Rules of the Road* (Bauer, 1998)

rules of the road, pg 40~57, 12:30 - 12:50, 1-17-0T today Jenna"s mom said "Yes". Jenna told her mom about not being scared. She told Faith to be brave and visit grandma everyday. Jenna and Mrs. Gladestone left and the made it to the first stop. The store didn't look or sell w/ heart. I also predicted - while Jenna's gone, something is going to happen with the grandma

peers can. Compare Ronald's and Alma's paper journal responses (Figures 1 and 2) with their threaded discussion posts in Tables 4 and 5.

Discussion

The First Class software was easy for students to learn and presented few problems. When students were given time to respond during school hours using the software, the process went smoothly. The Web browser interface available to students at home was less effective, however, and students had trouble accessing it from their homes. We made sure that students had adequate time in class for their responses.

We noted several implications for instruction. Leu et al. (2004) proposed 10 central principles around which research and theory of new literacies should be constructed. Four of these principles are of particular interest in this study:

First, the Internet and other ICTs (information and communication technologies) require new literacies to fully access their potential. Threaded discussions, as we configured them, are egalitarian and closed networks (Buchanan, 2002) with near equal distribution of links between the participants and not open to participants from outside the class. By *closed networks*, we mean that students were assigned to a group that did not change during the literature circle cycle, and they could only correspond with members of their own group online. By *egalitarian*, we mean that students had roughly equal opportunities to participate and post to the group.

Without the technology of the Internet, the power of the threaded discussion would have been very difficult, if not impossible, to achieve. When students began discussing books online we noted many instances of emoticons and font size and color changes. As the academic year proceeded, however, students became more engaged in the discussions themselves, and these novelty elements consumed less of the students' time online. We noted fewer emoticons and more substantive entries. Not all students were motivated by the opportunities to use computers for discussion of books. We found a number of students who, for various reasons (including a lack of keyboarding skills), found that they preferred the more traditional instructional sequences.

Analysis of electronic transcripts over time led us to conclude that the asynchronous nature of online discussion prompted students to think more deeply about their responses to the literature and to the members of their groups than did the paper journal or the face-to-face discussions. What students did in the electronic discussions was to read and thoughtfully respond to their peers' postings. Thus the entries provided for a far more authentic discussion than did the face-to-face discussions, where students (based upon observation) did just their parts, taking turns and failing to react or build upon others' offerings.

The second principle argues that critical literacies are central to the new literacies. As the reader can see in the sample discussions from *The Breadwinner*, students had the opportunity to examine the text from a variety of vantage points. They had to consider one another's point of view, build on it, and then place that in the context of a time and place about which they knew little. For *The Breadwinner* discussions, students had to displace their perceptions of Afghani culture as presented in popular stereotypes in the United States with more accurate descriptions presented in the book and the information they were able to gain from discussions online and face-to-face with one another and the researchers.

Third, learning is often socially constructed within new literacies. Students were able to construct meaning by customizing their learning experiences as they read and discussed the literature in much the same way that we now use road maps. We both possess many paper road maps, but in most instances when maps are needed we use the Internet. The customized maps produced show only the relevant portions of the terrain to be traversed and the route from start to finish. Level of detail can be increased or decreased, depending on our background knowledge of the terrain. Similarly, students used the threaded discussions to customize their reading experiences and mediate discussions with their peers.

Teachers become more important, though their role changes, within new literacy classrooms. As with the first three principles discussed, we found that our role as researchers and teachers was transformed, often in ways we didn't expect. As we became participants in, instead of directors of, the threaded discussions, we adjusted our expectations about what counted as academic language and the expected style of the written discourse students used. We were surprised, even though we shouldn't have been, at the quality of the student work once their voices were restored through social contact. Time online was provided, and time between posts, due to the nature of the technology, allowed for participation with peers. This created the opportunity to construct meaning that would have been far more difficult in a traditional I-R-E discourse. We also found that teacher participation in electronic discussions was critical to increasing the level and complexity of student response. We both responded to students' postings at various times. For example, Wolsey posted this electronic response dated January 30, 2002:

> Nice threaded discussion going on here, girls. Keep up the good work. Patty, your predictions are a model of good thinking :-) You don't always know what's next, but if you make a good guess then read ahead—you'll find out. Makes it more exciting, too. Elizabeth and Kathy had some pretty good observations about Jenna's [*Rules of the Road*, Bauer, 1998] motivation. We haven't talked much about motivation, but all characters (even fictional ones) have to have a reason for doing what they do. Keep exploring this.

When this scaffolding effect was missing, students made less effective responses. We found that the electronic discussions were more interactive and produced better literary responses than paper journals or face-to-face discussions when the teacher provided scaffolding in this manner.

In other pragmatic ways, we adjusted the demands of the literature circles to reduce the academic load on students. At first we asked them to do it all: write in paper journals, discuss face-to-face, and make electronic journal entries. As we gained confidence in the students' use of the technology, we were able to relax some of the other requirements. Wolsey gained confidence that the electronic discussions were contributing to students' academic development. In this sense, the online discussions facilitated other classroom face-to-face discussions.

Finally, the rigidity of literature circle protocol as we applied it appeared to cause a pro forma discussion. Students did their parts without much true engagement in the face-to-face discussions over time, but at the same time it was difficult for students to break away from the roles. The online discussions appear to have eased that rigidity and tended to produce more genuine responses both online and face-to-face. In face-to-face discussion, students often referred to their online posts. Because the students felt a sense of responsibility to their peers, we noted a form of positive peer pressure to keep up with reading. The electronic community created a sense of home where authentic student voices were encouraged; the social setting offered students comfort and context for their learning, the opportunity to demonstrate competence, and the chance to contribute to the learning of the group members. Threaded discussions allowed us to center our literature study on the student voices in ways that would have been nearly impossible without the technology.

References
Apple, M.W. (1975). The hidden curriculum and the nature of conflict. *Interchange*, 2, 4.

Bintz, W.P., & Shelton, K.S. (2004). Using written conversation in middle school: Lessons from a teacher researcher project. *Journal of Adolescent & Adult Literacy*, *47*, 482–507.

Borko, H. (2004). Professional development and teacher learning: Mapping the terrain. *Educational Researcher*, *33*, 3–15.

Buchanan, M. (2002). *Nexus: Small worlds and the groundbreaking science of networks*. New York: W.W. Norton.

Burniske, R. (2000). *Literacy in the cyber age: Composing ourselves online*. Arlington Heights, IL: Skylight Professional Development.

Christensen, R. (2002). Effects of technology integration education on the attitudes of teachers and students. *Journal of Research on Technology in Education, 34*, 411–434.

Csikszentmihalyi, M. (1990). Flow: *The psychology of optimal experience*. New York: Harper & Row.

Daniels, H. (1994). *Literature circles: Voice and choice in the student-centered classroom*. York, ME: Stenhouse.

Daniels, H. (2002). Literature circles: *Voice and choice in book clubs and reading groups* (2nd ed.). York, ME: Stenhouse.

Dillon, J.T. (1990). *The practice of questioning*. New York: Routledge.

Gee, J.P. (2003). *What video games have to teach us about learning and literacy*. New York: Palgrave MacMillan.

Glasser, W. (1986). *Control theory in the classroom*. New York: Harper & Row.

Goodlad, J.I. (1984). *A place called school*. New York: McGraw-Hill.

Grisham, D.L., & Wolsey, T.D. (2005). Improving writing: Comparing the responses of eighth graders, preservice teachers and experienced teachers. *Reading and Writing Quarterly, 21*, 315–330.

Guthrie, J.T., & Wigfield, A. (2000). Engagement and motivation in reading. In M.L. Kamil, P.B. Mosenthal, P.D. Pearson, & R. Barr (Eds.), *Handbook of reading research* (Vol. 3, pp. 403–422). Mahwah, NJ: Erlbaum.

Hillocks, G., Jr. (2002). *The testing trap: How state writing assessments control learning*. New York: Teachers College Press.

Ivey, G., & Broaddus, K. (2001). "Just plain reading": A survey of what makes students want to read in middle school classrooms. *Reading Research Quarterly, 36*, 350–377.

Leu, D.J., Jr., Kinzer, C.K., Coiro, J., & Cammack, D.W. (2004). Toward a theory of new literacies emerging from the Internet and other information and communication technologies. In R.B. Ruddell & N. Unrau (Eds.), *Theoretical models and processes of reading* (5th ed., pp. 1570–1613). Newark, DE: International Reading Association.

McEneaney, J. (2000). Ink to link: A hypertext history in 36 nodes. *Reading Online, 4*(5). Retrieved December 14, 2004, from http://www.readingonline.org/articles/art_index.asp?HREF=/articles/mceneaney2/index.html

Mehan, H. (1979). *Learning lessons: Social organization in the classroom*. Cambridge, MA: Harvard University Press.

Newburger, E.C. (2001, September). *Home computers and Internet use in the United States: August 2000*. Retrieved January 26, 2006, from http://www.census.gov/prod/2001pubs/p23%2D207.pdf

Norton-Meier, L.A. (2004). A technology user's bill of rights: Lessons learned in chat rooms. *Journal of Adolescent & Adult Literacy, 47*, 606–608.

Reinking, D. (1998). Synthesizing technological transformations of literacy in a post-typographic world. In D. Reinking, M.C. McKenna, L.D. Labbo, & R.D. Kieffer (Eds.), *Handbook of literacy and technology: Transformation in a post-typographic world* (pp. xi–xxx). Mahwah, NJ: Erlbaum.

Sherry, L. (2000). The nature and purpose of online conversations: A brief synthesis of current research as related to the WEB project. *International Journal of Educational Telecommunications, 6*(1), 19–52.

Smith, M.W., & Wilhelm, J.D. (2002). *"Reading don't fix no Chevys": Literacy in the lives of young men*. Portsmouth, NH: Heinemann.

Street, B.V. (1995). *Social literacies: Critical approaches to literacy development, ethnography, and education*. New York: Longman.

Vygotsky, L.S. (1978). *Mind in society: The development of higher psychological processes* (M. Cole, V. John-Steiner, S. Scribner, & E. Souberman, Eds. & Trans.). Cambridge, MA: Harvard University Press. (Original work published 1934)

Wenger, E. (2003). *Communities of practice*. Paper presented at the Fall 2003 conference of the California Council on Teacher Education, San Diego, CA, October 30–November 1, 2003.

Wertsch, J.V. (Ed.). (1985). *Culture, communication, and cognition: Vygotskian perspectives*. New York: Cambridge University Press.

Wolsey, T.D. (2004). Literature discussion in cyberspace: Young adolescents using threaded discussion groups to talk about books. *Reading Online, 7*(4). Retrieved January 26, 2006, from http://www.readingonline.org/articles/art_index.asp?HREF=wolsey/index.html

Young adult literature cited

Bauer, J. (1998). *Rules of the road*. New York: Penguin.

Bernall, M. (1999). *She said yes: The unlikely martyrdom of Cassie Bernall*. New York: Simon & Schuster.

Craven, M. (1973). *I heard the owl call my name*. New York: Dell.

Curtis, C.P. (1995). *The Watsons go to Birmingham—1963*. New York: Bantam Doubleday Dell Books for Young Readers.

Draper, S.M. (1999). *Romiette and Julio*. New York: Simon Pulse.

Ellis, D. (2001). *The breadwinner*. Toronto, ON: Groundwood.

Hemingway, E. (1952). *The old man and the sea*. New York: Macmillan.

Pelzer, D. (1995). *A child called it: One child's courage to survive*. Deerfield Beach, FL: Health Communications.

Ryan, P.M. (2000). *Esperanza rising*. New York: Scholastic.

Tolkien, J.R.R. (1965). *The fellowship of the ring*. Boston: Houghton Mifflin.

Questions for Reflection

- Technological innovations have changed the ways we communicate. For example, cell phones, iPods, and instant messaging have become widespread for most of us. Think about and share your thoughts regarding what has changed during your lifetime. What information and communication technologies were prevalent when you were growing up? Now think about what elements of your classroom reading comprehension instruction you might change to take advantage of recent technologies. Make a list of your ideas and share them with your colleagues.

- The authors write of online threaded discussion as allowing students to build their reading experiences and their understanding through interaction with others. Based on what you know about factors that influence comprehension, in what ways might online discussion enhance meaning construction?

- In this article, social components and supports for meaning construction are emphasized. How might technology enhance content reading tasks in your classroom? Do you think the use of technology is responsible for the successful learning community the authors describe? If you do not have access to comparable technology in your classroom, how might you adapt the techniques described in this article to encourage discussion that leads to making meaning from text?

Reading Literature, Reading Text, Reading the Internet: The Times They Are a'Changing

Linda B. Gambrell

erhaps one of the most significant trends to emerge during the past decade is the increasing attention that researchers and educators have devoted to the role of expository text in early literacy development. Although educators and theorists have long emphasized the importance of narrative in children's lives (Adams, 1990; Egan, 1998), a call has surfaced to give additional attention to expository or informational text in the early grades. A U.S. report last year titled *Reading at Risk* (National Endowment for the Arts, 2004) made me think about the current trend toward including more informational text in primary-grade classrooms and how such a trend might affect the reading habits of our youth.

The *Reading at Risk* report presents the findings from a survey that asked adults over the age of 18 about their leisure time reading habits. The findings revealed that, in 1992, 61% of adults reported reading books (of any kind) during leisure time, while in 2002 the percentage decreased to 57%. When asked specifically if they read novels, short stories, poetry, or plays during leisure time, 57% of respondents in 1982 reported they had done so. The percentage dropped to 54% in 1992 and again in 2002 to 48%, indicating that less than half of the adults surveyed read literary works for pleasure in that year. The question then arises: Are adults reading less or are they just reading differently?

MaryEllen Vogt (2004), current president of the International Reading Association, discussed *Reading at Risk* in a *Reading Today* column last summer and encouraged teachers to explore the meaning of the report's findings. Vogt posed some compelling questions for us to consider: Does "literary reading" only refer to the great works of literature, or is there a new and evolving definition that may supersede past definitions? Are children and young adults now engaging in many kinds of literate behaviors other than those that have been traditionally considered "literary"? A look at the increasing availability of informational text, its use in classroom instruction, and the expanding role of technology in U.S. culture might provide some insights and possible answers to these questions.

Early Literacy Instruction: Moving Toward a Balance

Reading educators have long been concerned about reading in the content areas, particularly the difficulty that some students experience around the fourth-grade level when expectations to independently negotiate content area textbooks increase. Only recently, however, have we begun to focus on the need to provide young students with exposure to, and strategic instruction in using, informational texts.

A number of studies conducted in the 1980s provided the underpinning and rationale for balancing young students' exposure to narrative

Reprinted from Gambrell, L.B. (2005, March). Reading literature, reading text, reading the Internet: The times they are a'changing. *The Reading Teacher, 58*(6), 588–591. doi: 10.1598/RT.58.6.8

and informational text. Research documented that students of all ages, from elementary to high school, experienced difficulty comprehending informational text (McGee, 1982; Meyer, Brandt, & Bluth, 1978; Taylor, 1980). Some reading researchers speculated that the problem was rooted in young students' lack of exposure to informational text, particularly given that they encounter primarily narrative forms in picture books and television shows. Another interesting finding during this period was that studies of international comparisons showed that students in Finland outperformed students from other countries in comprehending both narrative and informational text. A number of hypotheses have been put forth to explain Finland's reading proficiency. First, the sound–symbol relationship in the Finnish language is extremely consistent, with one letter representing one sound, making the decoding process much easier for young children to master. The second hypothesis has to do with the fact that from a very early age children in Finland are exposed to informational text, and much, if not most, of the early literacy instruction in classrooms uses informational text. An awareness of the need to introduce expository text in the early grades had begun, and interest has continued to develop in the following decades.

Two Classic Studies on Informational Text

There is little debate that prior to the 1990s U.S. culture and classrooms favored the use of narrative with young children; however, during the 1990s, research began to turn to young children's exposure to and comprehension of expository genres (Dreher, Davis, Waynant, & Clewell, 1998; Duke, 2000; Kamil & Lane, 1997; Pappas, 1993). Pappas's (1993) landmark study raised significant questions about whether narrative text should be the primary or dominant text used with young children. In her study, kindergarten children engaged in pretend readings of two stories and two informational books, which were then analyzed to gain insight about young children's strategies in dealing with these two genres. Pappas's study revealed that young children were just as successful in reenacting the informational books as they were the stories and that they preferred the informational text. Based on the findings of her study, Pappas challenged the "narrative as primary" notion, stating that an exclusive emphasis on reading "story" in the early grades limits children's experiences with other forms of text and may create a barrier to full access to literacy.

In a study that has become a classic, Duke (2000) explored the degree to which informational texts were actually included in classrooms and in what ways. Data were collected about the types of text on classroom walls, in the classroom library, and in classroom written-language activities. The results of the study revealed a scarcity of informational text in classroom print environments and activities. Few informational texts were included in the classroom libraries, very little informational text appeared on classroom walls and other surfaces, and a mean of only 3.6 minutes per day was spent with informational texts during classroom written-language activities. Perhaps even more revealing was the fact that the scarcity of the use of informational text was particularly acute for children in low-socioeconomic-status schools. Duke's research strongly suggested that young children in all of the classrooms she studied lacked the exposure to informational text needed to build the familiarity, comfort, and confidence required to become proficient readers of expository text in the later grades.

In discussing her results, Duke (2000) provided what I consider to be excellent advice. She cautioned that we should not attempt to increase time spent with informational text by decreasing the amount of time and attention given to narrative text. In other words, we should not pit narrative against informational text, but we should provide a balance.

Technology: Changes in the Culture of Reading

At about the same time that reading research began to emphasize the need for young children to have increased exposure to informational text, another phenomenon was occurring: The computer was becoming an integral tool in U.S. classrooms and culture. The computer and the Internet have put information literally at our fingertips. Perhaps the most significant impact on reading habits for children and adults is evidenced in our quest for information. We have shifted from leafing through traditional hardback encyclopedias and other resource books to logging on and "Googling" a topic. I suspect that the flexible access the Internet provides has resulted in an increase in the reading of informational text for children *and* adults. This brings me back to my experience with the *Reading at Risk* report.

As I stated earlier, my initial interest in the *Reading at Risk* report was piqued by a print article in *Reading Today*. Vogt's discussion of the key finding—that the reading of literary books in the United States was declining rapidly, especially among younger adults—spurred me to learn more. I went online to read the report in detail and then searched for the topic on the Internet to find what else was being said about the report in U.S. newspapers. Headlines in newspapers from New York to Seattle, Washington, included "Literary Reading in Dramatic Decline," "Book Reading Drops," "Fewer Noses Stuck in Books in America." I then logged on to several blogs (Web logs, or online journals) to find out what people were saying about the survey and discovered quite a range of interesting perspectives being discussed.

I began to think about how my reading experience on the Internet differed from simply reading a traditional print version of the *Reading at Risk* report. My interest was triggered by reading traditional print (a *Reading Today* column), but it was not a traditional book as defined by the *Reading at Risk* report. Because I have Internet access, I was able to quickly find the actual report and then read related newspaper columns, as well as a variety of blogs, in order to investigate what others thought about the report. Because I used the Internet, my reading on the topic was broader and I was exposed to multiple interpretations of the report. As a result, my understanding was expanded and enriched, much more so than

if I had only read the traditional printed version of *Reading at Risk*.

My reading of the *Reading at Risk* report, related newspaper articles, and websites occurred during a leisurely Sunday afternoon. Such reading would not have been reported in the *Reading at Risk* survey because not once did I read from a traditional book, and none of the text would have been considered literary. While the *Reading at Risk* report does acknowledge the contribution of electronic media in terms of information access and diversity, it also suggests that the Internet fosters short attention spans, accelerated gratification, and passive participation. Given my experience reading the report, I'd beg to differ.

Changing Times and Changing Texts

The reading of literature is vastly important to the cultural and intellectual development of all students, but they need to read and derive pleasure and knowledge from expository text as well. Reading literature and other text genres can enrich the mind and the soul. In U.S. classrooms and in U.S. culture, informational text is becoming more and more important. I agree with Duke (2000)—it is not a matter of one genre or the other, but rather it is a matter of balance, and this is as true for traditional books as it is for electronic media.

The *Reading at Risk* report contains much valuable information for anyone interested in literacy, and I encourage everyone to read it. Nevertheless, I urge caution in drawing the conclusion that reading is at risk. Perhaps reading as we have traditionally defined it is at risk. It seems that an expanded definition of reading should be developed that encourages a balance between narrative and exposition, hard copy and electronic media. While there may be a decline in the reading of literary books, the *Reading at Risk* survey has not convinced me that there is a decline in overall reading. I'm eternally optimistic that reading is, and will continue to be, highly valued in U.S. culture.

References

Adams, J.J. (1990). *Beginning to read: Thinking and learning about print*. Cambridge, MA: MIT Press.

Dreher, M.J., Davis, K.A., Waynant, P., & Clewell, S.F. (1998). Fourth-grade researchers: Helping children develop strategies for finding and using information. In T. Shanahan & F.V. Rodriques-Brown (Eds.), *47th yearbook of the National Reading Conference* (pp. 311–322). Chicago: National Reading Conference.

Duke, N. (2000). 3.6 minutes per day: The scarcity of informational texts in first grade. *Reading Research Quarterly, 35*, 202–224. doi:10.1598/RRQ.35.2.1

Egan, K. (1998). *Primary understanding: Education in early childhood*. New York: Routledge.

Kamil, M., & Lane, D. (1997, April). *A classroom study of the efficacy of using informational text for first grade reading instruction*. Paper presented at the American Educational Association meeting, San Diego, CA.

McGee, L. (1982). Awareness of text structure: Effects on children's recall of expository text. *Reading Research Quarterly, 17*, 581–589.

Meyer, B.J.F., Brandt, D.H., & Bluth, G.J. (1978, April). *Use of author's textual schema: Key for ninth graders' comprehension*. Paper presented at the annual meeting of the American Educational Research Association, Toronto, Canada.

National Endowment for the Arts. (2004). *Reading at risk: A survey of literary reading in America* (Rep. No. 46). Washington, DC: Author.

Pappas, C.C. (1993). Is narrative "primary"? Some insights from kindergartners' pretend readings of stories and information books. *Journal of Reading Behavior, 25*, 97–129.

Taylor, B.M. (1980). Children's memory for exposition text after reading. *Reading Research Quarterly, 15*, 399–411.

Vogt, M.E. (2004, August/September). Book reading drops, says new survey. *Reading Today, 22*, 6.

Questions for Reflection

- Think about texts found on the Internet. Are they fundamentally different from traditional print texts? Does constructing meaning from digital texts require different skills than those brought to bear in comprehension of traditional print forms?
- The author describes accessing online versions of reports, newspapers, blogs, and other texts—all of which use the online medium to deliver written language—but she does not mention multimedia. Do comprehension demands change when texts include audio, illustration, video, and interactivity—and, if so, how?

Constructing Anne Frank:
Critical Literacy and the Holocaust
in Eighth-Grade English

Karen Spector and Stephanie Jones

Knowing Anne, she was happy in the concentration camps. She didn't have to be quiet anymore; she could frolic outside. She could be in nature. She loved nature. I think this was a welcome relief for her. (Charlotte, a student in the study)

Every generation frames the Holocaust, represents the Holocaust, in ways that suit its mood. (Novick, 1999, p. 120)

There are few ambassadors of the Holocaust more deeply embedded in American adolescent consciousness than Anne Frank. Partly because of the uplifting Goodrich and Hackett (1956) play based upon her diary, Anne Frank has become an American icon of optimistic thinking and individual triumph (see Doneson, 1987; Novick, 1999; Ozick, 2000). In keeping with the Americanization of Anne Frank, students in this study liked to think of her as being hopeful, in love, frolicking, and—perhaps most surprising—still alive.

It is cause for concern, then, that through some version of her story (referred to simply as "the *Diary*" unless we are referencing a particular edition), school children first come into contact with the events of Nazi-occupied Europe, including the distortions that are part of the American version of Anne Frank's story. Teachers may suppose that by having students read the *Diary* they will become motivated to learn about the history. In fact, using first-person accounts is highly recommended for just that reason (Hernandez,

2004; Levstik, 1989; Totten, 2001; United States Holocaust Memorial Museum, 2006a, 2006b). But if the *Diary* and American cultural narratives lead students to construct an overarching narrative about the Holocaust that is redemptive, then this framing may delimit Holocaust construction rather than open it up for close scrutiny.

Representations are built toward some end (White, 1981), often a moral lesson that "accompanies" the Holocaust. Anne herself began building a representation of her life in hiding when she wrote in her diary and again when she began editing her diary on March 29, 1944 after she learned over their illegal radio that diaries would be sought at war's end. Because she didn't survive the Nazi onslaught, her father published *his* edited version of her diary in 1947 to fulfill her wish that she live on after death. *The Diary of Anne Frank: The Revised Critical Edition* (Barnouw & van der Stroom, 2001), prepared by the Netherlands Institute for War Documentation, clears up questions about the editing of the *Diary* by authenticating and positioning the three earliest versions along side one another: her original diary entries (version a), her edited entries (version b), and the version her father published in 1947 (version c). These three versions of the *Diary* create a multidimensional representation of Anne Frank.

The most persistent controversy surrounding the representation of the *Diary* has swirled around the Goodrich and Hackett play that was

Reprinted from Spector, K., & Jones, S. (2007). Constructing Anne Frank: Critical literacy and the Holocaust in eighth-grade English. *Journal of Adolescent & Adult Literacy, 51*(1), 36-48. doi: 10.1598/JAAL.51.1.4

first staged in the U.S. in 1955 and in Europe in 1956. The play was a huge success, winning a Pulitzer Prize and Tony Award. But it always had its detractors, foremost among them Meyer Levin who wanted to stage a *true* version of Anne's diary. According to Melnick (1997) and Ozick (2000), the play secularized Anne, emphasized the comical side of life in hiding, and set up Anne as an icon of optimism. These tendencies of the play even seem to have cast their light on students' readings of *other* versions of Anne Frank's diary. The lesson of the *Diary* for students in the study echoed the memorable refrain that ends the play: "I still believe that people are really good at heart" (Goodrich & Hackett, 1956, p. 174; students read the play from their textbook, Applebee et al., 1994). But lessons are not straightforward (Schweber, 2004), and as Novick (1999) claimed, people may take away from the Holocaust only what they bring to it. We argue that the enshrinement of Anne in American consciousness causes some students to repel thoughts that may shatter the culturally acquired uplifting vision they have of Anne Frank.

Our goal in this article is twofold: to complicate the practice of using the *Diary* as representative of the Holocaust in the classroom, and to demonstrate how teachers can bring critical literacy practices to the study of the *Diary* in ways that help students gain more nuanced views of Holocaust history and more robust views of historical actors. We are not postulating an anything-goes attitude toward historical events. Rather, we are encouraging a critical view of Holocaust representation and consumption via the *Diary* in English Language Arts classrooms.

Past Empirical Research

Despite the fact that Holocaust literature in general, and versions of the *Diary* in particular, are ubiquitous in secondary English classrooms, scant published empirical research is available to guide the practice. Much has been written about teaching and learning about the Holocaust in social studies classrooms, but most of this body of research deals with the evaluation of one curriculum, *Facing History and Ourselves* (Stern-Strom

& Parsons, 1982). Examining student gains in moral reasoning and prosocial thinking through exposure to this curriculum is the hallmark of these studies (Bardige, 1983, 1988; *Facing History and Ourselves*, 1993; Lieberman, 1981, 1986; Schultz, Barr, & Selman, 2001). However, the studies do not seem to take into account that as in all texts, Holocaust emplotment (the way events are sequenced) and enfigurement (the characterization of historical actors) position students to learn certain lessons rather than others.

One recent standout in the field of Holocaust education studies in classrooms is Schweber (2004) who studied four different Holocaust units. As in the other studies, Schweber began with the premise that moral lessons were inevitable, but unlike most of the other studies, she explored how the lessons were taught within each unit, not just whether students said they learned them. Her finding, that moral lessons do not simply "accompany" the study of the Holocaust but are constructed through the interaction of the texts teachers choose, the activities in which students participate, and the ideological narratives that teachers and students bring with them to the study of the Holocaust, is fundamental to this current research. Schweber found that emplotments varied widely from unit to unit and could be placed along three continua: particular to universal, insular to expanded, and tragic to redemptive. She also found that enfigurements of historical actors could be placed along three continua: individualized to collectively represented, normalized to exoticized, and personalized to depersonalized (see Table 1). Schweber's continua are important not only for understanding Holocaust representations, but also for critically viewing other socially constructed knowledge.

Holocaust literature has been the subject of few empirical studies. Hernandez (2004) looked at a unit of "witness narratives" in his own English classroom. Hernandez expected that his students would learn moral lessons, just as researchers in the social studies classroom had expected of their participants. In Schweber's terminology (2004), Hernandez used individualized Holocaust accounts to lead students to universal lessons, which tended to be redemptive (echoed

Table 1
Schweber's (2004) Continua of Emplotment and Enfigurement

Description of poles on the continua of emplotment

Particular	Emphasizing the uniqueness of Jewish suffering, anti-Semitism
Universal	Emphasizing universality of suffering, lessons, or racism
Insular	Teaching the Holocaust in historical isolation
Expansive	Teaching the Holocaust as parallel to other historical events (e.g., other genocides)
Tragic	The trajectory of meaning leans toward meaningless or "useless knowledge" (Delbo, 1995)
Redemptive	The trajectory of meaning leans toward hope, salvation, redemption, or something else that brings meaning to the Holocaust

Description of poles on the continua of enfigurement

Individualized	Focusing on particular historical actors (e.g., Anne Frank, Miep Gies)
Collectivized	Focusing on "the Jews," "the perpetrators," "the righteous gentiles"
Normalized	Focusing on ordinary people in extraordinary circumstances
Exoticized	Tending toward mythologizing victims or rescuers, demonizing perpetrators

in the title of his dissertation: *Voices of Witness, Messages of Hope*). His study showed that students can be limited in how they construct the Holocaust by the dictates of the teacher. This underscores the necessity for teachers to submit their intentions and plans for teaching the Holocaust to serious scrutiny. Britzman (1999) argued that a teacher's desire for "stable truth found in the insistence upon courage and hope" can shut out "the reverberations of losing and being lost" which are part of the "difficult knowledge" of the Holocaust (p. 304).

A Critical Literacy Approach

Instead of beginning with the assumption that particular lessons simply accompany the study of the Holocaust, a critical literacy approach to Holocaust literature attempts to make visible the sometimes invisible narratives that guide text choice, text authorship, and text consumption, all of which work together to open up or shut down particular avenues of meaning making. We use critical literacy in the sense that Haas-Dyson (2001) did, to include the participation "in activities or practices in which we use language, oral and written, to reflect on given words and most importantly, on their familiar relational backdrops (Freire, 1970; Weiler, 1991)" (Haas-Dyson, 2001, p. 5). "Given words" can be those given by the texts under consideration or by the students as they interact with the texts. Reflection on the words and on the backdrops they index is how meaning is constructed, and hence the place to focus critical literacy efforts. We shut down thinking about texts when we predetermine what students should be thinking instead of encouraging students to "(re-) construct" themselves and others through the process (Haas-Dyson, 2001). We argue that a critical literacy approach to the *Diary*, as opposed to a traditional one, may open up students to reconstructions that they may not be equipped to consider on their own. Although we certainly have our own preferred ways of constructing Anne Frank, we don't think it is wise to impose our views on students; rather, we choose to teach them to use the tools of critical literacy which can help them read multiple perspectives.

The Study

How do secondary students construct meaning about the Holocaust through Holocaust literature units? This question fueled the initial stages of this research when Karen (first author) entered the classroom of Mrs. Parker, an instructor well-known for teaching Holocaust literature in Adams Township, a primarily white, middle class, suburb outside of a large Midwestern city (the participants and the location have all been given pseudonyms). In the first year of the study, Karen spent 84 hours as a participant-observer in Mrs. Parker's accelerated English Language Arts classes during the length of the Holocaust unit. Forty-six of 47 students in Mrs. Parker's three classes participated in the study.

After analyzing the first-year data and finding that nearly all students saw the *Diary*, in the words of one eighth grader, as "more hopeful than sad," Karen in consultation with Stephanie (second author), devised a critical literacy unit revolving around the *Diary*. Karen then went to Mrs. Parker's new eighth-grade English classes the following year and asked the new set of students to participate in the study, including the critical literacy unit. Forty-five of Mrs. Parker's 52 eighth-grade students agreed to participate in the study. Karen spent 135 hours observing and teaching this group of students during the second year of the study. When she taught the critical literacy unit, she began by giving students short readings about the history of the Holocaust, anti-Semitism, Jews in Denmark, and the Frank family. After reading historical sources, the students read the Goodrich and Hackett (1956) play. Attempts to complicate students' readings of the *Diary* included showing students heavily edited video clips about Anne's deportation, imprisonment, and death (Dornheim, 2001) and comparing versions of the *Diary* (the Goodrich and Hackett, 1956, version and the *Definitive Edition*, Frank, 2001). The unit concluded with students engaging in critical discussion and writing about how they constructed the historical events and actors.

In the next section, using data from both years of the study, we demonstrate the following

two reasons why we thought a critical literacy unit was necessary.

1. Students in both years of the study came to the *Diary* with preconceived cultural narratives about Anne Frank; and
2. Students in both years of the study distorted the text in order to maintain these already present cultural narratives.

We include tips for teaching the *Diary* that evolved from each of these findings.

The Need for a Critical Literacy Lens

Already Knowing Anne Frank

In both years of the research, students felt as though they knew Anne Frank even before reading the Goodrich and Hackett (1956) version of her diary. They knew she was a young girl who hid from the Nazis. They knew she had a crush on Peter. They knew she was optimistic and brave. All of this could be chalked up to background knowledge (Fairclough, 1995), which "involves the representation of the 'the world' from the perspective of a particular interest" (p. 44). The construction of Anne that students knew mirrored the perky and sentimentalized Goodrich and Hackett (1956) Anne, even though most students hadn't yet read the play. In the words of one student, Anne's story presented the "Holocaust in a lighter kind of way" (Kylie).

In Anne's own words, and in her last diary entry ever, from Tuesday, August 1, 1944, she described herself as "a bundle of contradictions" who was "trying to find a way to become what [she'd] like to be and what [she] could be if...if only there were no other people in the world" (Frank, 2001, pp. 335–337; ellipsis in the original). But there were other people—namely Germans, the Dutch police, the Gestapo, and her betrayer—all of whom imposed their will on Anne, all of whom worked to cut her life woefully short. Most students weren't even aware that she vacillated between hope and despair while in hiding or that she perished in Bergen-Belsen a mere two months before the concentration camp was liberated. Their version of Anne Frank left her intact, still spreading her infectious spirit of optimism, still writing diary entries. The "snuffing out of her spirit" (Ozick, 2000, p. x), her death by typhus, her skeletal body dumped into a mass grave were not part of their versions of Anne Frank's story. The difficult knowledge of the Holocaust, and the pedagogic power of it, was bypassed (Britzman, 1999).

Even when students were explicitly told of her cruel death, they still tended to imagine her in hopeful ways. When students answered a question in their textbook (Applebee et al., 1994) that asked how Anne could have been happy in a concentration camp, Charlotte answered, "Knowing Anne, she was happy in the concentration camps. She didn't have to be quiet anymore; she could frolic outside. She could be in nature. She loved nature. I think this was a welcome relief for her." The basis for Charlotte's version was simply, "Knowing Anne...." When Karen asked Charlotte's classmates if they agreed with her, the room was filled with lifted arms; some had both hands raised, yet no one raised a voice or kept an arm down in protest of Charlotte's statement. No one. This is a testament to the powerful pull of the Americanized Anne Frank.

Teaching Tips

Before reading any version of the *Diary*, find out what students bring with them to the study of the text and the Holocaust in general. Ask students to discuss their knowledge of Anne Frank—and how they came to that knowledge—in small groups. Each group can create a poster depicting their version of Anne Frank using words and drawings and then present it to the whole class. This exercise serves several purposes. First, it activates students' prior knowledge and gets them to think about the sources of their prior knowledge. Many students in the study had sketchy understandings of how they came to know Anne Frank; some "just heard about" or "just knew about" her. Second, teachers can begin to talk about taken-for-granted understandings of Anne and how they are rooted

in ideologically inscribed narratives (the "relational backdrops") that co-produce meaning. Fiske (1989) argued that "Knowledge is never neutral, it never exists in an empiricist, objective relationship to the real. Knowledge is power, and the circulation of knowledge is part of the social distribution of power" (p. 149). In other words, get students thinking about the sources of their information—in what ways did the sources position students to understand Anne, and why? What ideological narratives did students possess that positioned them to accept only a happy and optimistic Anne? (See Table 2 for a list of critical literacy questions.)

After the initial reflection on what students bring with them to the study of the Holocaust, teachers can better plan what historical information will help students come to a more nuanced and robust understanding of the events and actors. Bos (2004) suggested that postsecondary instructors place the Jewish Frank family within the assimilationist milieu of prewar Germany and the Netherlands. Kopf (1997) provided excerpts from texts that give historical information about the Frank family, the Jews of Holland, and anti-Semitism in prewar and wartime Germany, and these excerpts are on target for secondary students. We do suggest that teachers explore brief histories of anti-Semitism and the Holocaust (United States Holocaust Memorial Museum, 2006b) in order to place in context the fate of Dutch Jews. The purpose of presenting the historical information is to contextualize the particularity of Jewish suffering. If you think of Schweber's continua (2004), adding historical information of this kind would slide students toward the poles of particularity and insularity. This can help to balance the presentation of the Holocaust because many teachers focus on expansive and universal representations of the Holocaust (cf. University of Cincinnati, 2003).

Within the next section, we discuss the ways that students attempted to maintain the hopeful and optimistic version of Anne Frank that they brought with them to the study of the *Diary*. Also within the section, we explore how questions grounded in critical literacy practices (Table 2)

Table 2
Critical Literacy Questions

About readers Questions/prompts that can be used with any text:
- Who might feel comfortable reading this text and why?
- Who might feel uncomfortable reading this text and why?
- Encourage readers to locate disconnections or feelings of disconnect as they read. This disconnect can lead to questioning and challenging of the text or their preexisting assumptions and beliefs.

Questions/prompts that can be used with various versions of Anne Frank's diary:
- What do you believe about the Holocaust? Anne Frank?
- From what source does your knowledge come?
- Can you think of other people who would view it differently?

About authors Questions/prompts that can be used with any text:
- What constraints on perspective does the author have?
- How is the author using his or her power in this text?
- Does the use of power lean more toward perpetuating stereotypes or toward challenging them?
- Is the author engaging in a dialogue with the reader, encouraging critical examination for example, or is the text positioned as "truth"?
- Who, or what, is given more power or privilege through this text?
- Who, or what, is given less power or privilege through this text?
- What power relations might the author have had to negotiate through the publishing of this text?

Questions/prompts that can be used with various versions of Anne Frank's diary:
- What is the author's perspective on Anne Frank?
- What does the author/editor want you to believe about Anne Frank?
- How did the author write the text to get you to believe this?
- What did the author/editor add to or take away from Anne Frank's diary?
- How does this revision change the way readers might interpret Anne Frank's experiences?

About texts Questions/prompts that can be used with any text:
- Who could have created this text?
- What can you guess about the perspective of the writer (composer, speaker)?
- Who are the intended audiences—and how can you tell?
- What assumptions are made about the intended audiences?
- What readers might have a similar perspective?
- What readers might have a very different perspective?
- What perspectives, practices, or people are marginalized or devalued in the text?
- Does this text position the reader as an "insider" or an "outsider" and how does that change the reading?

Questions/prompts that can be used with various versions of Anne Frank's diary:
- What information in the text does not match what you thought you knew about Anne Frank? (A focus on disconnection)
- Whose interests might be served by this representation of Anne Frank?
- Whose voices are not heard in the text?
- How does the text's beginning and ending push you to interpret it in a particular way?
- How does a redemptive or tragic ending change what you believe about Anne?
- What moral lessons does the text support or push toward its readers?
- Is the text more particular or more universal in orientation? Does the text focus on the particulars of Anne Frank's experiences or does it attempt to universalize them?
- Are groups of people portrayed as individuals or as collectives?
- Are the historical actors normalized or exoticized?
- Which version is Anne Frank's diary?

(continued)

can be used to complicate the enfigurement of Anne as only optimistic.

Distorting Anne and Her World

Students enfigured Anne in ways that accentuated her optimism, thus distorting her experiences and even, at times, obscuring her death. For example, during a group exercise, Brooke enfigured a hopeful Anne by expurgating material from the *Definitive Edition* (Frank, 2001) that didn't fit her thesis—that Anne Frank was optimistic.

Brooke: [Reading from a handout of questions the teacher gave each group] What kind of girl is Anne Frank? And what are her most noticeable characteristics?

Candace: She is very energetic.

Brooke: Optimistic.

Carl: Positive.

Brooke: Okay. [Writing this down] She's an optimist who loves talking. Where's our support?

[several turns pass as Brooke looks in her book]

Brooke: Here it is! [She reads] "It's utterly impossible for me to build my life on a foundation of chaos...." Blah, blah, blah. No, here it is, "...ideals, dreams and cherished hopes rise within us, only to be crushed." Blah, blah, blah, "...I still believe, in spite of everything, that people are truly good at heart" [p. 333]. That's it! That's the one. Someone else write that down.

While trying to find the one line that supersedes all other statements Anne Frank made in the *Diary*, Brooke literally drowned out with "blah, blah, blah" the contradictory material. She focused on "people are basically good at heart" rather than on hopes crushed, a "foundation of chaos," a "wilderness" with "approaching thunder that, one day, will destroy us too" (Frank, 2001, p. 333).

Others accentuated her optimism by casting the diary as a love story, a survival story, or simply "the hopeful side of the Holocaust" (Zoe). All of these characterizations contain partial truths. She *did* have a crush on Peter; she *did* have an optimistic side; she and the other seven Jews *did* survive for over two years. Moreover, the *Diary* itself did not (and could not) capture the horror of concentration camps or even provide details about the Gestapo and SD raid on August 4, 1944 that put Anne and the others on the road to destruction. Her last entry was made on Tuesday, August 1, 1944. Because of this, the teacher and some students forgot, if only for a while, that Anne perished at Bergen-Belsen. For example, in an interview with James, Karen asked him about his impressions of Anne Frank:

James: Optimistic, never giving up, never giving in.

Karen: Okay, optimistic, hmmm. What happens at the end of the play?

James: They are discovered.

Karen: And?

James: That's it, I think.

Karen: Does she live?

James: Yeah.

Karen: Yeah?

James: Wait, nnnn no. Wait, we wouldn't have her diary. No, no, she dies. I remember. Miep gives the dad the diary at the end when she is dead.

Karen: Okay, she dies.

There are text-based reasons why students enfigured Anne as optimistic, in love, and alive. But these impressions distort the complex picture of life in hiding that Anne's own words convey when considered in their entirety.

Teaching Tips

We don't want to suggest that there is only one way to view Anne and her world, but we argue that the questions suggested in Table 2 may equip students to consider more evidence than only that which conforms to their already present enfigurement of Anne Frank. For example, what information in the text does not match what you thought you knew about Anne Frank? This kind of question asks students to focus on disconnections with texts. Secondary students can be skilled in finding *support* for their positions, as Brooke was in the example above, but asking them to find *contradictory* evidence is a critical skill that will ultimately help them assess the viability of their original thesis. This question may also help students develop a more nuanced impression of Anne. With teacher help, they can find quotations that speak to Anne's disappointment in Peter, thus complicating the love story and exposing students to an intelligent and mature Anne, not someone simply captivated by romance (e.g., Frank, 2001, pp. 306, 324–332). They can find quotations that bring them face to face with Anne's fear and despair, thus encouraging them to amend their solely optimistic view of Anne (e.g., Frank, 2001, pp. 27, 48, 54–55, 57, 134–135, and 211, to list but a few).

Anne's perspective has limitations, and asking students to consider questions under "About Authors" (Table 2) will help bring those limitations to the fore. For example, one might ask students: What constraints on perspective did the author have? She wasn't allowed, as Ozick (2000) reminded us, to give readers her final word on the events she experienced. And the diary genre doesn't always allow for the retrospective appraisal of what was written earlier, and particularly not in this case because the events that caused her to go into hiding also caused her death at 15 years old. We have no record of what Anne Frank thought about the heart of mankind after experiencing Westerbork, Auschwitz, and Bergen-Belsen. The Critical Literacy Questions and Schweber's (2004) continua make useful tools for complicating and assessing the representations of Anne Frank and the Holocaust that students construct, and we think these tools can lead students to more nuanced and robust versions of historical actors and emplotments.

In the previous section, we showed interpretative inclinations students had as they read the *Diary*. We sought to disrupt these inclinations with our critical literacy unit, highlights of which we present below. We are not attempting to provide a comparison between a traditional and critical literacy unit. We have given teachers reasons to believe one is needed and now we will provide advice for constructing a critical literacy unit around the *Diary*.

A Selection of Elements in the Critical Literacy Unit

Hope Interrupted

Drawing attention to the way the students' textbook (Applebee et al., 1994) framed the play within a section called "The Invincible Spirit," Karen began a classroom discussion about how the readers are positioned by the publishing company. She asked, "What if I were the textbook author, and I called this section 'The Depravity of the Nazis,' or 'The horror'?" Students were quick to point out that the story was not about horror at all, but "the story itself makes it fit better in 'the invincible spirit'" (Ted). Students were initially resistant to efforts to complicate their reading of the play. Karen asked them if Anne Frank's spirit really was invincible in the end. We discussed how the play merely alluded to her death and that the *Diary* itself could not possibly include the final chapter of her life.

To make "the depravity of the Nazis" and "the horror" more real to the students, Karen brought in movie clips (Dornheim, 2001) that depicted Anne Frank's deportation and imprisonment—a graphic and competing narrative to the hopeful Goodrich and Hackett play (1956). At the end of the clips, the students were somber and silent.

Karen: Let's talk about Anne's experiences in the concentration camps.

Ted: It's awful.

Tom: Thanks a lot. You ruined it for us!

Annabelle: Um, I still think she thought people were good [at heart].

Karen: Why? Why do you think that?

Annabelle: I don't know.

Tom: I don't think any human can go through that and still remain optimistic.

In a matter of the 15 minutes it took to show movie clips, students went from a unanimously—and solely—optimistic view of Anne Frank's story, to some students like Ted and Tom making adjustments to their previous constructions of Anne. Tom mentions that the clips "ruined" Anne Frank's story for the class. That is, the clips ruined the "familiar relational backdrop" (Haas-Dyson, 2001, p. 5) of hope. Before the clips, Ted was sure that Anne Frank's story was about her invincible spirit and not about Nazi-induced horror, but after the clips he commented simply, "It's awful." Others, like Annabelle, still held on, however tenuously, to their original appraisal that Anne would still think people were good at heart, but she couldn't explain why she felt this way. Clearly, not all students accepted the alternative version Karen presented for them, and it could be argued that this new version should have a strong effect because it was visual and was sanctioned by the teacher-researcher.

Comparing the Play and the Definitive Edition

After students saw the movie clips, some started to get mad at Goodrich and Hackett (1956) for duping them. They wanted to see what else the playwrights covered up or got wrong. Working in groups and using the texts of the Goodrich and Hackett play (1956) and the *Definitive Edition* (Frank, 2001), students searched for ways that the playwrights had constructed Anne. Ted railed against the playwrights in an essay he wrote.

> They wanted to make Anne this heroic, amazing, optimistic person. She seems almost like a super human.... Super-Anne then stays optimistic even in death camps and believes everyone is good at heart. Anne though in real life was not a super human.... [They] wanted the audience to be lifted, not to learn about how terrible life was in the concentration camps. They didn't want to show Jews being dehumanized and disgraced, so, they made you think that the camps weren't really that bad and that Anne was happy there. They wanted to focus on the good and not on the bad.... I [also] wanted it to be happy and hopeful, though this is not the case. (Ted)

These excerpts from Ted's paper demonstrate his belief that the playwrights had exoticized Anne (mythologized her into Super-Anne), universalized her suffering ("they didn't want to show Jews being dehumanized"), and created a redemptive trajectory of Holocaust emplotment ("everyone is good at heart"). Interestingly, these are some of the very criticisms that scholars like Melnick (1997) and Ozick (2000) have leveled against the text.

Florence ended up finding "many discrepancies between the play version and [the *Definitive Edition* (Frank, 2001)]." She wrote in an essay that the playwrights had misled the audience by ripping the "good at heart" quotation from the context in which it was written (Frank, 2001, p. 333). Florence ended her essay by writing, "If she had survived, I believe she would not have written that all people are truly good. She would have known better."

Instead of passively consuming ideology, students like Ted and Florence were engaging in critical literacy practices through actively constructing meaning from several texts and challenging the familiar relational backdrops that they had formerly associated with Anne Frank. Although students were doing a pretty good job of finding discrepancies between texts, we wanted to make sure that they could apply critical literacy skills to other Holocaust representations and not just to the *Diary*. Using the foundation of their work with the play (Goodrich & Hackett, 1956), the movie (Dornheim, 2001), and the *Definitive Edition* (Frank, 2001), we introduced Schweber's continua (2004) and encouraged students to think about how they were interpreting the Holocaust throughout the unit. We explore what happened in the next section.

Raising Awareness About Enfigurement and Emplotment

We wanted students to consider how characterizations of historical actors and the sequencing of events pushed them to accept certain interpretations, and hence lessons, of the Holocaust. Karen introduced students to Schweber's (2004) continua of enfigurement (individualized to collectivized and normalized to exoticized), and to the collectivized terms commonly used for Holocaust actors: victims, survivors, bystanders, perpetrators, collaborators, and rescuers. Because students tended to enfigure perpetrators as collectivized and exoticized, often referring to Nazis as "demonic," Karen asked them to write monologues from a perpetrator's point of view that served to individualize and normalize them. By demonizing perpetrators, human responsibility for the atrocities of the Holocaust can be diminished or obscured. As the Holocaust unit continued, students were asked to consider the way that actors were depicted in the texts they read, using Schweber's (2004) continua.

We also challenged students to consider how the endings of the texts they read pushed them to accept redemptive or tragic interpretations of the Holocaust. Just like with the *Diary*, students originally tended to ascribe redemptive endings to the other literary texts they read—*Night* (Wiesel, 1982), *Maus II* (Spiegelman, 1991), and *The Sunflower* (Wiesenthal, 1997)—even

if redemptive readings seemed to overlook conflicting evidence. Students preferred to believe that after the Holocaust "things returned to normal," that the Holocaust was a blip that thankfully passed off the radar screen. In one student's words, "All the books end happy because the Holocaust is finally over" (Tess).

Within the next section, we provide some teaching tips that evolved out of the critical literacy unit. We give suggestions for points of comparison between the Goodrich and Hackett play (1956), the Kesselman (2001) adaptation of the Goodrich and Hackett play, and the *Definitive Edition* (Frank, 2001).

Teaching Tips

The Goodrich and Hackett play (1956) was a good choice, from a critical literacy perspective, to acquaint students with the *Diary*. It helped to make visible the inclination toward universal, redemptive, and expansive readings that students and the American public in general seem to gravitate toward. The play, Novick (1999) argued, was exactly the optimistic and sentimental schlock that Americans in the 1950s craved. Perhaps little has changed. We do not encourage the use of the play unless it is followed by critical comparisons to Anne Frank's own words.

In addition to the two topics we mentioned earlier in the article (Anne's optimism and her relationship with Peter), there are a few key scenes that present the opportunity for students to see the differences between what Anne wrote in her diary and the bricolage of distortions that amass into the hopeful and universal theme consciously constructed by the Hollywood screenwriters who authored the play (Goodrich & Hackett, 1956). The Kesselman adaptation (2001) provided an interesting example of an attempt to rectify shortcomings ascribed to the original screenplay (secularizing Anne, universalizing the theme, isolating Anne from her own fears and desperation, giving the impression that Anne may still be alive at the end).

One key scene to use for comparison purposes is the Hanukkah celebration within each of the three versions. The Hanukkah celebration in the Goodrich and Hackett (1956) version is the moral center of the play, according to the original director of the stage production, Garson Kanin (Melnick, 1997). In it, Anne wears a lampshade on her head (literally), passes out presents she made for everyone, and sings an upbeat Hanukkah song about playing with dreidels and eating latkes. At the end of the scene, a noise is heard and the audience is reminded that the inhabitants of the annex are happy despite the fact that Nazis want them dead. In the Kesselman version, fear frames the Hanukkah celebration. Before the celebration, Anne has a nightmare about being discovered and the sounds of airplanes and bombs are heard overheard. Anne, in this version sans lampshade, still hands out presents, and still sings a song, but this time she sings "Ma'oz Tzur" in Hebrew—a traditional hymn of Jewish suffering and God's protection. In the *Definitive Edition*, the Hanukkah celebration is barely mentioned. Anne writes, "We didn't make much of a fuss with Hanukkah, merely exchanging a few small gifts and lighting the candles" (Frank, 2001, p. 73). She then mentioned that they sang "the song," which Otto Frank later confirmed was "Ma'oz Tzur" (Melnick, 1997). The opening of each text and the end of each text equally lend themselves to such critical comparisons. The critical literacy questions and Schweber's (2004) continua will help when leading students to critical deconstructions and reconstructions.

Students in the study tended to construct hopeful versions of Anne Frank's story by distorting the texts they read in order to bend them into the shape of their already present cultural narratives. Through concerted efforts to equip students with critical literacy skills, some students were able to begin viewing the *Diary*, in several versions, as sites for investigating how texts position readers and readers position texts. As we interrupted the solely hopeful construction through which most students read the *Diary*, some were able to uncover a more nuanced and robust version of the writer whose diary is said to be the most widely read text after the Bible (Bos, 2004). Along the way, we provided teaching tips to help classroom teachers who were interested in equipping students to take a critical literacy stance toward the construction of Anne Frank.

Tom, a student in this study, claimed that problematizing the frolicking version of a happy, hopeful, and immortal Anne Frank "ruined" it for him. Critical literacy practices could be framed as spoiling naïve perceptions students of any age have of society in general, a sort of end of an age of innocence. The truth is, however, that such innocence has been socially constructed, and perpetuating practices that reinforce fairy-tale endings is not going to equip students with the tools and strategies they need to critically understand how texts operate to position readers. An extreme version of language wielding power to position readers is the Holocaust itself, where slogans, pamphlets, and speeches were used to position Jews as vermin and Germans as advanced human beings. Less extreme versions of this play out every day in the lives of young students in the form of advertising campaigns for products and services that are not necessarily promoting a healthy lifestyle, and more dangerous forms including recruitment for soldiers in a time of war by the U.S. government, where advertising positions readers and potential soldiers one particular way while the signed contract positions them very differently (Bigelow, 2005).

We want teachers to hear one resounding message, if nothing else: lessons and Holocaust meaning emerge from the interaction between texts, readers, and the ideological narratives that inspire both. Lessons are not conveyed through any simple formula of representation; emplotment and enfigurement create trajectories for meaning that once in motion collide with cultural narratives that people bring with them to the study of the Holocaust. And these things are not only true for the interpretation of the Holocaust, but also for other cultural narratives that frame the way we think about the world. Anstey (2002) argued "the availability of vast amounts of information and the ideologies represented in it will...require new and sophisticated literacy and social skills in order to examine, accept, or resist the variety of ideas presented" (p. 446). Engaging a critical literacy approach to representations of different sociocultural events will create powerful literacy through which students can begin to both deconstruct and reconstruct themselves and their worlds.

References

Anstey, M. (2002). "It's not all black and white": Postmodern picture books and new literacies. *Journal of Adolescent & Adult Literacy, 45*, 444–456.

Applebee, A., Bermúdez, A.B., Hynds, S., Langer, J.A., Marshall, J., & Norton, D.E. (Consultants) (1994). *McDougal Littell literature and language green level*. Evanston, IL: McDougal, Littell & Company.

Bardige, B.L. (1983). *Reflective thinking and prosocial awareness: Adolescents face the Holocaust and themselves*. Unpublished doctoral dissertation, Harvard University.

Bardige, B.L. (1988). Things so finely human: Moral sensibilities at risk in adolescence. In C. Gilligan, J.V. Ward, J.M. Taylor, & B.L. Bardige (Eds.), *Mapping the moral domain: A contribution of women's thinking to psychological theory and education* (pp. 87–110). Cambridge, MA: Harvard University Press.

Barnouw, D. & van der Stroom, G. (Eds.). (2001). *The diary of Anne Frank: The revised critical edition*. Prepared by The Netherlands Institute for War Documentation. New York: Doubleday.

Bigelow, B. (2005). The recruitment minefield. *Rethinking Schools, 19*(3), 42–48.

Bos, P. (2004). Reconsidering Anne Frank: Teaching the diary in its historical and cultural context. In M. Hirsch & I. Kacandes (Eds.), *Teaching the representation of the Holocaust* (pp. 348–359). New York: Modern Language Association.

Britzman, D. (1999). "Dimensions of a lonely discovery": Anne Frank and the question of pedagogy. In J. Robertson (Ed.), *Teaching for a tolerant world, grades K–6: Essays and resources* (pp. 294–309). Urbana, IL: National Council of Teachers of English.

Comber, B. (1992). Critical literacy: A selective review and discussion of recent literature. *South Australian Educational Researcher, 3*(1), 1–10.

Delbo, C. (1995). *Auschwitz and after*. New Haven, CT: Yale University Press.

Doneson, J. (1987). The American history of Anne Frank's diary. *Holocaust and Genocide Studies, 2*(1), 149–160.

Dornheim, R. (Director). (2001). *Anne Frank: The whole story* [Television movie]. New York: ABC.

Facing History and Ourselves. (1993, January). *Project submission to the program effectiveness panel*. Washington, DC: U.S. Department of Education.

Fairclough, N. (1995). *Critical discourse analysis: The critical study of language*. New York: Longman.

Fiske, J. (1989). *Reading the popular*. Boston: Unwin Hyman.

Frank, A. (2001). *The diary of a young girl: The definitive edition* (O.H. Frank, M. Pressler, & S. Massotty, Eds. & Trans.). New York: Doubleday.

Goodrich, F., & Hackett, A. (1956). *The diary of Anne Frank*. New York: Random House.

Haas-Dyson, A. (2001). Relational sense and textual sense in a U.S. urban classroom: The contested case of Emily, girl friend of a Ninja. In B. Comber & A. Simpson (Eds.), *Negotiating critical literacies in classrooms* (pp. 3–18). Mahwah, NJ: Erlbaum.

Hernandez, A.A. (2004). *Voices of witness, messages of hope: Moral development theory and transactional response in a literature-based Holocaust studies curriculum*. Unpublished doctoral dissertation, Ohio State University.

Jones, S. (2006). *Girls, social class, and literacy: What teachers can do to make a difference*. Portsmouth, NH: Heinemann.

Kesselman, W. (Adapter). (2001). *The diary of Anne Frank by Frances Goodrich and Albert Hackett*. New York: Dramatists Play Service.

Kopf, H.R. (1997). *Understanding Anne Frank's The Diary of a young girl: A student casebook to issues, sources, and historical documents*. Westport, CT: Greenwood.

Levstik, L. (1989). Historical narrative and the young reader. *Theory Into Practice, 28*, 114–119.

Lieberman, M. (1981). Facing history and ourselves: A project evaluation. *Moral Education Forum, 6*(2), 36–41.

Lieberman, M. (1986). *Evaluation report 78680D to the joint dissemination review panel*. Brookline, MA: Facing History and Ourselves Resource Center.

Melnick, R. (1997). *The stolen legacy of Anne Frank: Meyer Levin, Lillian Hellman, and the staging of the diary*. New Haven, CT: Yale University Press.

Novick, P. (1999). *The Holocaust in American life*. Boston: Houghton Mifflin.

Ozick, C. (2000). *Quarrel and quandary: Essays*. New York: Knopf.

Schultz, L.H., Barr, D.J., & Selman, R.L. (2001). The value of a developmental approach to evaluating character development programmes: An outcome study of Facing History and Ourselves. *Journal of Moral Education, 30*(1), 3–27.

Schweber, S.A. (2004). *Making sense of the Holocaust: Lessons from classroom practice*. New York: Teachers College Press.

Spiegelman, A. (1991). *Maus II: A survivor's tale: And here my troubles began*. New York: Pantheon Books.

Stern-Strom, M., & Parsons, W.S. (1982). *Facing history and ourselves*. Watertown, MA: International Education.

Totten, S. (2001). *Teaching Holocaust literature*. Boston: Allyn & Bacon.

United States Holocaust Memorial Museum. (2006a). *Guidelines for teaching about the Holocaust*. Retrieved April 24, 2007, from www.ushmm.org/education/for educators/guidelines/

United States Holocaust Memorial Museum. (2006b). *Teaching about the Holocaust: A resource book for educators.* Retrieved April 24, 2007, from www.ushmm.org/ education/foreducators/teachabo/teaching_holcaust .pdf

University of Cincinnati Evaluation Services Center. (2003). *An assessment of Holocaust education in Ohio, Indiana, and Kentucky.* Cincinnati, OH: University of Cincinnati Evaluation Services Center.

White, H. (1981). The value of narrativity in the representation of reality. In W.J.T. Mitchell (Ed.), *On narrative* (pp. 1–23). Chicago: University of Chicago.

Wiesel, E. (1982). Night. New York: Bantam.

Wiesenthal, S. (1997). *The sunflower: On the possibilities and limits of forgiveness.* New York: Schocken.

Wooldridge, N. (2001). Tensions and ambiguities in critical literacy. In B. Comber & A. Simpson (Eds.), *Negotiating critical literacies in classrooms* (pp. 259–270). Mahwah, NJ: Erlbau.

Questions for Reflection

• The authors argue that the way Hernandez (2004) constructed his unit on the Holocaust likely influenced the way his students came to understand the events. How actively do you examine your own understandings of the texts you teach? How may your background and membership in different groups (e.g., your race, class, gender, religion, ability groups) affect what texts you select and what students learn? How can you open up spaces for critical literacy in your classroom?

• Would encouraging students to challenge assumptions, examine personal beliefs and their roots, and consider texts from a variety of points of view be controversial in your school or district? How could you work to overcome possible objections to a critical approach to reading and writing? What important local issues would benefit from critical literacy habits of mind? How can you enlist the support of parents and caregivers in the process of teaching children to become critically literate consumers and producers of knowledge?

Appendix:
Further Reading on Selected Topics

In this appendix we share suggested readings about the processes of decoding, vocabulary development, and reading fluency which support comprehension. Also included are further readings on the topics of digital literacy and critical literacy.

Decoding

- Duffelmeyer, F. (2002). Alphabet activities on the Internet. *The Reading Teacher*, *55*(7), 631–635.
- Gill, S.R. (2006). Teaching rimes with shared reading. *The Reading Teacher*, *60*(2), 191–193.
- International Reading Association. (n.d.). *Phonics through shared reading* [Podcast]. Class Acts. www.reading.org/downloads/podcasts/CA-Gill.mp3
- Morrow, L.M., and Tracey, D.H. (1997). Strategies used for phonics instruction in early childhood classrooms. *The Reading Teacher*, *50*(8), 644–651.
- Prior, J. (n.d.). A is for apple: Building letter-recognition fluency [Lesson plan]. ReadWriteThink.org. www.readwritethink.org/lessons/lesson_view.asp?id=132
- Rosen, M. (n.d.). Getting the *ig* in pig: Helping children discover onset and rime [Lesson plan]. ReadWriteThink.org. www.readwritethink.org/lessons/lesson_view.asp?id=103

Vocabulary

- Bromley, K. (2007). Nine things every teacher should know about words and vocabulary instruction. *Journal of Adolescent & Adult Literacy*, *50*(7), 528–537.
- International Reading Association. (n.d.). *Teaching vocabulary in middle and high school* [Podcast]. Class Acts. www.reading.org/downloads/podcasts/CA-Bromley.mp3
- ReadWriteThink.org. (n.d.). My world of words: Building vocabulary lists [Lesson plan]. ReadWriteThink.org. www.readwritethink.org/lessons/lesson_view.asp?id=53
- Ruddell, M.R., and Shearer, B.A. (2002). "Extraordinary," "tremendous," "exhilarating," "magnificent": Middle school at-risk students become avid word learners with the Vocabulary Self-Collection Strategy (VSS). *Journal of Adolescent & Adult Literacy*, *45*(5), 352–363.

Fluency

- Hamner, D. (n.d.). Improving fluency through group literary performance [Lesson plan]. ReadWriteThink.org.

www.readwritethink.org/lessons/lesson_view.asp?id=793

- Hofsess, L. (n.d.). The reading performance: Understanding fluency through oral interpretation [Lesson plan]. ReadWriteThink.org. www.readwritethink.org/lessons/lesson_view.asp?id=28

- International Reading Association. (n.d.). *Phrasing for fluency* [Podcast]. Class Acts. www.reading.org/downloads/podcasts/CA-Ellery.mp3

- Martinez, M., Roser, N.L., and Strecker, S. (1998/1999). "I never thought I could be a star": A Readers Theatre ticket to fluency. *The Reading Teacher, 52*(4), 326–334.

- Rasinski, T.V., Padak, N.D., McKeon, C.A., Wilfong, L.G., Friedauer, J.A., and Heim, P. (2005). Is reading fluency a key for successful high school reading? *Journal of Adolescent & Adult Literacy, 49*(1), 22–27.

Digital Literacy

- Carroll, M. (2004). *Cartwheels on the keyboard: Computer-based literacy instruction in an elementary classroom.* Newark, DE: International Reading Association.

- Gee, J.P. (2000). Teenagers in new times: A new literacy studies perspective. *Journal of Adolescent & Adult Literacy, 43*(5), 412–420.

- Holum, A., and Gahala, J. (2001, October). *Critical issue: Using technology to enhance literacy instruction.* Naperville, IL: North Central Regional Educational Laboratory. www.ncrel.org/sdrs/areas/issues/content/cntareas/reading/li300.htm

- Lapp, D., Flood, J., and Fisher, D. (1999). Intermediality: How the use of multiple media enhances learning. *The Reading Teacher, 52*(7), 776–780.

- Larson, L.C. (2008). Electronic reading workshop: Beyond books with new literacies and instructional technologies.

Journal of Adolescent & Adult Literacy, 52(2), 121–131.

- Malloy, J.A., and Gambrell, L.B. (2006). Approaching the unavoidable: Literacy instruction and the internet. *The Reading Teacher, 59*(5), 482–484. doi: 10.1598/RT.59.5.8

- O'Brien, D., and Scharber, C. (2008). Digital literacies go to school: Potholes and possibilities. *Journal of Adolescent & Adult Literacy, 52*(1), 66–68. doi: 10.1598/JAAL.52.1.7

- Scharber, C. (2009). Online book clubs: Bridges between old and new literacies practices. *Journal of Adolescent & Adult Literacy, 52*(5), 433–437. doi: 10.1598/JAAL.52.5.7

Critical Literacy

- Ciardiello, A.V. (2004). A democracy's young heroes: An instructional model of critical literacy practices. *The Reading Teacher, 58*(2), 138–147. doi:10. 1598/RT. 58.2.2

- Hall, L.A. and Piazza, S.V. (2008). Critically reading texts: What students do and how teachers can help. *The Reading Teacher, 62*(1), 32–41.

- Henry, L.A. (2006, April). SEARCHing for an answer: The critical role of new literacies while reading on the internet. *The Reading Teacher, 59*(7), 614–627. doi: 10.1598/RT.59.7.1

- McLaughlin, M., and Allen, M.B. (2002). *Guided comprehension: A teaching model for grades 3–8.* Newark, DE: International Reading Association.

- McLaughlin, M., and DeVoogd, G. (2004). Critical literacy as comprehension: Expanding reader response. *Journal of Adolescent & Adult Literacy, 48*(1), 52–62.

- Stevens, L.P., and Bean, T.W. (2007). *Critical literacy: Context, research and practice in the K-12 classroom.* Thousand Oaks, CA: Sage.